TOOLS AND ENVIRONMENTS FOR PARALLEL AND DISTRIBUTED COMPUTING

WILEY SERIES ON PARALLEL AND DISTRIBUTED COMPUTING

Series Editor: Albert Y. Zomaya

Parallel and Distributed Simulation Systems / Richard Fujimoto

Surviving the Design of Microprocessor and Multimicroprocessor Systems: Lessons Learned / Veljko Milutinović

Mobile Processing in Distributed and Open Environments / Peter Sapaty

Introduction to Parallel Algorithms / C. Xavier and S. S. Iyengar

Solutions to Parallel and Distributed Computing Problems: Lessons from Biological Sciences / Albert Y. Zomaya, Fikret Ercal, and Stephan Olariu (*Editors*)

New Parallel Algorithms for Direct Solution of Linear Equations / C. Siva Ram Murthy, K. N. Balasubramanya Murthy, and Srinivas Aluru

Practical PRAM Programming / Joerg Keller, Christoph Kessler, and Jesper Larsson Traeff

Computational Collective Intelligence / Tadeusz M. Szuba

Parallel and Distributed Computing: A Survey of Models, Paradigms, and Approaches / Claudia Leopold

Fundamentals of Distributed Object Systems: A CORBA Perspective / Zahir Tari and Omran Bukhres

Pipelined Processor Farms: Structured Design for Embedded Parallel Systems / Martin Fleury and Andrew Downton

Handbook of Wireless Networks and Mobile Computing / Ivan Stojmenović (*Editor*)

Internet-Based Workflow Management: Toward a Semantic Web / Dan C. Marinescu

Parallel Computing on Heterogeneous Networks / Alexey L. Lastovetsky

Tools and Environments for Parallel and Distributed Computing / Salim Hariri and Manish Parashar (*Editors*)

TOOLS AND ENVIRONMENTS FOR PARALLEL AND DISTRIBUTED COMPUTING

Edited by

Salim Hariri
Manish Parashar

A JOHN WILEY & SONS, INC., PUBLICATION

Copyright © 2004 by John Wiley & Sons, Inc. All rights reserved.

Published by John Wiley & Sons, Inc., Hoboken, New Jersey.
Published simultaneously in Canada.

No part of this publication may be reproduced, stored in a retrieval system, or transmitted in any form or by any means, electronic, mechanical, photocopying, recording, scanning, or otherwise, except as permitted under Section 107 or 108 of the 1976 United States Copyright Act, without either the prior written permission of the Publisher, or authorization through payment of the appropriate per-copy fee to the Copyright Clearance Center, Inc., 222 Rosewood Drive, Danvers, MA 01923, 978-750-8400, fax 978-646-8600, or on the web at www.copyright.com. Requests to the Publisher for permission should be addressed to the Permissions Department, John Wiley & Sons, Inc., 111 River Street, Hoboken, NJ 07030, (201) 748-6011, fax (201) 748-6008.

Limit of Liability/Disclaimer of Warranty: While the publisher and author have used their best efforts in preparing this book, they make no representations or warranties with respect to the accuracy or completeness of the contents of this book and specifically disclaim any implied warranties of merchantability or fitness for a particular purpose. No warranty may be created or extended by sales representatives or written sales materials. The advice and strategies contained herein may not be suitable for your situation. You should consult with a professional where appropriate. Neither the publisher nor author shall be liable for any loss of profit or any other commercial damages, including but not limited to special, incidental, consequential, or other damages.

For general information on our other products and services please contact our Customer Care Department within the U.S. at 877-762-2974, outside the U.S. at 317-572-3993 or fax 317-572-4002.

Wiley also publishes its books in a variety of electronic formats. Some content that appears in print, however, may not be available in electronic format.

Library of Congress Cataloging-in-Publication Data:

Hariri, Salim.
  Tools and environments for parallel and distributed
computing / Salim Hariri & Manish Parashar.
     p. cm.
  ISBN 0-471-33288-7 (Cloth)
  1. Parallel processing (Electronic computers) 2. Electronic data processing—Distributed processing. I. Parashar, Manish, 1967– II. Title.
  QA76.58.H37 2004
  004'.35—dc21   2003014209

Printed in the United States of America.

10 9 8 7 6 5 4 3 2 1

CONTENTS

Preface		xi
1. Parallel and Distributed Computing		1
S. Hariri and M. Parashar		
1.1	Introduction: Basic Concepts	1
1.2	Promises and Challenges of Parallel and Distributed Systems	4
	1.2.1 Processing Technology	5
	1.2.2 Networking Technology	5
	1.2.3 Software Tools and Environments	6
1.3	Distributed System Design Framework	6
	References and Further Reading	8
2. Message-Passing Tools		11
S. Hariri and I. Ra		
2.1	Introduction	11
2.2	Message-Passing Tools versus Distributed Shared Memory	12
	2.2.1 Distributed Shared Memory Model	12
	2.2.2 Message-Passing Model	12
2.3	Message-Passing System: Desirable Features	13
2.4	Classification of Message-Passing Tools	15
	2.4.1 Classification by Implementation	17
2.5	Overview of Message-Passing Tools	19
	2.5.1 Socket-Based Message Passing	19
	2.5.2 p4	20
	2.5.3 Parallel Virtual Machine	20
	2.5.4 Message-Passing Interface	21
	2.5.5 Nexus	22
	2.5.6 Madeleine I and II	22
	2.5.7 Active Messages	23
2.6	ACS	23
	2.6.1 Multithread Communications Services	24
	2.6.2 Separation of Data and Control Functions	24

		2.6.3	Programmable Communication, Control, and Management Service	26
		2.6.4	Multiple Communication Interfaces	28
		2.6.5	Adaptive Group Communication Services	29
	2.7	Experimental Results and Analysis		29
		2.7.1	Experimental Environment	30
		2.7.2	Performance of Primitives	30
		2.7.3	Application Performance Benchmarking	39
		2.7.4	Performance Results of Adaptive Schemes	44
	2.8	Conclusions		50
	References			52

3. Distributed Shared Memory Tools 57
M. Parashar and S. Chandra

	3.1	Introduction		57
	3.2	Cache Coherence		59
		3.2.1	Directory-Based Cache Coherence	59
	3.3	Shared Memory Consistency Models		60
	3.4	Distributed Memory Architectures		61
	3.5	Classification of Distributed Shared Memory Systems		62
		3.5.1	Hardware-Based DSM Systems	64
		3.5.2	Mostly Software Page-Based DSM Systems	69
		3.5.3	All-Software Object-Based DSM Systems	72
	References			76

4. Distributed-Object Computing Tools 79
R. Raje, A. Kalyanaraman, and N. Nayani

	4.1	Introduction		79
	4.2	Basic Model		80
		4.2.1	RMI	80
		4.2.2	CORBA	81
		4.2.3	DCOM	85
	4.3	Examples		86
		4.3.1	Experimental Setup	87
		4.3.2	Developing Applications under RMI, CORBA, and DCOM	87
		4.3.3	Experiment 1: Ping	90
		4.3.4	Experiment 2: Producer–Consumer Problem	103
		4.3.5	Experiment 3: Numerical Computation	118
	4.4	Comparison of the Three Paradigms		142
		4.4.1	Dependency Issues	142
		4.4.2	Implementation Details	142

		4.4.3 Architecture Details	142
		4.4.4 Support for Additional Features	144
		4.4.5 Performance Comparison	144
	4.5	Conclusions	146
	References		146

5. Gestalt of the Grid — 149
G. von Laszewski and P. Wagstrom

5.1	Introduction		149
	5.1.1	Motivation	150
	5.1.2	Enabling Factors	151
5.2	Definitions		152
5.3	Multifaceted Grid Architecture		154
	5.3.1	N-Tiered Grid Architecture	155
	5.3.2	Role-Based Grid Architecture	155
	5.3.3	Service-Based Grid Architecture	157
	5.3.4	Grid Challenges	158
5.4	Grid Management Aspects		158
	5.4.1	Managing Grid Security	159
	5.4.2	Managing Grid Information	161
	5.4.3	Managing Grid Data	161
	5.4.4	Managing Grid Execution and Resources	162
	5.4.5	Managing Grid Software	162
	5.4.6	Managing Grid Hardware	163
5.5	Grid Activities		163
	5.5.1	Community Activities	164
	5.5.2	Grid Middleware	166
	5.5.3	High-Throughput Computing	171
5.6	Grid Applications		175
	5.6.1	Astrophysics Simulation Collaboratory	175
	5.6.2	Particle Physics Data Grid	176
	5.6.3	NEESgrid	177
5.7	Portals		177
	5.7.1	HotPage	179
	5.7.2	Webflow and Gateway	179
	5.7.3	XCAT	180
	5.7.4	UNICORE	180
	5.7.5	JiPANG	181
	5.7.6	PUNCH	181
	5.7.7	Access Grid	182
	5.7.8	Commercial Grid Activities	182
5.8	Conclusions		183
References			183

6. Software Development for Parallel and Distributed Computing   189
M. Parashar and S. Hariri

6.1	Introduction		189
6.2	Issues in HPC Software Development		189
	6.2.1	Models for Parallel Computation	190
	6.2.2	Portable Application Description Medium	190
	6.2.3	Parallel Algorithm Development	191
	6.2.4	Program Implementation and Runtime	191
	6.2.5	Visualization and Animation	191
	6.2.6	Maintainability	192
	6.2.7	Reliability	192
	6.2.8	Reusability	192
6.3	HPC Software Development Process		192
6.4	Parallel Modeling of Stock Option Pricing		192
6.5	Inputs		194
6.6	Application Analysis Stage		195
6.7	Application Development Stage		198
	6.7.1	Algorithm Development Module	198
	6.7.2	System-Level Mapping Module	199
	6.7.3	Machine-Level Mapping Module	200
	6.7.4	Implementation/Coding Module	200
	6.7.5	Design Evaluator Module	201
6.8	Compile-Time and Runtime Stage		201
6.9	Evaluation Stage		202
6.10	Maintenance/Evolution Stage		202
6.11	Existing Software Support		203
	6.11.1	Application Specifications Filter	203
	6.11.2	Application Analysis Stage	204
	6.11.3	Application Development Stage	204
	6.11.4	Compile-Time and Runtime Stage	204
	6.11.5	Evaluation Stage	204
	6.11.6	Maintenance/Evolution Stage	205
	References		205

Index   **209**

CONTRIBUTORS

Sumir Chandra, Department of Electrical and Computer Engineering, Rutgers University, Piscataway, NJ 08854 (*E-mail*: sumir@caip.rutgers.edu)

Salim Hariri, Department of Electrical and Computer Engineering, University of Arizona, Tucson, AZ 85721 (*E-mail*: hariri@ece.arizona.edu)

A. Kalyanaraman, Department of Computer and Information Science, Indiana University Purdue University, Indianapolis, IN (*E-mail*: akalyana@cs.iupui.edu)

N. Nayani, Department of Computer and Information Science, Indiana University Purdue University, Indianapolis, IN (*E-mail*: nnayani@cs.iupui.edu)

Manish Parashar, Department of Electrical and Computer Engineering, Rutgers University, Piscataway, NJ 08854 (*E-mail*: parashar@caip.rutgers.edu)

Ilkyeun Ra, Department of Computer Science and Engineering, University of Colorado at Denver, Denver, CO 80217 (*E-mail*: ikra@carbon.cudenver.edu)

Rajeev Raje, Department of Computer and Information Science, Indiana University Purdue University, Indianapolis, IN (*E-mail*: rraje@cs.iupui.edu)

G. von Laszewski, Argonne National Laboratory, 9700 South Cass Avenue, Argonne, IL 60439 (*E-mail*: gregor@mcs.anl.gov)

P. Wagstrom, Department of Engineering and Public Policy, Carnegie Mellon University, Pittsburgh, PA 15213 (*E-mail*: pwagstro@andrew.cmu.edu)

PREFACE

The primary focus of this book is the rapidly evolving software technology for supporting the development, execution, management, and experimentation with parallel and distributed computing environments. The design, development, and utilization of parallel and distributed computing environments that can efficiently support a wide range of scientific and engineering applications remains a challenging research problem due to the complexity and varying requirements of the applications, heterogeneity of the computing systems and their networks, asynchronous complex interactions among the system and application components, and the heterogeneity of the software tools and environments. However, recent advances in processing and network technology and software tools have addressed successfully many of the obstacles hindering the wide deployment of parallel and distributed computing environments.

Active research in parallel processing has resulted in advances in all aspects of the computing technologies, including processing technology, computer networking technology, and software technology. Advances in processing technology have resulted in faster, more powerful processors with increased functionality. Advances in computer networking technology have introduced reliable high-speed networks capable of providing high transfer rates. Advances in software technology have provided easy-to use tools and environments for the development of parallel applications. These advances have resulted in the proliferation of a large number of different architectural classes, such as SIMD computers, MIMD computers, vector computers, and data flow computers, where each class represents a set of different trade-offs in design decisions such as coarse-grained (MIMD) parallelism versus fine-grained (SIMD) parallelism, shared memory MIMD versus distributed memory MIMD, hypercube topology versus mesh topology, and circuit-switched versus packet-switched communication. Each architectural class is tuned to deliver maximum performance to a specific set of applications. However, it remains a fact that none of the existing computing systems are general enough to address all classes of applications and provide the desired performance levels. In addition, these architectures are not scalable and their relatively narrow applicability has prevented them from being cost-effective.

Furthermore, the development of efficient application software capable of exploiting the available computing potential is nontrivial and requires a thorough understanding not only of the application, but also of the target computing environment. Given the diversity of current computing systems and their architectural complexity, this is not a reasonable proposition, especially since application developers are not, in general, computer engineers. Even porting existing applications to high-performance systems is nontrivial and usually involves extensive redevelopment. As a result, the future of parallel and distributed computing will be governed to a large extent by the availability of sufficiently high-level languages, tools, and development environments that can support application developers.

A key factor contributing to the complexity of parallel software development is the increased degrees of freedom that have to be resolved and tuned in such an environment. Typically, during the course of parallel software development, the developer is required to select between available algorithms for the particular application, between possible hardware configurations and among possible decompositions of the problem onto the hardware configuration selected, and between different communication and synchronization strategies. The set of reasonable alternatives that have to be evaluated is very large, and selecting the best alternative among these is a formidable task.

The current user has to spend considerable time in understanding the details of the overall system as well as specific system aspects such as data distribution, problem partitioning and scheduling, routing, load balancing, efficient vectorization, efficient utilization of the memory hierarchy, and synchronization, in order to achieve even a fraction of the theoretical peak performance offered by the system. Consequently, there exists a significant disproportion between the effort involved in developing an application algorithm and in its efficient realization on any high-performance system.

It is this realization that has motivated the writing of this book. The goal of the book is to serve as a reference for current software tools and technologies that can be used to develop, implement, and support high-performance parallel and distributed computing environments and applications. In this book we review promising software tools and environments that play an important role in the development of high-performance parallel/distributed systems and applications, and highlight the salient features and limitations of these tools and environments. Consequently, this book can serve as a useful reference for researchers, educators, and practitioners in the field of parallel and distributed computing, supercomputing, and networking.

The book is organized into six chapters; a brief summary is as follows.

Chapter 1: Parallel and Distributed Computing

This chapter provides an introduction to parallel and distributed systems and their benefits in performance, resource sharing, extendibility, reliability, and cost-effectiveness. It outlines parallel and distributed computing approaches and paradigms and the opportunities and challenges of parallel and distributed computing. Finally, it presents a three-tiered distributed system design framework to highlight architectural issues, services, and candidate technologies for implementing parallel/distributed computing systems and applications.

Chapter 2: Message-Passing Tools

This chapter briefly reviews message-passing models for network-centric applications. It presents the advantages of message-passing tools and their classification with respect to the application domain, programming model supported, communication model, portability, and adaptability. The chapter describes hardware- and software-based approaches to improve the performance of message-passing tools. This is followed by an overview of existing message-passing tools such as socket-based message passing, p4, Parallel Virtual Machine (PVM), Message-Passing Interface (MPI), Nexus, Madeleine, and Active Messages. The chapter then describes the design of ACS (Adaptive Communication System), a multithreaded message-passing tool, and presents an experimental evaluation of ACS and three different message-passing tools (p4, PVM, and MPI) with respect to primitives and application performance.

Chapter 3: Distributed Shared Memory Tools

This chapter presents tools and environments for distributed shared memory (DSM), a software abstraction of shared memory on a distributed memory multiprocessor or cluster of workstations. It outlines the properties and features of DSM systems and classifies them based on their architectures. The chapter then describes cache coherence protocols for hardware-based DSM systems, including CC-NUMA, COMA, and S-COMA; hybrid schemes, including R-NUMA and AS-COMA; and hardware-based environments, such as the MIT Alewife Machine and the Stanford FLASH multiprocessor. Finally, existing DSM systems such as TreadMarks, Brazos, Mirage+, Orca, SAM, Midway, CRL, and fine-grained Shasta DSM are described.

Chapter 4: Distributed-Object Computing Tools

This chapter provides an overview of popular distributed-object approaches such as Java RMI, CORBA, and DCOM and presents the basic model underlying each approach followed by example applications with code segments from different domains. An experimental evaluation of these approaches is presented followed by a comparison of the approaches with respect to language and platform dependency, implementation, architecture, additional feature support, and performance. The proposed Unified Metaobject Model is discussed.

Chapter 5: Gestalt of the Grid

The gestalt of the Grid presented in this chapter provides an overview of important influences, developments, and technologies that are shaping state-of-the-art Grid computing. The motivation and enabling factors for the development of the Grid are described, followed by various Grid definitions. Common architectural views such as N-tiered, role-based, and service-based Grid architectures are presented, followed by Grid management aspects that include managing Grid security, Grid information, Grid data, Grid execution and resources, and Grid software and hardware. The Grid activities presented in this chapter are classified into community activities such as Global Grid Forum and production Grids; development toolkits and middleware, such as the Globus project, OGSA, Legion, Storage Resource Broker, Akenti, and NWS; high-throughput computing, such as Condor, NetSolve, Ninf, SETI@Home, and Nimrod-G; and applications such as ASC, PPDG, and NEESgrid. Popular Grid portals and their toolkits, such as HotPage, Webflow and Gateway, XCAT, UNICORE, JiPANG, PUNCH, and Access Grid, are presented.

Chapter 6: Software Development for Parallel and Distributed Computing

This chapter presents a study of the software development process in high-performance parallel and distributed computing (HPC) environments and investigates the nature of support required at each stage of development. The objective is to illustrate the significance of tools and environments discussed in this book during software development. The chapter first highlights some of the issues that must be addressed during HPC software development. The HPC software development process is then described. A parallel stock option pricing model is used as a running example in this discussion. Finally, some existing tools applicable at each stage of the development process are identified.

Acknowledgments

This book has been made possible due to the efforts and contributions of many people. First and foremost, we would like to acknowledge all the contributors for their tremendous effort in putting together excellent chapters that are comprehensive and very informative. We would like to thank the reviewers for their excellent comments and suggestions. We would also like to thank Val Moliere, Kirsten Rohstedt, and the team at John Wiley & Sons, Inc. for getting this book together. Finally, we would like to dedicate this book to our families.

SALIM HARIRI
MANISH PARASHAR

CHAPTER 1

Parallel and Distributed Computing

S. HARIRI

Department of Electrical and Computer Engineering, University of Arizona, Tucson, AZ

M. PARASHAR

Department of Electrical and Computer Engineering, Rutgers University, Piscataway, NJ

1.1 INTRODUCTION: BASIC CONCEPTS

The last two decades spawned a revolution in the world of computing; a move away from central mainframe-based computing to network-based computing. Today, servers are fast achieving the levels of CPU performance, memory capacity, and I/O bandwidth once available only in mainframes, at a cost orders of magnitude below that of a mainframe. Servers are being used to solve computationally intensive problems in science and engineering that once belonged exclusively to the domain of supercomputers. A distributed computing system is the system architecture that makes a collection of heterogeneous computers, workstations, or servers act and behave as a single computing system. In such a computing environment, users can uniformly access and name local or remote resources, and run processes from anywhere in the system, without being aware of which computers their processes are running on. Distributed computing systems have been studied extensively by researchers, and a great many claims and benefits have been made for using such systems. In fact, it is hard to rule out any desirable feature of a computing system that has not been claimed to be offered by a distributed system [24]. However, the current advances in processing and networking technology and software tools make it feasible to achieve the following advantages:

- *Increased performance.* The existence of multiple computers in a distributed system allows applications to be processed in parallel and thus

---

Tools and Environments for Parallel and Distributed Computing, Edited by Salim Hariri and Manish Parashar
ISBN 0-471-33288-7 Copyright © 2004 John Wiley & Sons, Inc.

improves application and system performance. For example, the performance of a file system can be improved by replicating its functions over several computers; the file replication allows several applications to access that file system in parallel. Furthermore, file replication distributes network traffic associated with file access across the various sites and thus reduces network contention and queuing delays.

- *Sharing of resources.* Distributed systems are cost-effective and enable efficient access to all system resources. Users can share special purpose and sometimes expensive hardware and software resources such as database servers, compute servers, virtual reality servers, multimedia information servers, and printer servers, to name just a few.
- *Increased extendibility.* Distributed systems can be designed to be modular and adaptive so that for certain computations, the system will configure itself to include a large number of computers and resources, while in other instances, it will just consist of a few resources. Furthermore, limitations in file system capacity and computing power can be overcome by adding more computers and file servers to the system incrementally.
- *Increased reliability, availability, and fault tolerance.* The existence of multiple computing and storage resources in a system makes it attractive and cost-effective to introduce fault tolerance to distributed systems. The system can tolerate the failure in one computer by allocating its tasks to another available computer. Furthermore, by replicating system functions and/or resources, the system can tolerate one or more component failures.
- *Cost-effectiveness.* The performance of computers has been approximately doubling every two years, while their cost has decreased by half every year during the last decade [3]. Furthermore, the emerging high-speed network technology [e.g., wave-division multiplexing, asynchronous transfer mode (ATM)] will make the development of distributed systems attractive in terms of the price/performance ratio compared to that of parallel computers.

These advantages cannot be achieved easily because designing a general purpose distributed computing system is several orders of magnitude more difficult than designing centralized computing systems—designing a reliable general-purpose distributed system involves a large number of options and decisions, such as the physical system configuration, communication network and computing platform characteristics, task scheduling and resource allocation policies and mechanisms, consistency control, concurrency control, and security, to name just a few. The difficulties can be attributed to many factors related to the lack of maturity in the distributed computing field, the asynchronous and independent behavior of the systems, and the geographic dispersion of the system resources. These are summarized in the following points:

- There is a lack of a proper understanding of distributed computing theory—the field is relatively new and we need to design and experiment with a large number of general-purpose reliable distributed systems with different architectures before we can master the theory of designing such computing systems. One interesting explanation for the lack of understanding of the design process of distributed systems was given by Mullender [2]. Mullender compared the design of a distributed system to the design of a reliable national railway system that took a century and half to be fully understood and mature. Similarly, distributed systems (which have been around for approximately two decades) need to evolve into several generations of different design architectures before their designs, structures, and programming techniques can be fully understood and mature.
- The asynchronous and independent behavior of the system resources and/or (hardware and software) components complicate the control software that aims at making them operate as one centralized computing system. If the computers are structured in a master–slave relationship, the control software is easier to develop and system behavior is more predictable. However, this structure is in conflict with the distributed system property that requires computers to operate independently and asynchronously.
- The use of a communication network to interconnect the computers introduces another level of complexity. Distributed system designers not only have to master the design of the computing systems and system software and services, but also have to master the design of reliable communication networks, how to achieve synchronization and consistency, and how to handle faults in a system composed of geographically dispersed heterogeneous computers. The number of resources involved in a system can vary from a few to hundreds, thousands, or even hundreds of thousands of computing and storage resources.

Despite these difficulties, there has been limited success in designing special-purpose distributed systems such as banking systems, online transaction systems, and point-of-sale systems. However, the design of a general-purpose reliable distributed system that has the advantages of both centralized systems (accessibility, management, and coherence) and networked systems (sharing, growth, cost, and autonomy) is still a challenging task [27]. Kleinrock [7] makes an interesting analogy between the human-made computing systems and the brain. He points out that the brain is organized and structured very differently from our present computing machines. Nature has been extremely successful in implementing distributed systems that are far more intelligent and impressive than any computing machines humans have yet devised. We have succeeded in manufacturing highly complex devices capable of high-speed computation and massive accurate memory, but we have not gained sufficient understanding of distributed systems; our systems are still highly

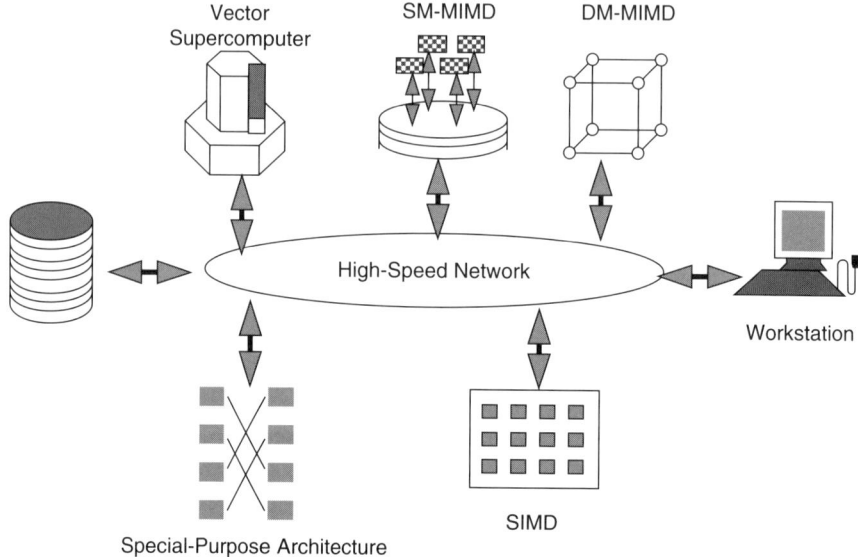

Fig. 1.1 High-performance distributed system.

constrained and rigid in their construction and behavior. The gap between natural and man-made systems is huge, and more research is required to bridge this gap and to design better distributed systems.

In the next section we present a design framework to better understand the architectural design issues involved in developing and implementing high-performance distributed computing systems. A *high-performance distributed system* (HPDS) (Figure 1.1) includes a wide range of computing resources, such as workstations, PCs, minicomputers, mainframes, supercomputers, and other special-purpose hardware units. The underlying network interconnecting the system resources can span LANs, MANs, and even WANs, can have different topologies (e.g., bus, ring, full connectivity, random interconnect), and can support a wide range of communication protocols.

1.2 PROMISES AND CHALLENGES OF PARALLEL AND DISTRIBUTED SYSTEMS

The proliferation of high-performance systems and the emergence of high-speed networks (terabit networks) have attracted a lot of interest in parallel and distributed computing. The driving forces toward this end will be (1) the advances in processing technology, (2) the availability of high-speed network, and (3) the increasing research efforts directed toward the development of software support and programming environments for distributed computing.

Further, with the increasing requirements for computing power and the diversity in the computing requirements, it is apparent that no single computing platform will meet all these requirements. Consequently, future computing environments need to capitalize on and effectively utilize the existing heterogeneous computing resources. Only parallel and distributed systems provide the potential of achieving such an integration of resources and technologies in a feasible manner while retaining desired usability and flexibility. Realization of this potential, however, requires advances on a number of fronts: processing technology, network technology, and software tools and environments.

1.2.1 Processing Technology

Distributed computing relies to a large extent on the processing power of the individual nodes of the network. Microprocessor performance has been growing at a rate of 35 to 70 percent during the last decade, and this trend shows no indication of slowing down in the current decade. The enormous power of the future generations of microprocessors, however, cannot be utilized without corresponding improvements in memory and I/O systems. Research in main-memory technologies, high-performance disk arrays, and high-speed I/O channels are, therefore, critical to utilize efficiently the advances in processing technology and the development of cost-effective high-performance distributed computing.

1.2.2 Networking Technology

The performance of distributed algorithms depends to a large extent on the bandwidth and latency of communication among the network nodes. Achieving high bandwidth and low latency involves not only fast hardware, but also efficient communication protocols that minimize the software overhead. Developments in high-speed networks provide gigabit bandwidths over local area networks as well as wide area networks at moderate cost, thus increasing the geographical scope of high-performance distributed systems.

The problem of providing the required communication bandwidth for distributed computational algorithms is now relatively easy to solve given the mature state of fiber-optic and optoelectronic device technologies. Achieving the low latencies necessary, however, remains a challenge. Reducing latency requires progress on a number of fronts. First, current communication protocols do not scale well to a high-speed environment. To keep latencies low, it is desirable to execute the entire protocol stack, up to the transport layer, in hardware. Second, the communication interface of the operating system must be streamlined to allow direct transfer of data from the network interface to the memory space of the application program. Finally, the speed of light (approximately 5 microseconds per kilometer) poses the ultimate limit to latency. In general, achieving low latency requires a two-pronged approach:

1. *Latency reduction.* Minimize protocol-processing overhead by using streamlined protocols executed in hardware and by improving the network interface of the operating system.
2. *Latency hiding.* Modify the computational algorithm to hide latency by pipelining communication and computation.

These problems are now perhaps most fundamental to the success of parallel and distributed computing, a fact that is increasingly being recognized by the research community.

1.2.3 Software Tools and Environments

The development of parallel and distributed applications is a nontrivial process and requires a thorough understanding of the application and the architecture. Although a parallel and distributed system provides the user with enormous computing power and a great deal of flexibility, this flexibility implies increased degrees of freedom which have to be optimized in order to fully exploit the benefits of the distributed system. For example, during software development, the developer is required to select the optimal hardware configuration for the particular application, the best decomposition of the problem on the hardware configuration selected, the best communication and synchronization strategy to be used, and so on. The set of reasonable alternatives that have to be evaluated in such an environment is very large, and selecting the best alternative among these is a nontrivial task. Consequently, there is a need for a set of simple and portable software development tools that can assist the developer in appropriately distributing the application computations to make efficient use of the underlying computing resources. Such a set of tools should span the software life cycle and must support the developer during each stage of application development, starting from the specification and design formulation stages, through the programming, mapping, distribution, scheduling phases, tuning, and debugging stages, up to the evaluation and maintenance stages.

1.3 DISTRIBUTED SYSTEM DESIGN FRAMEWORK

The distributed system design framework (DSDF) highlights architectural issues, services, and candidate technologies to implement the main components of any distributed computing system. Generally speaking, the design process of a distributed system involves three main activities: (1) designing the communication system that enables the distributed system resources and objects to exchange information, (2) defining the system structure (architecture) and the system services that enable multiple computers to act as a system rather than as a collection of computers, and (3) defining the distributed computing programming techniques to develop parallel and distributed applications. Based on this notion of the design process, the distributed system design framework can be described in terms of three layers (Figure 1.2): (1) *network, protocol, and interface (NPI) layer*, (2) *system architecture and services (SAS) layer*, and (3) *distributed computing paradigms (DCP) layer*. In what follows, we describe the main design issues to be addressed in each layer.

- *Communication network, protocol, and interface layer.* This layer describes the main components of the communication system that will be used for passing control and information among the distributed system resources. This layer is decomposed into three sublayers: network type, communication protocols, and network interfaces.
- *Distributed system architecture and services layer.* This layer represents the designer's and system manager's view of the system. SAS layer defines the structure and architecture and the system services (distributed file system, concurrency control, redundancy management, load sharing and balancing, security service, etc.) that must be supported by the distributed system in order to provide a single-image computing system.
- *Distributed computing paradigms layer.* This layer represents the programmer (user) perception of the distributed system. This layer focuses on the programming paradigms that can be used to develop distributed applications. Distributed computing paradigms can be broadly characterized based on the computation and communication models. Parallel and distributed computations can be described in terms of two paradigms: functional parallel and data parallel paradigms. In functional parallel paradigm, the computations are divided into distinct functions which are then assigned to different computers. In data parallel paradigm, all

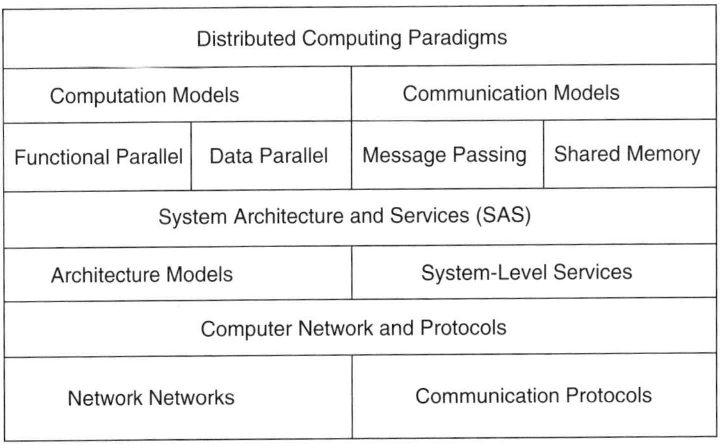

Distributed Computing Paradigms			
Computation Models		Communication Models	
Functional Parallel	Data Parallel	Message Passing	Shared Memory
System Architecture and Services (SAS)			
Architecture Models		System-Level Services	
Computer Network and Protocols			
Network Networks		Communication Protocols	

Fig. 1.2 Distributed system design framework.

the computers run the same program, the same program multiple data (SPMD) stream, but each computer operates on different data streams. One can also characterize parallel and distributed computing based on the technique used for intertask communications into two main models: message-passing and distributed shared memory models. In message passing, tasks communicate with each other by messages, while in distributed shared memory, they communicate by reading/writing to a global shared address space.

The primary objective of this book is to provide a comprehensive study of the software tools and environments that have been used to support parallel and distributed computing systems. We highlight the main software tools and technologies proposed or being used to implement the functionalities of the SAS and DCP layers.

REFERENCES AND FURTHER READING

1. S. Mullender, *Distributed Systems*, Addison-Wesley, Reading, MA, 1989.
2. S. Mullender, *Distributed Systems*, 2nd ed., Addison-Wesley, Reading, MA, 1993.
3. Patterson and J. Hennessy, *Computer Organization Design: The Hardware/Software Interface*, Morgan Kaufmann, San Francisco, 1994.
4. B. H. Liebowitz and J. H. Carson, *Multiple Processor Systems for Real-Time Applications*, Prentice Hall, Upper Saddle River, NJ, 1985.
5. A. Umar, *Distributed Computing*, Prentice Hall, Upper Saddle River, NJ, 1993.
6. P. H. Enslow, What is a "Distributed" data processing system? *IEEE Computer*, January 1978.
7. L. Kleinrock, Distributed systems, *Communications of the ACM*, November 1985.
8. H. Lorin, *Aspects of Distributed Computer Systems*, Wiley, New York, 1980.
9. A. S. Tannenbaum, *Modern Operating Systems*, Prentice Hall, Upper Saddle River, NJ, 1992.
10. *ANSA Reference Manual Release 0.03* (draft), Alvey Advanced Network Systems Architectures Project, Cambridge, 1997.
11. G. Bell, *Ultracomputer a teraflop before its time*, Communications of the ACM, pp. 27–47, August 1992.
12. A. Geist, *PVM 3 User's Guide and Reference Manual*, Oak Ridge National Laboratory, Oak Ridge, TN, 1993.
13. K. Birman and K. Marzullo, *ISIS and the META Project*, Sun Technology, Summer 1989.
14. K. Birman et al., *ISIS User Guide and Reference Manual*, Isis Distributed Systems, Inc., Ithaca, NY, 1992.
15. J. D. Spragins, J. L. Hammond, and K. Pawlikowski, *Telecommunications Protocols and Design*, Addison-Wesley, Reading, MA, 1991.
16. D. R. McGlynn, *Distributed Processing and Data Communications*, Wiley, New York, 1978.

17. C. B. Tashenberg, *Design and Implementation of Distributed-Processing Systems*, American Management Associations, 1984.
18. K. Hwang and F. A. Briggs, *Computer Architecture and Parallel Processing*, McGraw-Hill, New York, 1984.
19. F. Halsall, *Data Communications, Computer Networks and Open Systems*, 3rd ed., Addison-Wesley, Reading, MA, 1992.
20. A. Danthine and O. Spaniol, *High Performance Networking, IV*, International Federation for Information Processing, 1992.
21. U. M. Borghoff, *Catalog of Distributed File/Operating Systems*, Springer-Verlag, New York, 1992.
22. T. F. LaPorta and M. Schwartz, Architectures, features, and implementations of high-speed transport protocols, *IEEE Network*, May 1991.
23. H. T. Kung, Gigabit local area networks: a systems perspective, *IEEE Communications*, April 1992.
24. D. E. Comer, *Internetworking with TCP/IP*, Vol. I, Prentice Hall, Upper Saddle River, NJ, 1991.
25. A. S. Tannenbaum, *Computer Networks*, Prentice Hall, Upper Saddle River, NJ, 1988.
26. G. F. Coulouris and J. Dollimore, *Distributed Systems: Concepts and Design*, Addison-Wesley, Reading, MA, 1988.
27. J. A. Stankovic, A perspective on distributed computer systems, *IEEE Transactions on Computers*, December 1984.
28. G. Andrews, Paradigms for interaction in distributed programs, *Computing Surveys*, March 1991.
29. R. Chin and S. Chanson, Distributed object based programming systems, *Computing Surveys*, March 1991.
30. *Random House College Dictionary*, Random House, New York, 1975.
31. S. Shatz, *Development of Distributed Software*, Macmillan, New York, 1993.
32. N. Jain, M. Schwartz, and T. R. Bashkow, Transport protocol processing at GBPS rates, *Proceedings of the SIGCOMM Symposium on Communication Architecture and Protocols*, August 1990.
33. D. A. Reed and R. M. Fujimoto, *Multicomputer Networks Message-Based Parallel Processing*, MIT Press, Cambridge, MA, 1987.
34. J. B. Maurice, *The Design and Implementation of the UNIX Operating System*, Prentice Hall, Upper Saddle River, NJ, 1986.
35. Ross, An overview of FDDI: the fiber distributed data interface, *IEEE Journal on Selected Areas in Communications*, pp. 1043–1051, September 1989.
36. C. Weitzman, Distributed Micro/minicomputer Systems: Structure, Implementation, and Application, Prentice Hall, Upper Saddle River, NJ, 1980.
37. W. D. Hillis and G. Steele, Data parallel algorithms, *Communications of the ACM*, Vol. 29, p. 1170, 1986.
38. P. J. Hatcher and M. J. Quinn, *Data-Parallel Programming on MIMD Computers*, MIT Press, Cambridge, MA, 1991.
39. M. Singhal, *Advanced Concepts in Operating Systems: Distributed, Database, and Multiprocessor Operating Systems*, McGraw-Hill, New York, 1994.

40. IBM, *Distributed Computing Environment: Understanding the Concepts*, IBM Corporation, Armonk, NY, 1993.
41. M. Stumm and S. Zhou, Algorithms implementing distributed shared memory, *Computer*, Vol. 23, No. 5, pp. 54–64, May 1990.
42. B. Nitzberg and V. Lo, Distributed shared memory: a survey of issues and algorithms, *Computer*, pp. 52–60, August 1991.

CHAPTER 2

Message-Passing Tools

S. HARIRI

Department of Electrical and Computer Engineering, University of Arizona, Tucson, AZ

I. RA

Department of Computer Science and Engineering, University of Colorado at Denver, Denver, CO

2.1 INTRODUCTION

Current parallel and distributed software tools vary with respect to the types of applications supported, the computational and communication models supported, the implementation approach, and the computing environments supported. General-purpose message-passing tools such as p4 [11], MPI [46], PVM [64], Madeleine [41], and NYNET Communication System (NCS) [53] provide general-purpose communications primitives, while dedicated systems such as BLACS (Basic Linear Algebra Communication System) [70] and TCGMSG (Theoretical Chemistry Group Message-Passing System) [31] are tailored to specific application domains. Furthermore, some systems provide higher level abstractions of application-specific data structures (e.g., GRIDS [56], CANOPY [22]). In addition, these software tools or programming environments differ in the computational model they provide to the user, such as loosely synchronous data parallelism, functional parallelism, or shared memory. Different tools use different implementation philosophies such as remote procedure calls, interrupt handlers, active messages, or client/server-based, which makes them more suitable for particular types of communication. Finally, certain systems (such as CMMD and NX/2) are tied to a specific system, in contrast to portable systems such as PVM and MPI.

Given the number and diversity of available systems, the selection of a particular software tool for an application development is nontrivial. Factors

---

Tools and Environments for Parallel and Distributed Computing, Edited by Salim Hariri and Manish Parashar
ISBN 0-471-33288-7 Copyright © 2004 John Wiley & Sons, Inc.

governing such a selection include application characteristics and system specifications as well as the usability of a system and the user interface it provides. In this chapter we present a general evaluation methodology that enables users to better understand the capacity and limitations of these tools to provide communications services, control, and synchronization primitives. We also study and classify the current message-passing tools and the approaches used to utilize high-speed networks effectively.

2.2 MESSAGE-PASSING TOOLS VERSUS DISTRIBUTED SHARED MEMORY

There are two models of communication tools for network-centric applications: message passing and distributed shared memory. Before we discuss message-passing tools, we briefly review distributed shared memory models and compare them to message-passing models.

2.2.1 Distributed Shared Memory Model

Distributed computing can be broadly defined as "the execution of cooperating processes which communicate by exchanging messages across an information network" [62]. Consequently, the main facility of distributed computing is the message-exchanging system, which can be classified as the shared memory model and the message-passing model.

As shown in Figure 2.1, the distributed shared memory model (DSM) provides a virtual address space that is shared among processes on loosely coupled processors. That is, the DSM is basically an abstraction that integrates the local memory of different machines in a networking environment into a single local entity shared by cooperating processes executing on multiple sites. In the DSM model, the programmer sees a single large address space and accesses data elements within that address space much as he or she would on a single-processor machine. However, the hardware and/or software is responsible for generating any communication needed to bring data from remote memories. The hardware approaches include MIT Alewife [3], Princeton Shrimp [20], and KSR [35]. The software schemes include Mirage [43], TreadMarks [67], and CRL [12].

In a distributed computing environment, the DSM implementation will utilize the services of a message-passing communication library in order to build the DSM model. This leads to poor performance compared to using the low-level communication library directly.

2.2.2 Message-Passing Model

Message-passing libraries provide a more attractive approach than that of the DSM programming model with respect to performance. Message-passing

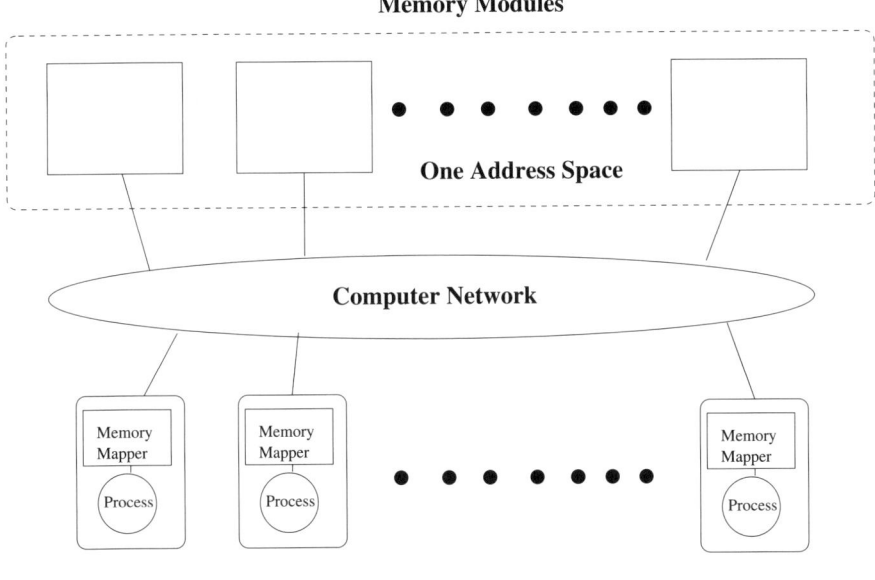

Fig. 2.1 Distributed shared memory model.

libraries provide Inter Process Communication (IPC) primitives that shield programmers from handling issues related to complex network protocols and heterogeneous platforms (Figure 2.2). This enables processes to communicate by exchanging messages using *send* and *receive* primitives.

It is often perceived that the message-passing model is not as attractive for a programmer as the shared memory model. The message-passing model requires programmers to provide explicit message-passing calls in their codes; it is analogous to programming in assembly language. In a message-passing model, data cannot be shared—they must be copied. This can be a problem in applications that require multiple operations across large amounts of data. However, the message-passing model has the advantage that special mechanisms are not necessary for controlling an application's access to data, and by avoiding using these mechanisms, the application performance can be improved significantly. Thus, the most compelling reason for using a message-passing model is its performance.

2.3 MESSAGE-PASSING SYSTEM: DESIRABLE FEATURES

The desirable functions that should be supported by any message-passing system can be summarized as follows:

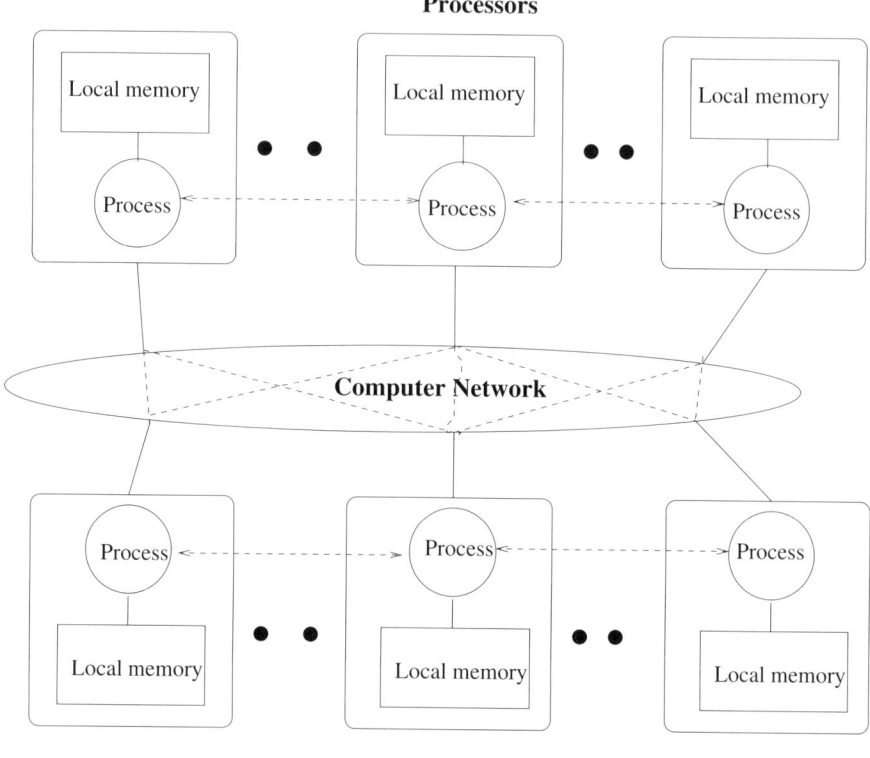

Fig. 2.2 Message-passing model.

1. *Simplicity*. A message-passing system should be simple and easy to use.
2. *Efficiency*. A message-passing system should be as fast as possible.
3. *Fault tolerance*. A message-passing system should guarantee the delivery of a message and be able to recover from the loss of a message.
4. *Reliable group communication*. Reliable group communication facilities are important for many parallel and distributed applications. Some required services for group communications are atomicity, ordered delivery, and survivability.
5. *Adaptability*. Not all applications require the same degree of quality of service. A message-passing system should provide different levels or types of services to meet the requirements of a wide range of applications. Furthermore, message-passing services should provide flexible and adaptable communication services that can be changed dynamically at runtime.
6. *Security*. A message-passing system should provide a secure end-to-end communication service so that a message cannot be accessed by any

users other than those to whom it is addressed and the sender. It should support authentication and encryption/decryption of messages.
7. *Heterogeneity*. Programmers should be free from handling issues related to exchanging messages between heterogeneous computers. For instance, data representations between heterogeneous platforms should be performed transparently.
8. *Portability*. A message-passing system should be easily portable to most computing platforms.

2.4 CLASSIFICATION OF MESSAGE-PASSING TOOLS

In this section we classify message-passing tools and discuss the techniques used to improve their performance. Message-passing tools can be classified based on application domain, programming model, underlying communication model, portability, and heterogeneity (Figure 2.3).

- *Application domain*. This criterion classifies message-passing tools as either *general-purpose* or *application-specific*, according to the targeted application domain. General-purpose tools such as p4, PVM, and MPI provide a wide range of communication primitives for implementing a variety of applications, while some general-purpose tools such as ISIS [10], Horus [55], Totem [45], and Transis [14] provide efficient group communication services that are essential to implement reliable and fault-tolerant distributed applications. On the other hand, dedicated systems such as the Basic Linear Algebra Communication System (BLACS) and the Theoretical Chemistry Group Message-Passing System (TCGMSG) are tailored to specific application domains. Furthermore, some tools provide higher-level abstractions of application-specific data structures (e.g., GRIDS [56], CANOPY [22]).
- *Programming model*. Existing message-passing tools also differ with respect to the programming models that are supported by the tool. The programming model describes the mechanisms used to implement computational tasks associated with a given application. These mechanisms can be broadly classified into three models: *data parallel*, *functional parallel*, and *object-oriented models*. Most message-passing tools support a data-parallel programming model such as ACS [1,2], MPI, p4, and PVM. There are some message-passing tools, such as ACS, MPI, and PVM, that offer functional programming. Agora [4] and OOMPI [50] were developed to support object-oriented programming models.
- *Communication model*. Message-passing tools can be grouped according to the communication services used to exchange information between tasks. Three communication models have been supported by message-passing tools: *client–server*, *peer-to-peer*, and *Active Messages*. MPF [44]

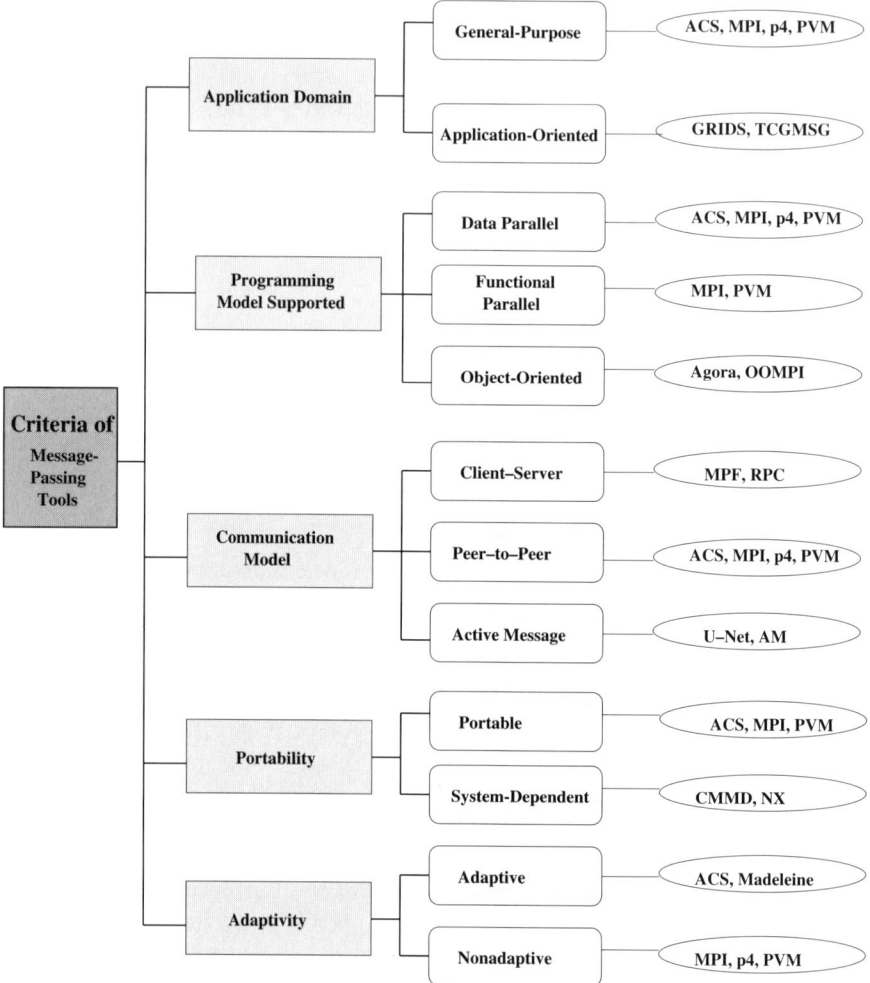

Fig. 2.3 Classification of current message-passing tools.

and *Remote Procedure Call* (RPC) [49] are classified as client–server models. Peer-to-peer message-passing tools include ACS, MPI, p4, and PVM. Many message-passing tools are supported by this peer-to-peer communication model. A new communication model, Active Messages (AM) [19], reduces communication latency and response time. The techniques used to exploit the high bandwidth offered by a high-speed network are discussed in detail later in this section.

- *Portability*. Message-passing tools can be either *portable* to different computing platforms or *tied to a particular system*. Message-passing tools written by using standard communication interfaces are usually portable,

but cannot fully utilize the benefits of the underlying communication network. Such tools as CMMD [65] or NX/2 [54] are specially designed to support message-passing for particular systems (e.g., CMMD for CM5 and NX/2 for Intel parallel computers). Since these tools use proprietary communication hardware and software, their performance is better than that of general-purpose message-passing tools.
- *Adaptability.* Supporting adaptability is becoming increasingly important for implementing applications. ACS and Madeleine [41] were developed to provide adaptable message-passing models that can adjust their communication primitives to reflect changes in network traffics and computer loads. In fact, most message-passing tools such as MPI, p4, and PVM do not support adaptability.

2.4.1 Classification by Implementation

Message-passing tools can be classified based on the techniques used to improve their performance. These techniques can be classified into two categories (Figure 2.4): a *hardware-based approach* and a *software-based approach*.

Hardware-Based Approach In the hardware-based approach, such as Nectar [5], Afterburner [13], OSIRIS [15], Shrimp [20], Memory Channel [38], and Parastation [69], research efforts have focused on building special hardware to reduce communication latency and to achieve high throughput. The developers of communication hardware develop device drivers and proprietary application programming interfaces (APIs) to access their communication hardware. By porting well-known programming interfaces (e.g., the BSD *socket*) or standard message-passing libraries (e.g., MPI) into their implementations, existing applications written using these standards can achieve high throughput. This approach is useful for building a high-performance tightly coupled homogeneous workstation cluster. However, the use of special communication hardware makes it difficult to port these implementations to different computing platforms. Furthermore, this approach cannot be easily adapted to support different schemes.

Software-Based Approach The main focus of the software-based approach is either to incorporate special software techniques (e.g., deploying adaptive techniques, multithreading, utilizing middle-ware services) into existing message-passing tools or to fine-tune the performance of critical parts of the low-level communication interfaces (e.g., device driver, firmware codes of the network adapter cards) for the existing high-speed networks (e.g., ATM, Myrinet). This approach can be summarized as follows:

1. *Multithreading.* This has been proven to be an efficient technique to overlap computations with communications or I/O operations and to

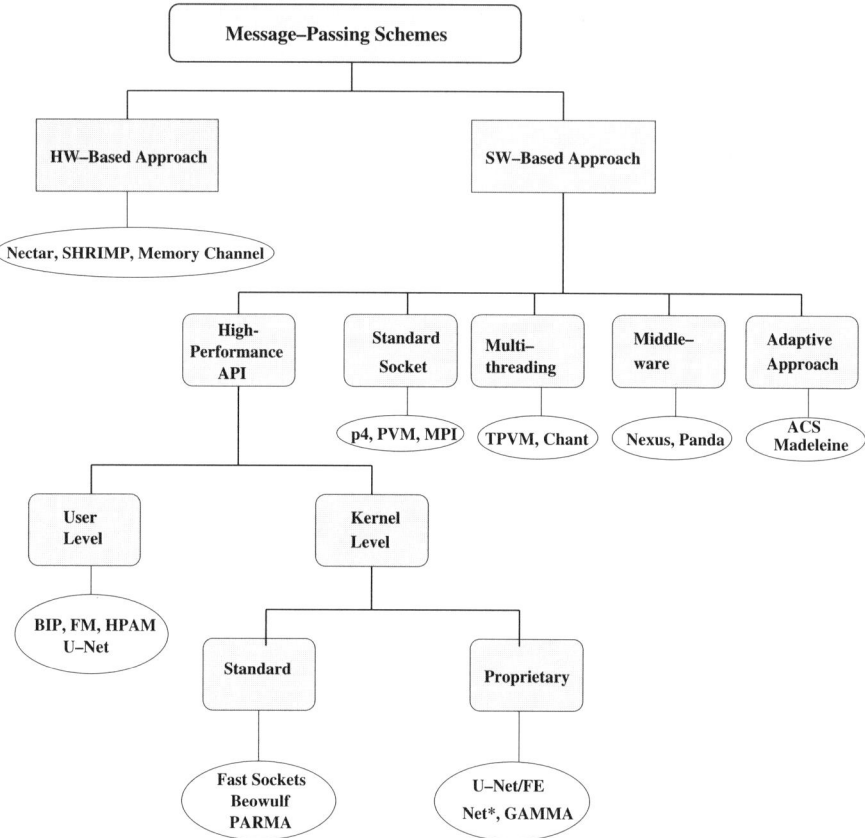

Fig. 2.4 Classification of message-passing schemes by implementation techniques.

support asynchronous events in applications. The research efforts in this category incorporate multithreading into existing message-passing tools or develop a new message-passing tool using multithreading [39] techniques. TPVM [21] is a multithreaded message-passing tool built on top of PVM without making any changes in the original implementation. LPVM [71] is an experimental PVM version that modifies the original PVM implementation to make it thread-safe and then adds thread-related functions. Chant [30] is an extension of Pthreads [47] that allows threads in a distributed environment to communicate using message-passing tools (e.g., MPI).

2. *High-performance API.* This technique is used to improve the performance of message-passing tools by replacing standard communication interfaces (e.g., the BSD Socket) used in existing message-passing tools with high-performance communication interfaces (e.g., ATM API,

Active Messages (AM), U-Net [18], Fast Message (FM) [52], Fast Sockets [57], and NCS). These techniques can be grouped into two groups based on the place where the high-performance interface is implemented: kernel level and user level. In the kernel-level approach the message-passing system is supported by an operating system (OS) kernel with a set of low-level communication mechanisms. These kernel-level techniques can be compatible with *standard interfaces* (e.g., Fast Socket [57], Beowulf [7], PARMA [51]) or with *proprietary interface*s (e.g., GAMMA [26], Net* [48], U-Net/FE [17]). The user-level approach is designed to improve performance by avoiding the invoking of system calls. Currently developed message-passing systems with user-level techniques are BIP [8], Fast Message(FM) [52], HPAM [40], and U-Net for ATM [18].

3. *Middleware.* Another technique is to modify existing message-passing tools so that they can utilize special middleware services (e.g., Panda [9], Nexus [23]). This technique is used mainly for incorporating portability and heterogeneity support into existing message-passing tools rather than improving the performance of each system. The Nexus-based MPI [24] and Panda-based PVM [58] implementations are examples of this category.

2.5 OVERVIEW OF MESSAGE-PASSING TOOLS

2.5.1 Socket-Based Message Passing

The most popular and accepted standard for interprocess communication (IPC) is the socket-based communication *socket*. Socket is a generalized networking capability introduced in 4.1cBSD and subsequently refined into their current form with 4.2BSD [63]. Since socket allows communication between two different processes that could be running on the same or different machines, socket-based communication is widely developed for both UNIX and PC Windows environments. For a programmer, a socket looks and behaves much like a low-level file descriptor. Thus, commands such as read() and write() work with sockets in the same way as they do with files and pipes. There are two different types of sockets: (1) *connection-* or *stream-oriented*, and (2) *connectionless* or *datagram*. In general, the connection-oriented socket is used with Transfer Control Protocol (TCP), and the connectionless socket is used with User Datagram Protocol (UDP).

For any process to communicate with another process, a socket should be created in each communicating process by invoking the *socket()* system call, which contains the type of communicating protocol and *socket* types (e.g., stream socket, datagram socket, raw socket, etc.). The *socket()* system call returns a descriptor that we can use for subsequent system calls. Once a *socket* has been created, the servers or clients should bind their well-known addresses or specific addresses into the *socket* using the *bind()* system call to identify themselves.

Sockets can be compatible with almost every computing platform and use the underlying networks directly without injecting extra overhead between the application layer and networks, which is faster than other message-passing tools that are implemented on top of the socket API. However, socket programming does not have a rich set of communication primitives and cannot be used easily by application programmers.

2.5.2 p4

The Argonne National Laboratory developed p4 [11] as a portable library of C and Fortran subroutines for programming parallel computers. It includes features to explicit parallel programming of shared memory machines and networked workstations via message passing. p4 is a library of routines designed to express a wide variety of parallel algorithms.

The main feature of p4 is its support for multiple models of parallel and distributed computations. For the shared memory model of parallel computation, p4 provides a set of useful monitors for coordinating access to shared data. Users of p4 can also construct the monitors using p4 primitives. For the distributed memory model, p4 provides message-passing functions such as typed send and receive operations, global operations, and the creation of processes according to a text file describing group and process structures.

It is easy to port p4 to different computing platforms and to run tasks in heterogeneous computing environments. To support this, the *process management* of p4 is essential. In p4, there are hierarchies between the processes of *master* and *slave* when they are created. One of the limitations of p4 is due to the static creation of processes. In addition, buffer allocation and management are complicated and p4 is not user friendly.

2.5.3 Parallel Virtual Machine

The Parallel Virtual Machine (PVM) was developed as a software package to support an ongoing heterogeneous network-computing research project involving Oak Ridge National Laboratory and several research institutions [27]. PVM provides users with an integrated set of software tools and libraries that enables a collection of heterogeneous computer systems to be viewed as a single parallel virtual machine. It transparently handles all message-passing routing, data conversion, and tasks scheduling across a network of incompatible computer architectures.

PVM runs efficiently on most distributed systems, as well as on shared memory systems and massively parallel processors (MPPs). In PVM, users decompose the application into separate tasks and write their applications as collections of cooperating tasks. A PVM application runs on a virtual machine created by the PVM environment, which starts and terminates tasks and provides communication and synchronization services between tasks.

The PVM message-passing primitives are oriented toward heterogeneous operations, involving strongly typed constructs for buffering and transmission. Communication constructs include those for sending and receiving data structures, as well as high-level primitives such as broadcast, barrier synchronization, and global sum. The interprocess communications in PVM can be done either by using message passing or shared memory similar to the UNIX shared memory. To support shared memory primitives, PVM must emulate a shared memory model using PVM message-passing primitives, which leads to high overhead for its DSM primitives. PVM supports group communication operations such as dynamic group create, join, and leave operation. PVM is widely used in heterogeneous distributed computing environments because of its efficiency in handling heterogeneity, scalability, fault tolerance, and load balancing.

2.5.4 Message-Passing Interface

Unlike other message-passing tools, the first version of MPI was completed in April 1994 by a consortium of more than 40 advisory members in high-performance parallel and distributed computing. This effort has resulted in defining both the syntax and semantics of a core of message-passing library routines that is useful for a wide range of users and can be efficiently implemented on a wide range of MPPs. The main advantages of establishing a message-passing standard are portability and ease of use. In a distributed memory environment in which the higher-level routines and/or abstractions are built upon lower-level message-passing routines, the benefits of standardization are particularly apparent. Furthermore, the definition of a message-passing standard provides vendors with a set of routines that they can implement efficiently or, in some cases, provides hardware support.

MPI provides a uniform high-level interface to the underlying hardware, allowing programmers to write portable programs without compromising efficiency and functionality. The main features of MPI are:

1. *Communication services.* MPI has a large set of collective communication services and point-to-point communication services. In addition, it provides operations for creating and managing groups in a scalable way.
2. *Full asynchronous communications.*
3. *User-defined data types.* MPI has an extremely powerful and flexible mechanism for describing data movement routines by both predefined and derived data types.
4. *Well-supported MPP and clusters.* A virtual topology reflecting the communication pattern of the application can be associated with a group of processes. MPI provides a high-level abstraction for the message-passing

topology such that general application topologies are specified by a graph, and each communication process is connected by an arc.

2.5.5 Nexus

Nexus consists of a portable runtime system and communication libraries for task parallel programming languages [23]. It was developed to provide integrated multiple threads of control, dynamic processes management, dynamic address space creation, a global memory model via interprocessor references, and asynchronous events. It also supports heterogeneity at multiple levels, allowing a single computation to utilize different programming languages, executables, processors, and network protocols. The core basic abstractions provided by Nexus are as follows:

- *Nodes*. In the Nexus environment, a *node* represents a physical processing resource. It provides a set of routines to create nodes on named computational resources. A node specifies only a computational resource and does not imply any specific communication medium or protocol.
- *Contexts*. A *context* is an object on which computations run. It contains an executable code and one or more data segments to a node. Nexus supports the separation of context creation and code execution.
- *Threads*. In Nexus, a computation is done in one or more threads of control. Nexus creates a thread in two different modes: within the same context and in a different context, and provides a routine for creating threads within the context of the currently executing thread.
- *Global pointers*. Nexus creates any address within a context that allows contexts to move between them and intercontext reference. Global pointers are used in conjunction with remote service requests to enable actions to take place on a different context.
- *Remote service requests*. In Nexus, a thread can invoke an action in a remote context via a remote service request. The result of the remote service request is returned by a handler that is in the context pointed to by a global pointer.

2.5.6 Madeleine I and II

Madeleine I [41] has been implemented as an RPC-based multithreaded message-passing environment by *Laboratoire de l'Informatique du Parallélisme* in 1999. It aims at providing both efficient and portable interprocess communications, and consists of two layers:

- *Portability layer:* an interface with network protocol such as TCP and Virtual Interface Architecture (VIA) [68]

- *RPC layer:* a higher layer that provides advanced generic communication facilities to optimize RPC operations

Madeleine II [42] is an adaptive multiprotocol extension of the Madeleine I portable communication interface. It provides multiple network protocols such as VIA, Scalable Coherent Interface (SCI) [61], TCP, MPI, and mechanisms to dynamically select the most appropriate transfer method for a given network protocol according to various parameters, such as data size or responsiveness to user requirements. Although the Madeleine is a portable and adaptive message-passing tool, it does not have rich communication primitives such as group communication primitives.

2.5.7 Active Messages

Standard asynchronous message passing is so inefficient on commercial parallel processors that except for very large messages, applications achieve little overlap of communication and computation in practice. This performance deficiency is due primarily to message startup costs. Message-passing systems typically have a great deal of overhead, most significantly as a result of message copying from the user memory to communication buffers, and back.

Active Messages [19] is designed to overcome those types of communication overhead and achieve high performance in large-scale multiprocessors. To reduce the time span from when a message starts sending until an action is performed on the destination processor, AM messages contain the address of the handler to be invoked on the message. This handler extracts the message from the network in an application-specific way. Thus, the message can be processed immediately or it can be integrated into an ongoing computation.

The performance measurement of AM on the nCube/2 shows that active messages perform slightly over the minimum suggested by hardware, which is an order of magnitude lower than existing messaging systems. There have been several efforts to develop message-passing tools based on the Active Message model, namely, UNet-ATM [16], Generic Active Messages (GAM) [25], and HPAM [40].

2.6 ACS

ACS [1,2] (Adaptive Communication Systems) is a multithreaded message-passing tool developed at Syracuse University, University of Arizona, and University of Colorado at Denver that provides application programmers with multithreading (e.g., thread synchronization, thread management), and communication services (e.g., point-to-point communication, group communication, synchronization). Since ACS is developed as a proof-of-concept message-passing tool, it does not provide the full capabilities required if it were to be used as a programming environment. However, we chose ACS as one of the tools for evaluation because the implementation philosophy is unique and provides a flexible environment that is not supported by other message-passing tools.

ACS is architecturally compatible with the ATM technology, where both control (e.g., signaling or management) and data transfers are separated and each connection can be configured to meet the quality of service (QoS) requirements of that connection. Consequently, the ACS architecture is designed to support various classes of applications by providing the following architectural supports.

2.6.1 Multithread Communications Services

The advantage of using a thread-based programming paradigm is that it reduces the cost of context switching, provides efficient support for fine-grained applications, and allows the overlapping of computation and communication. Overlapping computation and communication is an important feature in network-based computing. In wide area network (WAN)-based distributed computing, the propagation delay (limited by the speed of light) is several orders of magnitude greater than the time it takes to actually transmit the data [34]. Therefore, the transmission time of a small file—1 kilobyte (kB)—is insignificant when compared to the propagation delay. Reducing the impact of the propagation delay requires that we modify the structure of computations so that they overlap communications.

2.6.2 Separation of Data and Control Functions

In high-speed networks very little time is available to decode, process, and store incoming packets at a gigabit per second rate. Also, the bandwidth provided by high-speed networks is generally enough to be allocated to multiple connections. Therefore, the software architectures of communication systems for highspeed networks should be designed to exploit these requirements fully. The communication process can be divided into two major functions: control and data. The control functions are responsible for establishing and maintaining connections to provide efficient and reliable communication links. The data-transferring functions are responsible for reliably sending and receiving data. In general, these two functions cannot run simultaneously, because they were designed to share the communication link with each other. As Thekkath, Levy, and Lazowska did for distributed operating systems [66], we designate a channel for control and management and a data channel, and operate them concurrently. Thus, by separating control/management and data, we accomplish better performance, as will be shown later. What follows is a detailed description of the two planes.

Control Management Plane This plane provides the appropriate control and management functions, including error control (EC), flow control (FC), fault tolerance control (FTC), QoS control (QC), security control (SC), connection control management (CCM), and application control management (ACM). For each application, ACS establishes one or more connections that meet the application requirements in terms of the type of flow control mechanism (rate-based or window-based), error control (parity check field or selective retransmission), connection control (connection oriented or connectionless service), fault tolerance, security, and the type of functions required to control send/receive and multicast operations. We use multithreaded agents to implement the control mechanisms selected for any given application at runtime. For instance, in a collaborative environment that connects nodes using wireless and wired networks, the nodes communicating by using wireless networks will select the appropriate flow and error control mechanisms for wireless networks, while the nodes communicating over wired networks use different control mechanisms. The ACS CMP provides all the capabilities required to select these control management functions at runtime in order to achieve this adaptability.

Data Communication Plane This plane provides a rich set of communication services that allows applications or tasks to cooperate and exchange information. These communication services include the following:

- *Point-to-point communication primitives* that are responsible for data transmission between two nodes. The attributes of these primitives can be tailored to meet the application requirements by providing various types of communication primitives: blocking versus nonblocking, buffered versus nonbuffered.
- *Group communication services* (e.g., multicast, broadcast, gathering/scattering) that can be implemented using different algorithms. For example, by selecting the appropriate multicast algorithm for a particular application (rooted tree, spanning tree, etc.), the cost of group communications can be reduced significantly and thus improve the application performance.
- *Multiple communication interfaces* enable applications to choose the appropriate communication technology when there are several types, depending upon availability and capability. In this architecture, three types of communication interface are supported:
  - *Socket communication interface* (SCI). SCI is provided mainly for achieving high portability over a heterogeneous network of computers (e.g., workstations, PCs, parallel computers).
  - *ATM communication interface* (ACI). ACI provides applications with more flexibility to fully exploit the high speed and functionality of ATM networks. Since ATM API does not define flow control and error control schemes, programmers can select the appropriate communication

services according to the QoS, quality of protection (QoP), and quality of fault tolerance (QoF) requirements of the applications.
- *Wireless communication interface* (WCI). WCI offers a wireless access backbone network whose quality is close to that of wired access, thus extending broadband services to mobile users.

Providing different implementation mechanisms that can be selected dynamically at runtime will lead to a significant improvement in application performance, security, and fault tolerance. In a multimedia collaborative application (videoconferencing) over a wide area network where multiple end nodes and intermediate nodes cooperate, reliable multicasting service can be supported by selecting the appropriate multicast algorithm suitable for the application requirements.

2.6.3 Programmable Communication, Control, and Management Service

Each network-centric application requires different schemes for flow control, error control, and multicasting algorithms. One of the main goals of the adaptive communication architecture is to provide an efficient modular approach to support these requirements dynamically. Thus the proposed ACS architecture should be able to support multiple flow control (e.g., window-based, credit-based, or rate-based), error control (e.g., go-back N or selective repeat), and multicasting algorithms (e.g., repetitive send/receive or a multicast spanning tree) within the *control plane* to meet the QoS requirements of a wide range of network-centric applications. Each algorithm is implemented as a thread, and programmers select the appropriate control thread that meets the performance and QoS requirements of a given network-centric application at runtime. In ACS, the application requirements can be represented in terms of QoS, QoP, and QoF requirements. Figure 2.5 illustrates an example of how ACS dynamically build a protocol for each connection and adaptively manages the application execution environment when several end systems that are connected through different network technologies (wired ATM and wireless) with different capabilities and performance can communicate with each other collaboratively. Figure 2.5 shows two sessions that are configured with different parameters. Session 1 is a connection over a wired network that is relatively more reliable and has higher bandwidth, and session 2 is a connection on a wireless network that is less secure and has lower bandwidth than that of the wired network. Hence, these sessions need different protocol mechanisms to implement their flow and error control. For example, the protocol for session 1 can be built by invoking the following ACS primitives:

- *ACS_add_agent (dest, session, &agent, selective_repeat_error_control)*
- *ACS_add_agent (dest, session, &agent, credit_based_flow_control)*

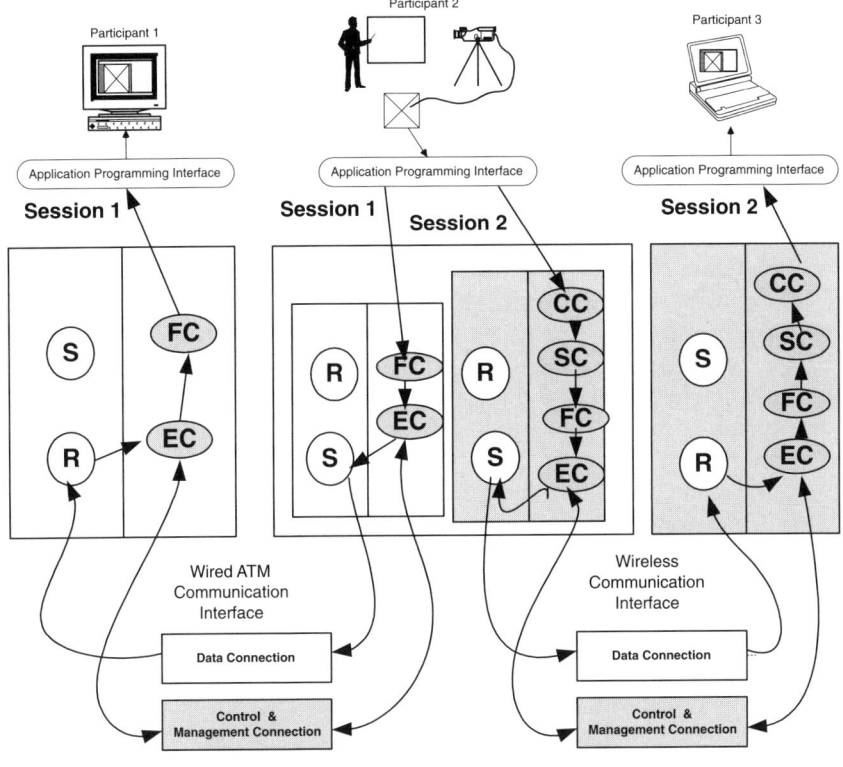

Fig. 2.5 Adapting to an application execution environment.

The advantages of using this approach to build a specific protocol is that the established connection does not have to be disconnected to change the protocol attributes during execution. If the user wants to use a different compression algorithm to reduce the amount of data transmitted (e.g., increase the compression level over session 2 since it is using a low-bandwidth wireless network) the user can invoke the appropriate ACS primitive. For example, the user can change the Qos, QoP, and QoF requirements of any open session by invoking the corresponding ACS primitives:

- *int ACS_QoS_change (int dest, int session, QoS_t qos)*
- *int ACS_QoP_change (int dest, int session, QoP_t qop)*
- *int ACS_QoF_change (int dest, int session, QoF_t qof)*

2.6.4 Multiple Communication Interfaces

Some parallel and distributed applications demand low-latency and high-throughput communication services to meet their QoS requirements, whereas others need portability across many computing platforms more than performance. Most message-passing systems cannot dynamically support a wide range of QoS requirements because their protocol architectures and communication interfaces are fixed. The proposed adaptive communication architecture is flexible and can be used to build a large heterogeneous distributed computing environment that consists of several high-speed local clusters. In the environment shown in Figure 2.6, each homogeneous local cluster can be configured to use the appropriate application communication interface that is supported by the underlying computing platforms and is appropriate for the computations running on the that cluster. In addition, each cluster can be interconnected by using the socket interface which is supported by all the clusters. For example, the user can open a session within cluster 1 that uses the Ethernet connection interface [socket interface (SCI)], a session within cluster 2 that uses the ATM communication interface (ACI), and a session within cluster 3 that is connected by wireless communication interface (WCI).

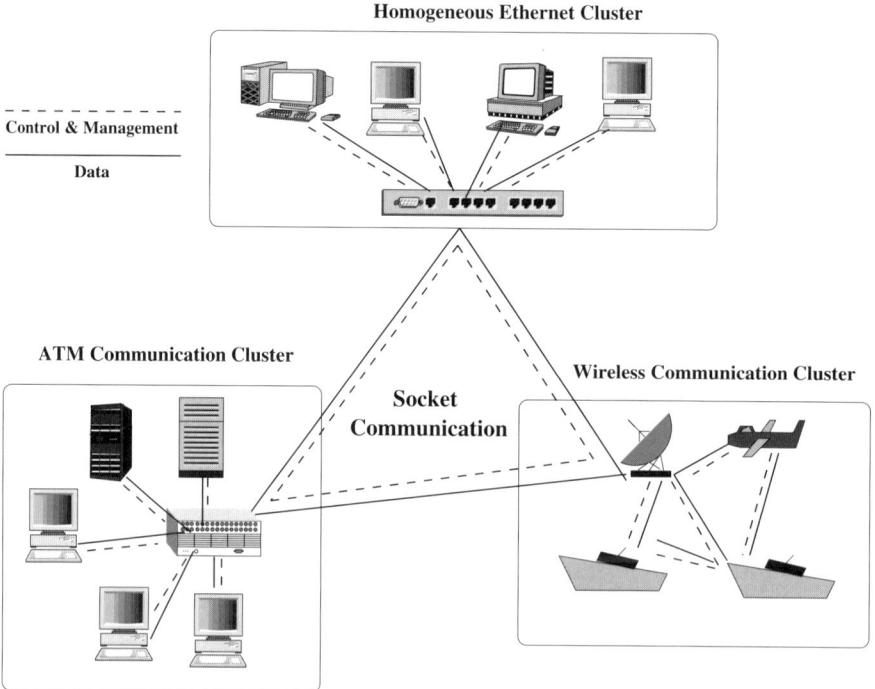

Fig. 2.6 Use of multiple communication interfaces in ACS.

The connection between clusters is set up with the SCI. The syntax for defining a session in ACS is as follow:

```
Session_ID ACS_open_session
           (int dest, Comm_t comm, QoS_t qos, Sec_t qop,
            Fault_t qof)
```

where dest denotes the destination machine, comm denotes communication interface type (e.g., SCI, ACI, WCI), qos, qop, and qof denote quality of service, security, and fault tolerance requirements for an application, respectively.

Once a session is established, an ACS application can exchange messages according to the session attributes specified by session-open primitives. The syntax for ACS send/receive primitives is:

- *int ACS_send(int dest, int dest_id, int session, char *buf, int len, int type)*
- *int ACS_recv(int *src, int *src_id, int *session, char **buf, int len, int *type)*

The facility allows ACS to improve the overall performance of an application because ACS can optimize the performance of local applications with the best available network infrastructure in each cluster.

2.6.5 Adaptive Group Communication Services

ACS allows the dynamic formation of groups so that any process can join and/or leave a group dynamically. All the communications related to a group are handled by a single group server. Within each group there is a single group server that is responsible for intergroup and multicasting communications. The default implementation of ACS multicasting is a tree-based protocol, which is more efficient than repetitive techniques for large group sizes. The ACS architecture, which separates the data and control/management transfer, allows multicasting operations to be implemented efficiently by using control connections to transfer status information (e.g., membership change, acknowledgment to maintain reliability). This separation optimizes the data path and improves the performance of ACS applications. To support adaptive group communication services, ACS use two types of algorithms: resource aware scheduling algorithm (RAA) and application aware scheduling algorithm (AAA). RAA uses network characteristics and computing resource powers to build the appropriate multicasting algorithm; AAA uses size and pattern of group communications to set up a group communication schedule.

2.7 EXPERIMENTAL RESULTS AND ANALYSIS

We evaluate the performances of the ACS primitives and those of three different message-passing tools (p4, PVM, and MPI) and evaluate them from two different perspectives: primitives performance and applications performance. All experiments were conducted over two different computing platforms (SUN workstations running Solaris and IBM workstations running AIX 4.1) interconnected by an ATM network and Ethernet. In all measurements, we used the ACS version implemented over the *socket* interface. For the PVM benchmarking we used the PVM direct mode, where the direct TCP connection is made between two endpoints. The MPICH [28] was used to evaluate the performance of MPI.

2.7.1 Experimental Environment

The current ACS has been implemented and tested at the HPDC laboratory and Sun workstation clusters at Syracuse University. The HPDC laboratory has been constructed to provide cutting-edge communication system testing environments and to encourage faculties and students to research and develop noble technologies in high-performance and distributed computing and high-speed communication system research fields. The HPDC laboratory is configured with an IBM 8260 ATM switch [32] and an IBM 8285 workgroup ATM switch [33]. The IBM 8260 ATM switch offers twelve 155-Mbps multiple ATM connections to Sun workstations and PCs via UNI 3.1 [6] and classical IP over ATM standards [36]. The IBM 8285 ATM concentrator is connected to IBM 8260 ATM switch and provides twelve 25-Mbps ATM connections to PCs. The current configuration of the HPDC laboratory is shown in Figure 2.7. There are several Sun workstation clusters in the Department of Electrical Engineering and Computer Science at Syracuse University. They are located in different rooms, floors, and buildings and are connected via 10-Mbps Ethernet (Figure 2.8). Most of the machines are Sun Ultra 5 workstations, some are Sun SPARCs, some are Sun SPARC classic, and there are some Sun Ultra 4 workstations. With both the HPDC laboratory and the Sun workstation clusters, we measured the performance of ACS, p4, PVM, and MPI in terms of their primitives and applications. We present and discuss experimental results in the following sections.

2.7.2 Performance of Primitives

We benchmark the performance of the basic communication primitives provided by each message-passing tool as point-to-point communication primitives (e.g., send and receive) and group communication primitives (e.g., broadcast).

Point-to-Point Communication Performance In order to compare the performance of point-to-point communication primitives, the round-trip performance is measured using an echo program. In this echo program the client transmits a message of proper size that is transmitted back once it is received at the receiver side. Figures 2.9 and 2.11 show the performance of point-to-

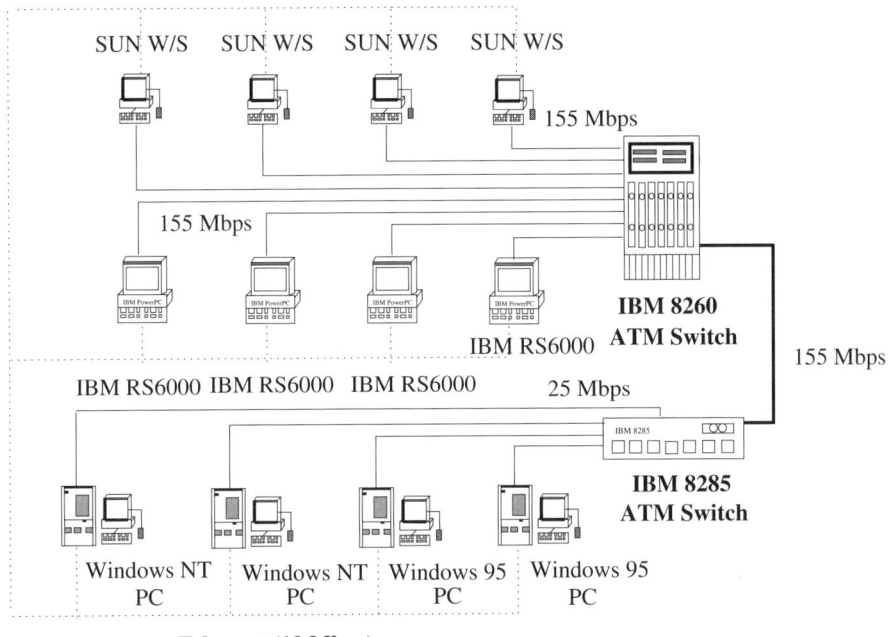

Fig. 2.7 HPDC laboratory at Syracuse University.

point (send/receive) communication primitives of four message-passing tools for different messages of sizes up to 64 kB when they are measured using different computing platform (i.e., Sun Solaris workstations to IBM AIX workstations). To measure the round-trip time, the timer starts in the client code before transmitting a message and stops after receiving the message back. The difference in time is used to calculate the round-trip time of the corresponding message size. The time was averaged over 100 iterations after discarding the best and worst timings. As we can see from Figures 2.9 and 2.11, ACS outperforms other message-passing tools in any message sizes, while p4 has the best performance on the IBM AIX platform (Figure 2.10). For message size smaller than 1 kB, the performance of all four tools is the same, but the performance of p4 on the Sun Solaris platform and the performance of PVM on the IBM AIX get worse as the message size gets bigger.

Consequently, it should be noted that the performance of send/receive primitives of each message-passing tool varies according to the computing platform (e.g., hardware or kernel architecture of the operating system) on which the tools are implemented. ACS gives a good performance on either the same computing platform or on a different platform. PVM performs worst on the IBM AIX platform, but shows performance comparable to ACS on both the Sun Solaris platform and the heterogeneous environment. The

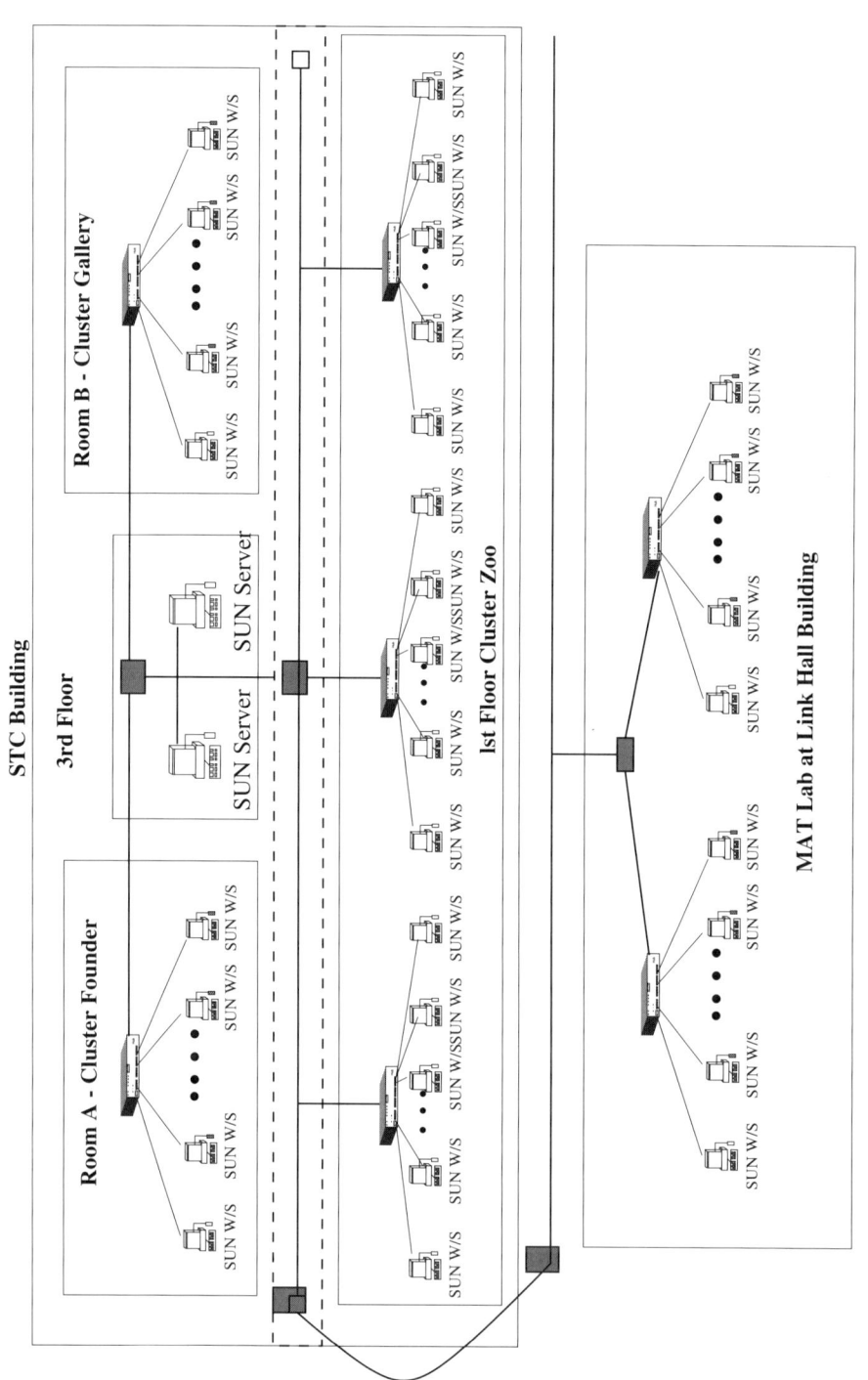

Fig. 2.8 Sun workstation cluster at Syracuse University.

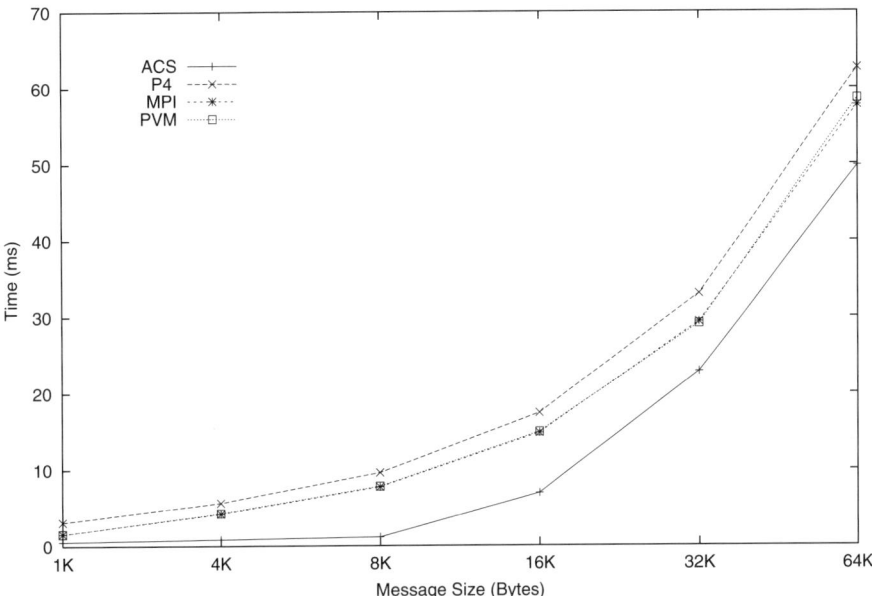

Fig. 2.9 Point-to-point communication performance in a Sun cluster environment.

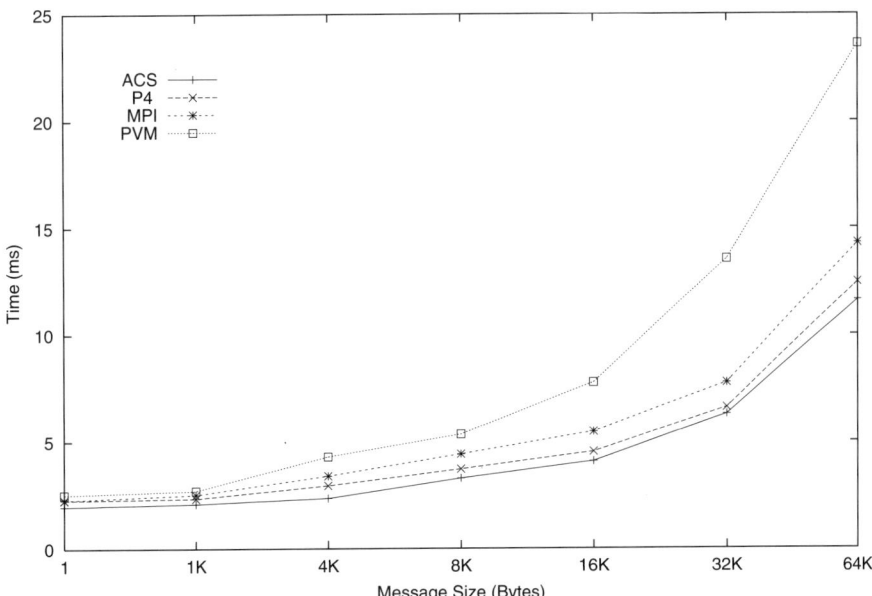

Fig. 2.10 Point-to-point communication performance in an IBM cluster environment.

34 MESSAGE-PASSING TOOLS

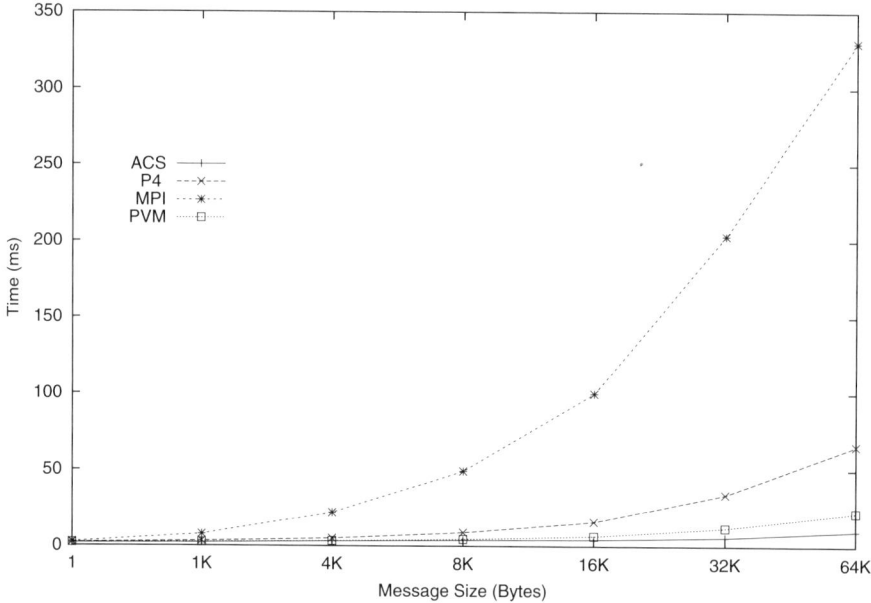

Fig. 2.11 Point-to-point communication performance over ATM in a heterogeneous environment.

performance of p4 was worst on the Sun workstation running Solaris. MPI and p4 give a better performance on the IBM workstation running AIX than on either the Sun workstation running Solaris or the heterogeneous machines running different operating systems. This implies that the performance of applications written by using these two tools over the Sun Solaris platform and the heterogeneous environment will be inferior to that written of applications using other message-passing tools.

Group Communication Performance Figures 2.12 to 2.18 show the performance of broadcasting primitives [i.e., *ACS_mcast()*, *p4_broadcast()*, *pvm_mcast()*, and *MPI_Bcast()*] over an Ethernet network for message sizes from 1 byte to 64 kB. The group size varies from 2 to 16, and up to 16 Sun Solaris workstations were used for measuring the timings. As we can see from Figures 2.12 to 2.18, the execution time of each broadcasting primitive increases linearly for small message sizes up to 1 kB but shows different patterns when we increase message and group size. The ACS primitive [*ACS_mcast()*] gives the best performance for various message and group sizes. Furthermore, the *ACS_mcast()* primitive shows its broadcasting time is smoothly increased as we increase size of group over eight members and message size over 4 kB. ACS can outperform when the group size and message get larger because the *ACS_mcast()* primitive where most of the information

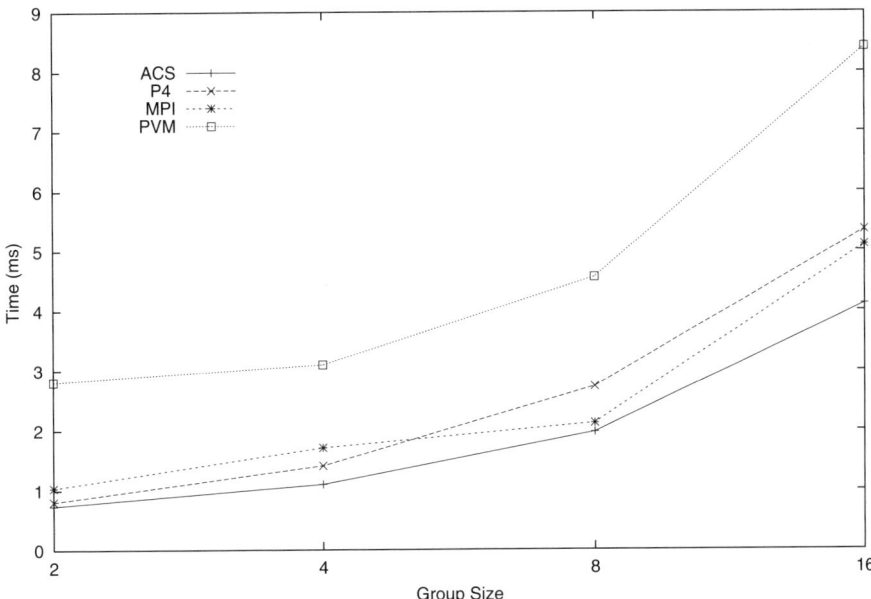

Fig. 2.12 Comparison of broadcasting performance (message = 1 byte).

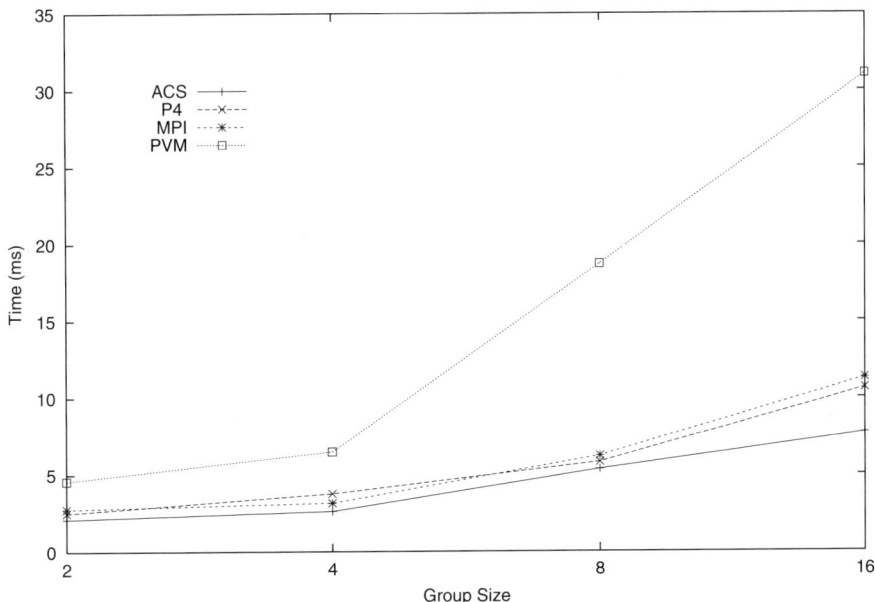

Fig. 2.13 Comparison of broadcasting performance (message = 1 kB).

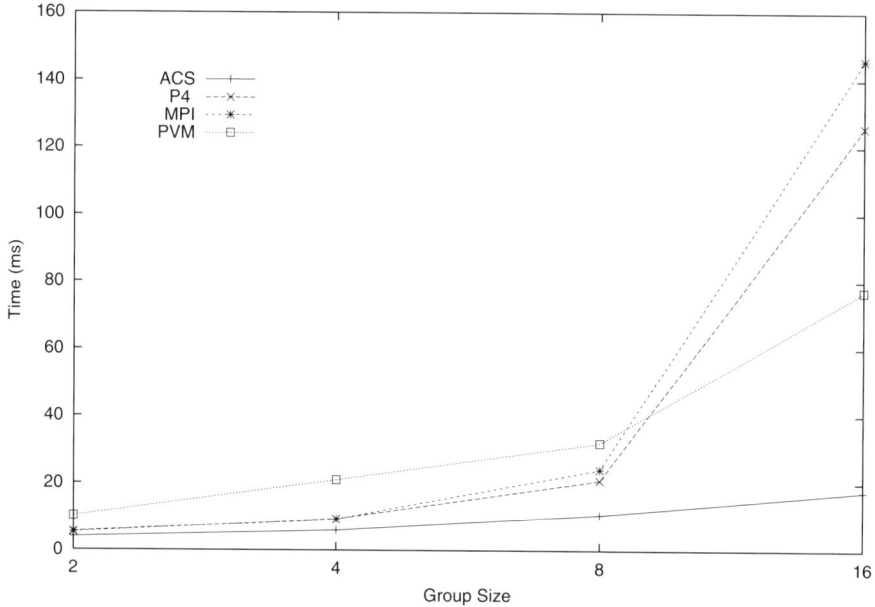

Fig. 2.14 Comparison of broadcasting performance (message = 4 kB).

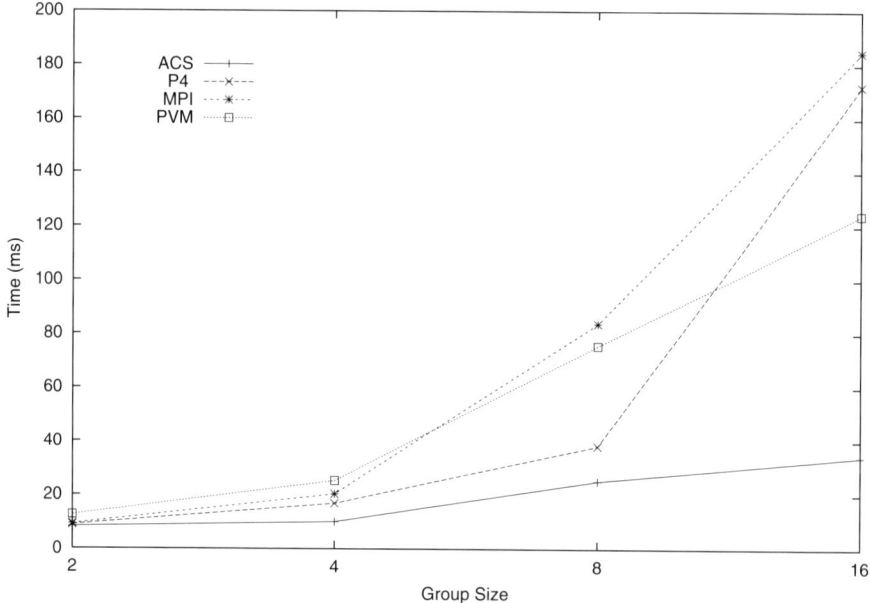

Fig. 2.15 Comparison of broadcasting performance (message = 8 kB).

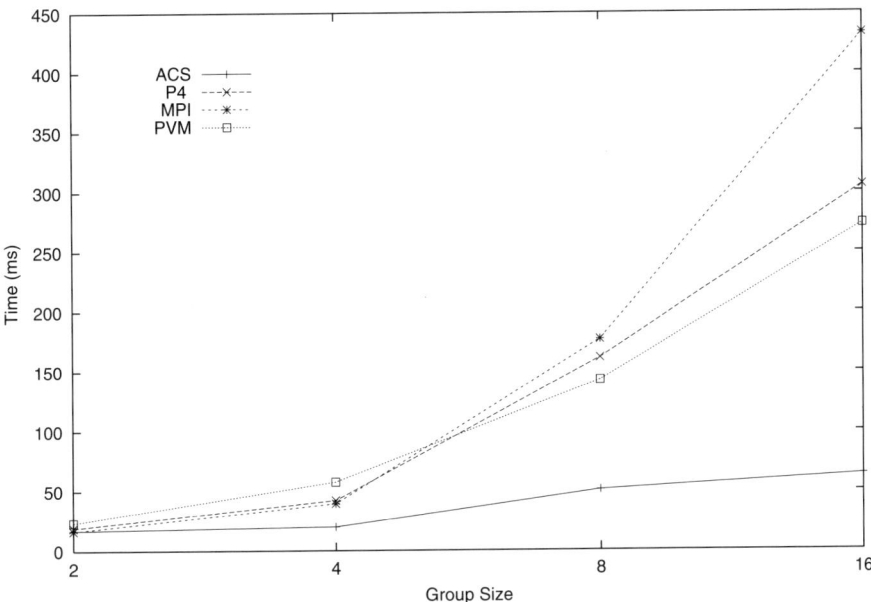

Fig. 2.16 Comparison of broadcasting performance (message = 16 kB).

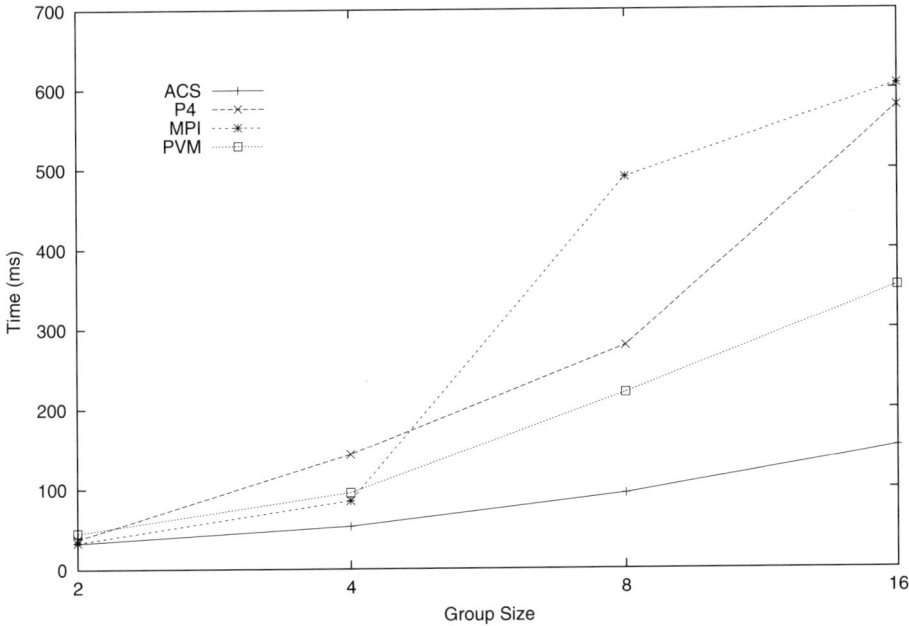

Fig. 2.17 Comparison of broadcasting performance (message = 32 kB).

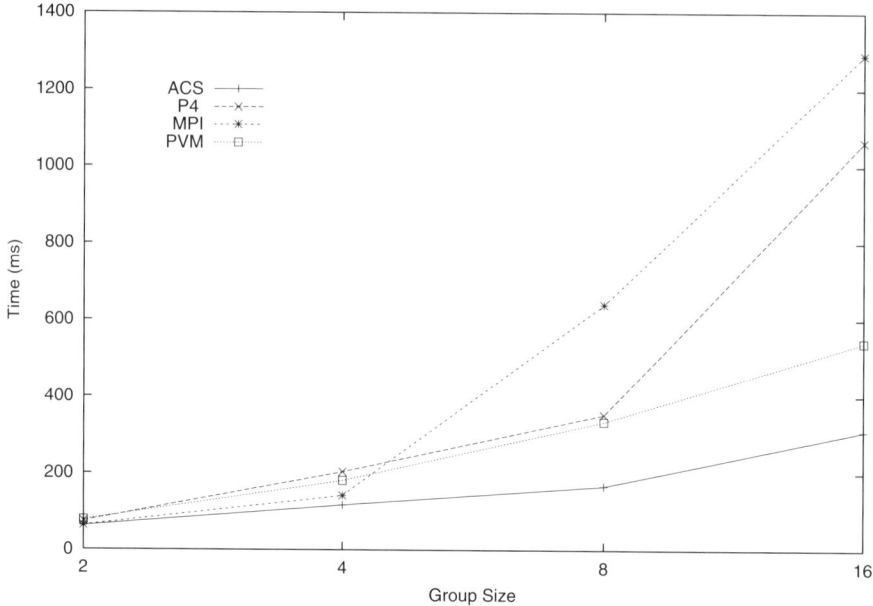

Fig. 2.18 Comparison of broadcasting performance (message = 64 kB).

for performing group communications (e.g., set up binary tree, set up routing information) is set up in advance by using separate connections, and the start-up time for the broadcasting operations is very small. Also, the tree-based broadcasting improves performance as the group size gets bigger. Consequently, the larger the message and group sizes, the bigger the difference of execution time between ACS and other tools. The performance of the p4 primitive (*p4_broadcast()*) is comparably good except for the message size of 32 kB for which the p4 performance rapidly gets worse as we increase the group size. One reason for this is that p4 shows a poorer performance for point-to-point communication with large message sizes than that of the Sun Solaris platform, as shown in Figure 2.9. The performance of the PVM primitive [*pvm_mcast()*] is not very good for small message sizes, and as the message and group size increase, the performance improves very little. In the *pvm_mcast()*, where the broadcasting operation is implemented by invoking a send primitive repeatedly, the performance is expected to increase linearly as we increase the group size. Moreover, *pvm_mcast()* constructs a multicasting group internally for every invocation of the primitive, which results in a high start-up time when transmitting small messages, as shown in Figures 2.12 and 2.13 (message size 1 byte and 1 kB). The MPI primitive [*MPI_Bcast()*] shows a performance comparable to that of ACS and p4 for relatively small message sizes (up to 4 kB) and small group sizes (up to eight group members), but it gets rapidly worse when it is running for large message sizes (over 8 kB) and large group sizes (over six members). This is because MPI and p4 perform their broadcasting by calling a point-to-point primitive repeatedly, which is not scalable.

2.7.3 Application Performance Benchmarking

We evaluate message-passing tools by comparing the execution time of four applications [i.e., fast Fourier transform (FFT), Joint Photographic Experts Group (JPEG) compression/decompression, parallel sorting with regular sampling (PSRS), back-propagation neural network (BPNN) learning, voting] that are commonly used in parallel and distributed systems. Most of the application results shown in Figures 2.19 to 2.28 are almost identical to the results of primitive performances shown in Figures 2.9 to 2.18. This means that the tool with the best performance in executing its communication primitives will also give the best performance results for a large number of network-centric applications. For example, ACS applications outperform other implementations, regardless of the platform used. For applications that require many communications with small messages (e.g., FFT), the performance improvement is modest; for applications with a large amount of data exchange, the performance improvement is greater (e.g., JPEG, PSRS). Furthermore, for applications where a lot of broadcasting with a large amount of data is performed

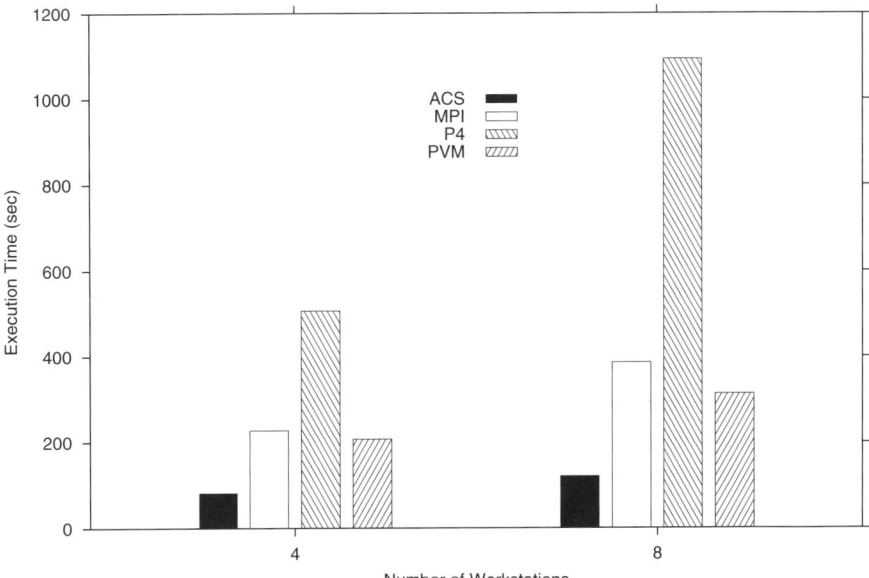

Fig. 2.19 Back-propagation neural network performance in a heterogeneous environment.

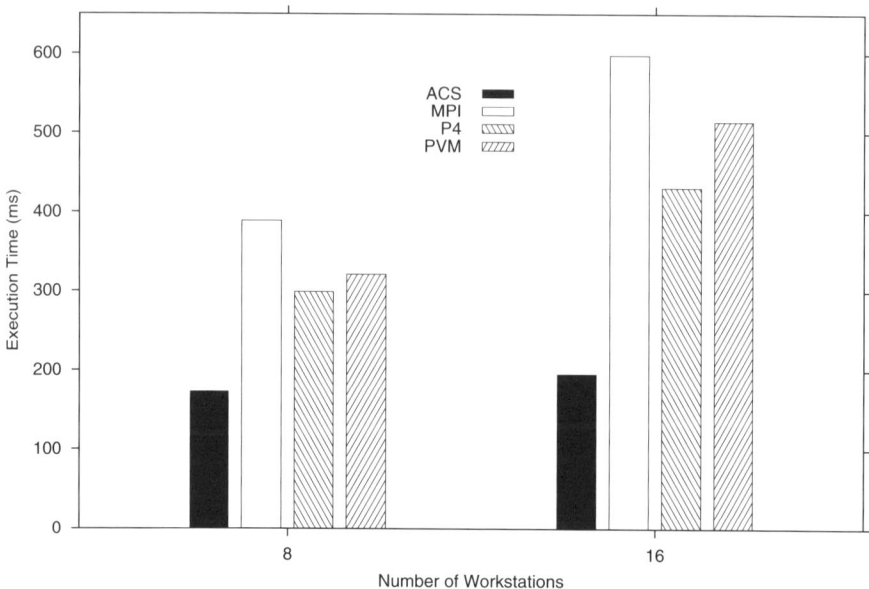

Fig. 2.20 Fast Fourier transform performance in a heterogeneous environment.

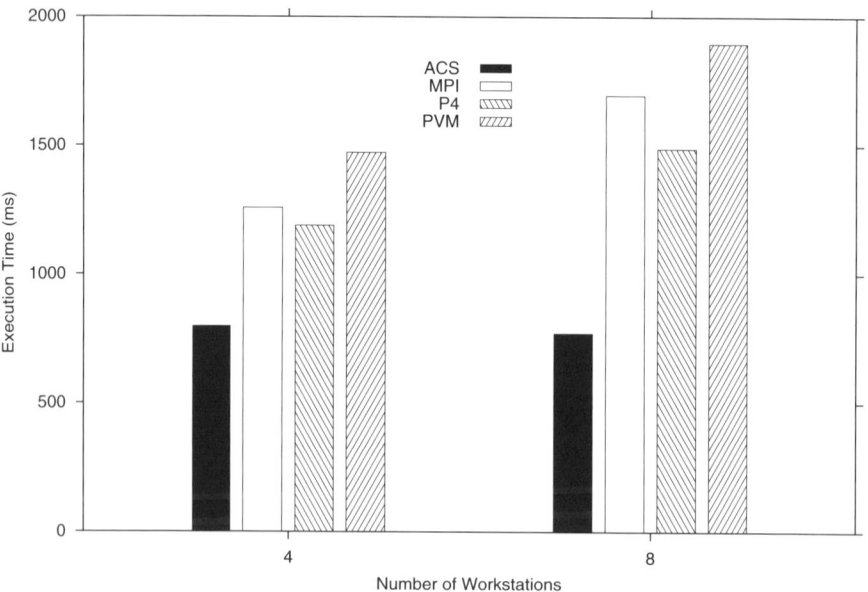

Fig. 2.21 JPEG performance in a heterogeneous environment.

EXPERIMENTAL RESULTS AND ANALYSIS 41

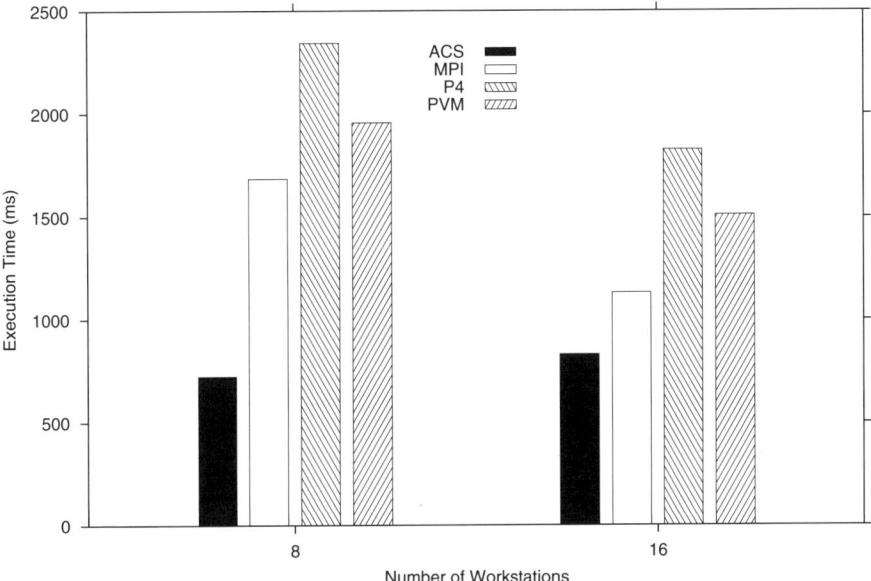

Fig. 2.22 Parallel sorting performance in a heterogeneous environment.

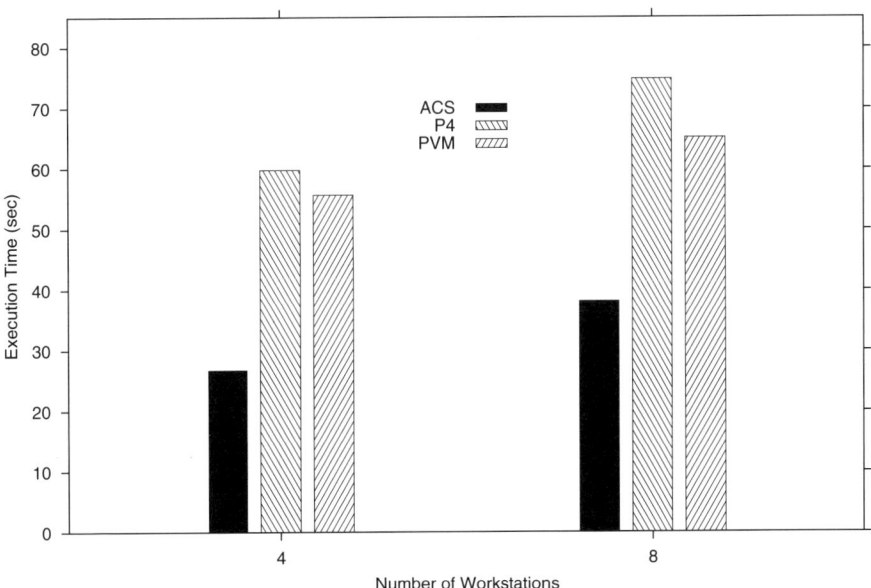

Fig. 2.23 Voting performance in a heterogeneous environment.

42 MESSAGE-PASSING TOOLS

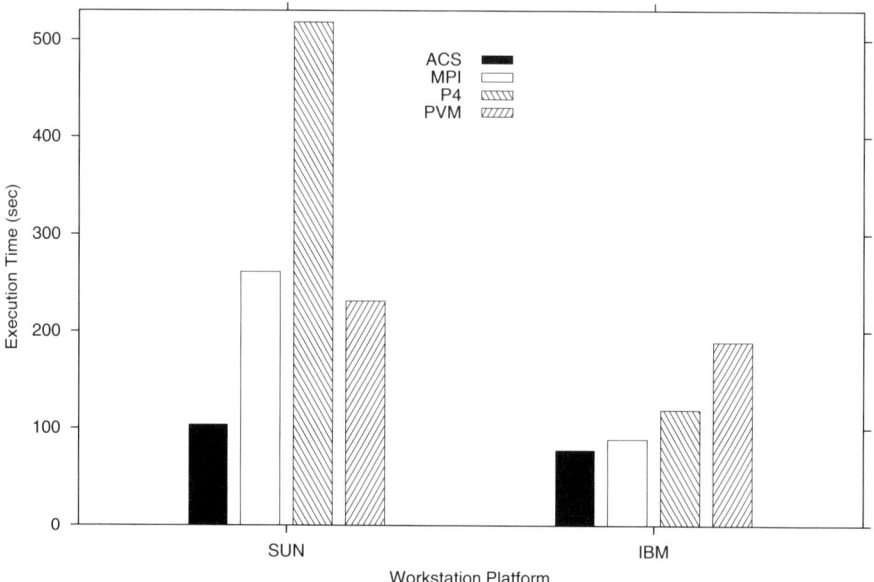

Fig. 2.24 Back-propagation neural network performance in a homogeneous environment.

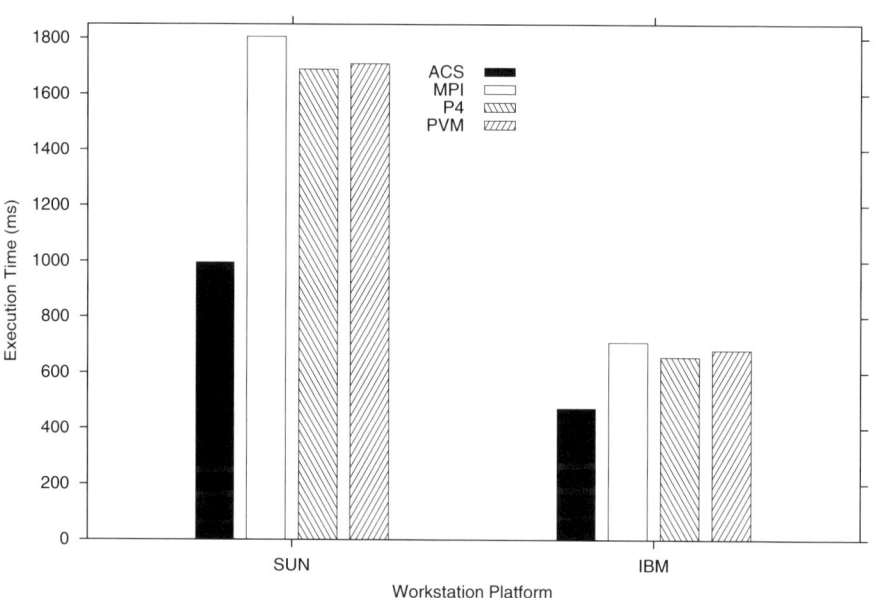

Fig. 2.25 Fast Fourier transform performance in a homogeneous environment.

EXPERIMENTAL RESULTS AND ANALYSIS 43

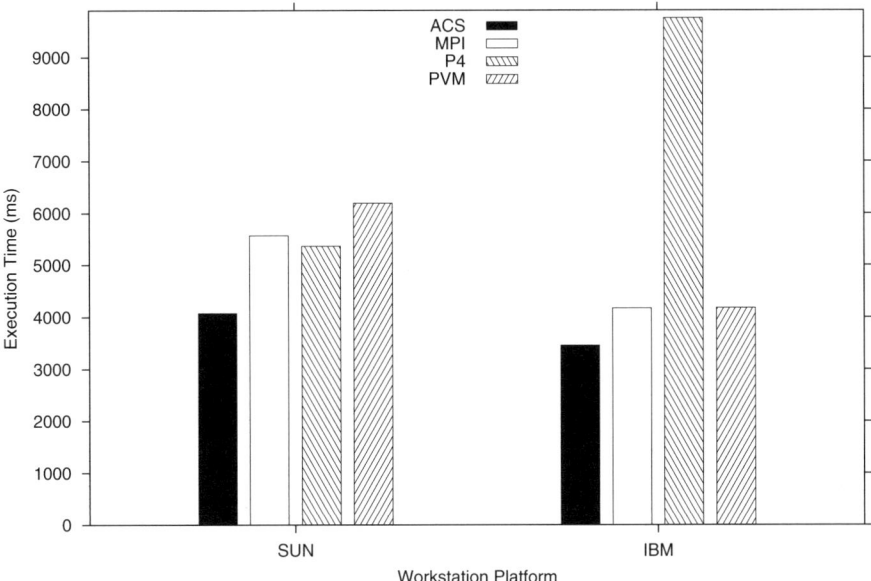

Fig. 2.26 JPEG performance in a homogeneous environment.

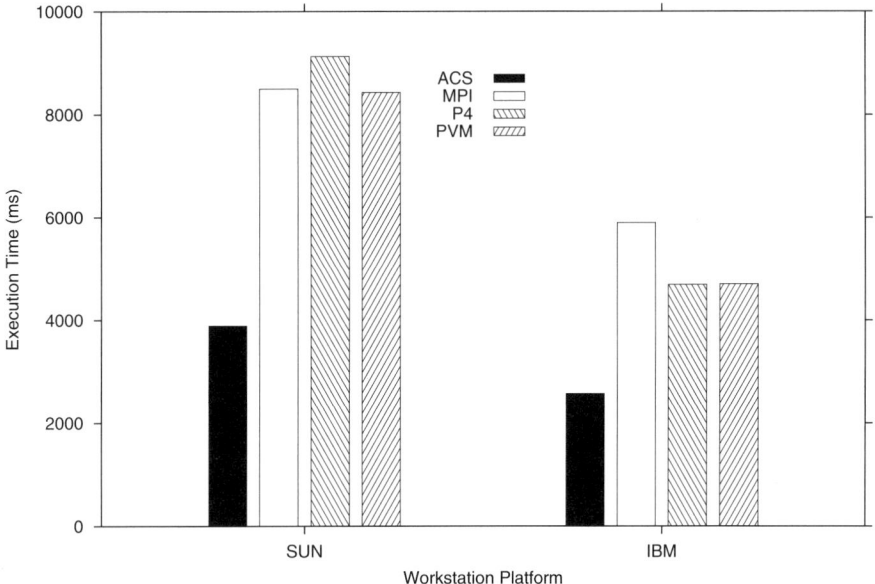

Fig. 2.27 Parallel sorting performance in a homogeneous environment.

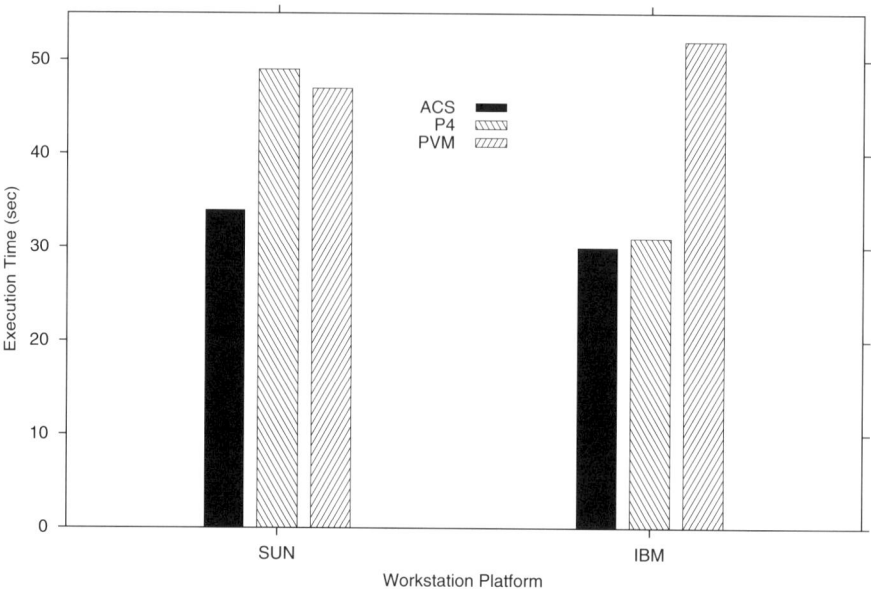

Fig. 2.28 Voting performance in a homogeneous environment.

(e.g., BPNN), ACS shows outstanding performance. We believe that most of the improvements of ACS in this case are due to the overlapping of communications and computations and the tree-based broadcasting primitive. Figures 2.19 through 2.23 compare the performance of each message-passing tool, using up to 16 Sun Solaris workstations interconnected by an Ethernet network.

In general, PVM implementations perform better than MPI and p4 implementations in a heterogeneous environment, whereas in a homogeneous environment the performance of MPI implementations is comparable to that of PVM implementations. The performance of a p4 implementation in a BPNN application is not good over four Sun Solaris workstations, but is better over four IBM AIX workstations, due to the fact that p4 has the worst broadcasting performance for large message sizes on a Sun Solaris platform, as shown in Figure 2.12 through 2.18.

2.7.4 Performance Results of Adaptive Schemes

Performance Result of Application-Aware Multicasting Assume that there is an application that has one group and three subgroups for multicasting requests (Figure 2.29). We evaluate the performance of this application with respect to two multicasting trees: (1) a binary tree algorithm, and (2) a two-level tree. These two multicasting trees are constructed when the *ACS_group_create()* is called:

Multicasting Application:
/* Assume $G0 = \{m_1, m_2,..., m_{16}\}$,
$G1 = \{m_1, m_2,..., m_8\}$, $G2 = \{m_9, m_{10}, m_{11}, m_{12}\}$,
$G3 = \{m_{15}, m_{16}\}$
  Thus, $G1, G2, G3 \subset G0$
  $|G0| = 16, |G1| = 8, |G2| = 4, |G3| = 2$
  msgsize = {1,8,16,32,64,128,256,512,1K,2K,4K,8K,
  16K,32K,64K,72K } */,
.....
  for i= 1 to10
    /* multicasts a message 10 times to group G0 */
    ACS_mcast(G0,int,10,msgbuf,msgsize);
  endfor
...
  for j= 1 to 25
    /* multicasts a message 25 times to group G1 */
    ACS_mcast(G1,int,10,msgbuf,msgsize);
  endfor
...
  for k= 1 to 50
    /* multicasts a message 50 times to group G2 */
    ACS_mcast(G2,int,10,msgbuf,msgsize);
  endfor
...
  for l= 1 to 100
    /* multicasts a message 100 times to group G3 */
    ACS_mcast(G3,int,10,msgbuf,msgsize);
  endfor
...
End Multicasting Application

Fig. 2.29 Application of ACS multicasting.

- Binary tree:
  *ACS_group_create(G0,TCP,none,err1,**Binary**,QoS)*
- Two-level tree:
  *ACS_group_create(G0,TCP,none,err1,**2-Level**,QoS)*

The corresponding trees for these two calls are shown in Figures 2.30 and 2.31, respectively.

We evaluate two different types of trees using the ACS multicasting communication service in order to:

1. Determine the performance difference between a binary tree and other trees.
2. Check the effectiveness of the multicasting performance function that we derived in Section 2.6.3.

46 MESSAGE-PASSING TOOLS

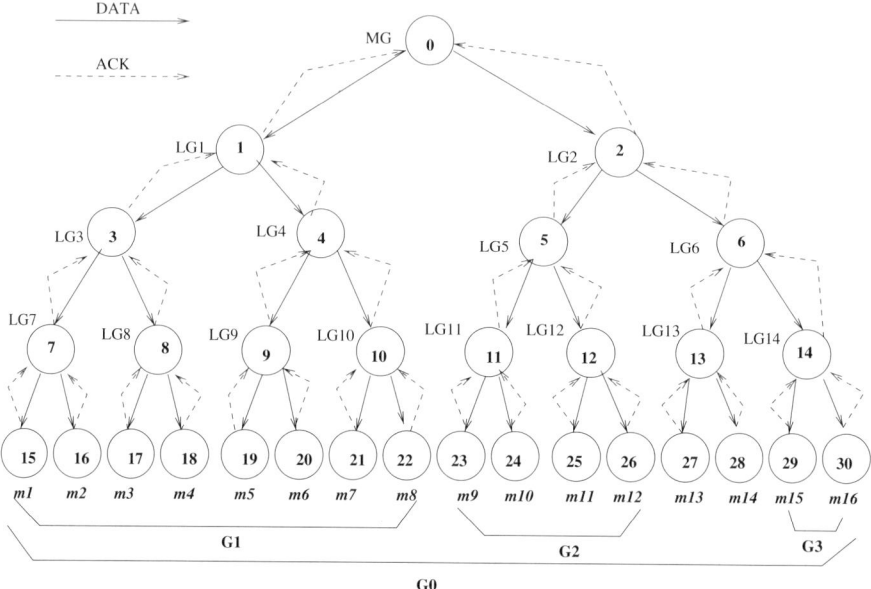

Fig. 2.30 Binary tree configuration.

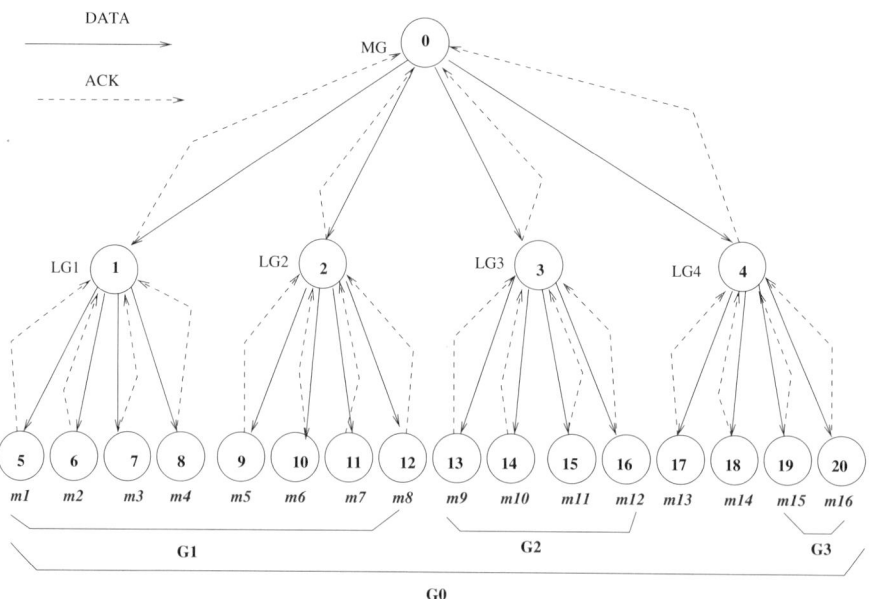

Fig. 2.31 Two level tree configuration.

In this example, we compare the performance of the ACS multicast algorithm with our analytical performance function $MP_k(m)$ for various message sizes. The multicast performance can be described in terms of the delays related to data transfer, message processing delays at each receiver node, and the delay related to acknowledgments for each group (G0, G1, G2, and G3), as shown in Table 2.1. We substitute the values of the delays related to $T_k^n(m)$, $D_k^n(m)$, and $A_k^n(c)$ (in Table 2.1) and get the MPFs for two different multicasting trees:

$$MP_2(m) = 740 \times t(m) + 315 \times o(m) + 740 \times a(c) + f_2(m)$$
$$MP_{2L}(m) = 370 \times t(m) + 410 \times o(m) + 370 \times a(c) + f_{2L}(m)$$

To evaluate the application multicast performance for the two trees, we use the data transfer time [$(T_k^n(m))$, receiving delay $(D_k^n(m))$, acknowledgment delay $(A_k^n(c))$, and congestion delay $(f_k(m))$] shown in Table 2.2.

The application performance for both the measurement and prediction functions are shown in Table 2.3. The error between predicted multicasting time and measurement is mostly within less than a 2% range. The multicast function can be used to predict the performance of the multicast algorithm and thus can be used to identify the appropriate multicast tree structure suitable for any given application.

TABLE 2.1 Group Multicast Component Delays

| Delay Time | | Group | | | | Total |
Time	Tree	G0	G1	G2	G3	Time
Data transfer	$T_2^{xi}(m)$	$4t(m) \times 10$	$4t(m) \times 25$	$4t(m) \times 50$	$4t(m) \times 100$	$740t(m)$
	$T_{2L}^{xi}(m)$	$2t(m) \times 10$	$2t(m) \times 25$	$2t(m) \times 50$	$2t(m) \times 100$	$370t(m)$
Receiving	$D_2^i(m)$	$4o(m) \times 10$	$3o(m) \times 25$	$2o(m) \times 50$	$1o(m) \times 100$	$315o(m)$
	$D_{2L}^i(m)$	$6o(m) \times 10$	$4o(m) \times 25$	$3o(m) \times 50$	$1o(m) \times 100$	$410o(m)$
Acknowledge	$A_2^i(c)$	$4a(c) \times 10$	$4a(c) \times 25$	$4a(c) \times 50$	$4a(c) \times 100$	$740a(c)$
	$A_{2L}^i(c)$	$2a(c) \times 10$	$2a(c) \times 25$	$2a(c) \times 50$	$2a(c) \times 100$	$370a(c)$

TABLE 2.2 Experimental Functions to Predict Application Multicast Performance (Milliseconds)

Time	1 B	64 B	1 kB	64 kB
$t(m)$	0.184	0.238	1.033	57.216
$o(m)$	0.036	0.037	0.040	45.937
$f_2(m)$	133.7137	191.2738	1,048.2170	13,408.0111
$f_{2L}(m)$	70.3830	110.9276	563.8934	8,855.4217

$a(4\,\text{B}) = 0.185\,\text{ms}$, where acknowledgment is 4 bytes only

TABLE 2.3 Application Multicast Performance Using Measurement and Analytical Techniques

Message Size (bytes)	Adaptive			Binary		
	Measured (ms)	Predict (ms)	Error (%)	Measured (ms)	Predict (ms)	Error (%)
1	225.434	221.673	1.668	420.610	418.114	0.594
8	228.649	229.664	0.444	423.889	424.177	0.068
16	235.464	234.819	0.274	431.246	431.068	0.041
32	254.525	251.831	1.058	456.688	460.861	1.037
64	276.409	282.608	2.243	504.950	515.949	2.178
128	328.443	324.557	1.183	598.115	591.269	1.145
256	750.875	720.197	4.086	788.042	787.010	0.131
512	774.726	834.860	7.762	1,196.972	1,200.553	0.299
1k	1,066.281	1,030.952	3.313	1,965.269	1,962.135	0.159
2k	2,212.446	2,169.975	1.920	3,499.494	3,493.880	0.160
4k	3,560.471	3,694.210	3.756	5,460.176	5,475.537	0.281
8k	6,575.173	6,459.763	1.755	9,057.693	9,047.092	0.117
16k	13,032.535	1,2680.382	2.702	17,841.220	17,597.816	1.364
32k	24,291.679	24,978.197	2.826	35,096.075	35,707.110	1.741
64k	49,023.240	48,927.978	0.194	70,447.749	70,354.916	0.132
72k	55,140.776	54,853.013	0.522	79,189.362	78,843.504	0.437

Performance of Application by Resource-Aware Scheduling Algorithm

We present some performance results of applications to show performance gains made by deploying adaptive schemes such as resource-aware scheduling.

Voting Application We have also compared the performance of ACS with other message-passing tools by measuring the execution time of a static voting application that requires intensive group communications. Replicating data at different locations is a common approach to achieving fault tolerance in distributed computing systems. One well-known technique to manage replicated data is a voting mechanism. The algorithm used in this experiment is based on the static voting scheme proposed by Gifford [29] and shown in Figure 2.32. In this experiment we assumed that there are 50 different files replicated at each node and that each file server process generates 500 *read* or *write* requests for arbitrary files. As we show in Figure 2.33, in a static voting application where the sizes of the broadcasting messages are small and the communications take place randomly, the performance of resource-aware multicasting ACS is comparable to that of non-resource-aware multicasting ACS for small groups. However, the performance gap gets wider as we increase group size. We believe that most of the improvements in the ACS resource aware scheduling algorithm are also due to utilizing the heterogeneity in computers.

Linear Equation Solver A linear equation solver application finds the solution vector x in the equation $Ax = b$, where A is a known $N \times N$ matrix and b is a known vector. The problem size in the experiments is 128×128. Each task was executed with one, two, and four Solaris machines interconnected by ATM over IP and Ethernet networks. The performance results of the individual tasks [LU (LU decomposition), INV (matrix inversion), and MULT (matrix multiplication)] that were executed over different networks are shown in Table 2.4.

LU gives better performance for sequential execution than do the two- and four-node cases, because its implementation is communication-bound. For an $N \times N$ problem size and P processors, an LU task requires N/P all-to-all communication and two one-to-all communication steps. For an INV task, four-node is the best, and for a MULT task, two-node is the best among others, since INV and MULT implementations require communication only for the data distribution and result gathering phases. Thus their implementations require only two one-to-all communication steps. An ATM-based network gives better results than an Ethernet-based case for all task implementations. According to these results, if the ACS user chooses one node for LU, four nodes for INV, and two nodes for MULT while developing his/her application, this combination will achieve a better performance than will other possibilities. These results show that the performance of any application can be improved significantly by the resource-aware scheduling algorithm provided by our newly developed ACS.

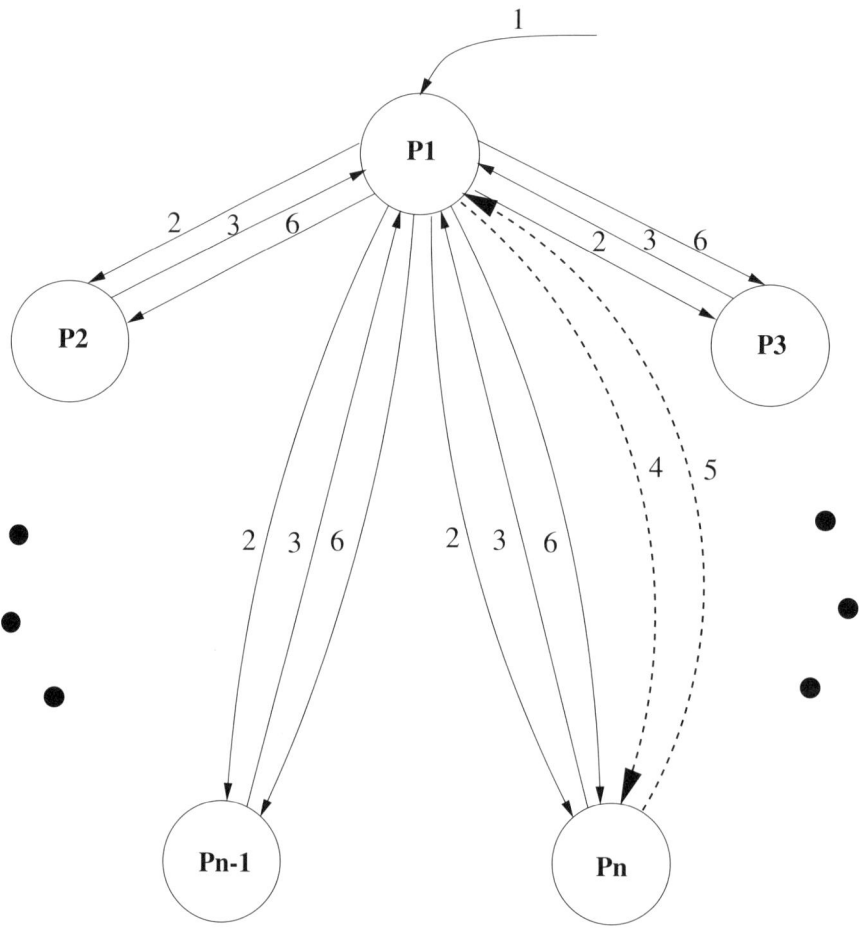

1=Read/Write Request, 2=Vote_Request, 3=Version Number and Votes
4=Request Latest Copy, 5=Return Latest Copy, 6=Release_Lock

Fig. 2.32 Static voting algorithm.

2.8 CONCLUSIONS

Applications running on networked workstations must use the underlying network to communicate with their parties on remote machines; thus they should be able to establish communication channels via a protocol for exchanging data. Message-passing tools have been developed to provide a reliable and efficient data transmission mechanism on top of the underlying network. In addition, they should be able to offer programming interfaces so that users can easily develop their applications. A summary of the usefulness and efficiency of popular message-passing tools is shown in Table 2.5.

CONCLUSIONS

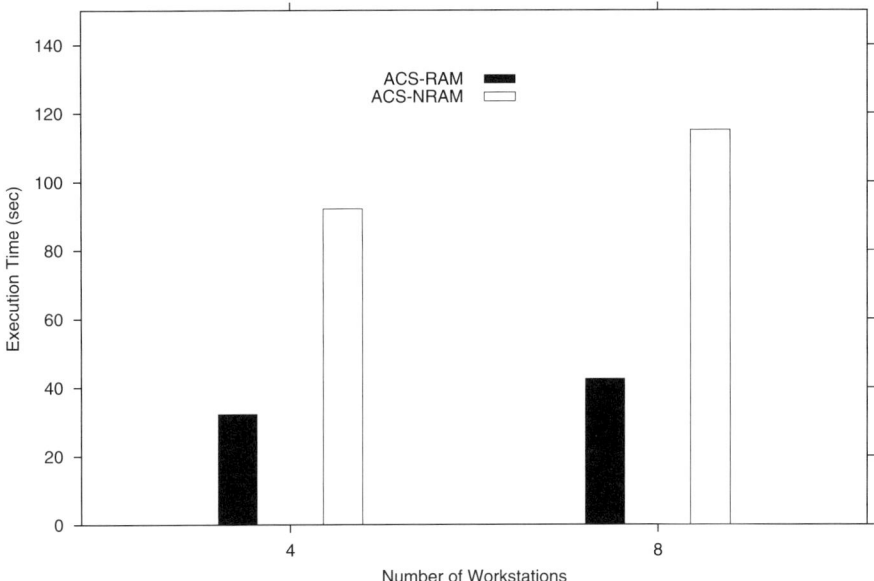

Fig. 2.33 Comparison of application performance.

TABLE 2.4 Performance of Linear Equation Solver Tasks on ATM and Ethernet (Milliseconds)

No. of Nodes	LU Ethernet	LU ATM	INV Ethernet	INV ATM	MULT Ethernet	MULT ATM
1	226,073	217,191	280,626	278,534	49,903	48,392
2	236,180	233,573	276,193	273,654	49,205	44,091
4	253,731	253,089	274,421	270,139	53,088	50,311

TABLE 2.5 Summary of Message-Passing Tools

Feature	p4	PVM	MPI	Madeleine	ACS
Richness of communication	$\sqrt{}_{ok}$	$\sqrt{}_{rich}$	$\sqrt{}_{very\ rich}$	$\sqrt{}_{poor}$	$\sqrt{}_{ok}$
Simplicity	$\sqrt{}$	$\sqrt{}$	$\sqrt{}$	$\sqrt{}$	$\sqrt{}$
Efficiency	$\sqrt{}_{low}$	$\sqrt{}_{low}$	$\sqrt{}_{ok}$	$\sqrt{}_{low}$	$\sqrt{}_{high}$
Fault tolerance		$\sqrt{}_{ok}$			$\sqrt{}_{ok}$
Reliable group communication		$\sqrt{}_{low}$	$\sqrt{}_{ok}$		$\sqrt{}_{high}$
Adaptability				$\sqrt{}_{ok}$	$\sqrt{}_{high}$
Security			$\sqrt{}_{low}$		$\sqrt{}_{ok}$
Heterogeneity		$\sqrt{}_{ok}$	$\sqrt{}_{ok}$		$\sqrt{}_{high}$
Portability		$\sqrt{}_{ok}$	$\sqrt{}_{high}$		$\sqrt{}_{high}$

REFERENCES

1. I. Ra, S. Park, and S. Hariri, Design and evaluation of an adaptive communication system for high performance distributed computing applications, *Proceedings of the International Workshop on Cluster Computing—Technologies, Environments, and Applications (CC-TEA'2000)*, Las Vegas, NV, June 2000.
2. I. Ra, S. Hariri, and C. Raghavendra, An adaptive communication system for heterogeneous network computing, *Proceedings of the 10th Heterogeneous Computing Workshop (HCW 2001)*, San Francisco, April 2001.
3. J. Kubiatowicz and A. Agarwal, The anatomy of a message in the Alewife multiprocessor, *Proceedings of the International Conference on Supercomputing (ICS 1993)*, pp. 195–206, July 1993.
4. W. Codenie, K. D. Hondt, T. D'Hondt, and P. Steyaert, Agora: message passing as a foundation for exploring OO language concepts, *SIGPLAN Notices*, Vol. 29, No. 12, pp. 48–57, December 1994.
5. E. Arnould, F. Bitz, E. Cooper, H. T. Kung, R. Sansom, and P. Steenkiste, The design of Nectar: a network backplane for heterogeneous multicomputers, *Proceedings of the 3rd International Conference on Architectural Support for Programming Languages and Operating Systems*, pp. 205–216, April 1989.
6. ATM Forum, *ATM User–Network Interface Specification, Version 3.1*, Prentice Hall, Upper Saddle River, NJ, 1994.
7. T. Sterling, D. J. Becker, D. Savarese, U. A. Ranawake, and C. V. Packer, BEOWULF: a parallel workstation for scientific computation. *Proceedings of the 24th International Conference on Parallel Processing*, Oconomowoc, WI, August 1995.
8. L. Prylli and B. Tourancheau, BIP: a new protocol designed for high performance networking on Myrinet, *Proceedings of the Workshop PC-NOW, IPPS/SPDP'98*, LNCS 1388, pp. 472–485, Springer-Verlag, Orlando, FL, April 1998.
9. R. Bhoedjang, T. Ruhl, R. Hofman, K. Langendoen, H. Bal, and F. Kaashoek, Panda: a portable platform to support parallel programming languages, *Proceedings of the Symposium on Experiences with Distributed and Microprocessor Systems IV*, pp. 213–226, September 1993.
10. K. Birman, R. Cooper, T. A. Joseph, K. P. Kane, F. Schmuck, and M. Wood, *Isis—A Distributed Programming Environment: User's Guide and Reference Manual*, Cornell University, Sthaca, NY, June 1990.
11. R. Butler and E. Lusk, Monitors, message, and clusters: the p4 parallel programming system, *Parallel Computing*, Vol. 20, pp. 547–564, April 1994.
12. K. L. Johnson, M. F. Kasshoek, and D. A. Wallach, CRL: high-performance all software distributed shared memory. *Proceedings of the 15th Symposium on Operating Systems Principles*, December 1995.
13. C. Dalton, G. Watson, D. Banks, C. Calamvokis, A. Edwards, and J. Lumley, Afterburner, *IEEE Network*, Vol. 7, No. 4, pp. 36–43, July 1993.
14. D. Dolev and D. Malki, The Transis approach to high availability cluster communication, *Communications of the ACM*, Vol. 39, No. 4, pp. 64–70, 1996.
15. P. Druschel, L. L. Peterson, and B. S. Davie, Experiences with a high-speed network adaptor: a software perspective, *Proceedings of SIGCOMM*, 1994.

16. T. Eicken, V. Avula, A. Basu, and V. Buch, Low-latency communication over ATM networks using active messages, *IEEE Micro*, Vol. 15, No. 1, pp. 46–53, February 1995.
17. M. Welsh, A. Basu, and T. Eicken, Low-latency communication over fast Ethernet, *Proceedings Euro-Par '96*, Lyon, France, August 1996.
18. T. Eicken, A. Basu, V. Buch, and W. Vogels, U-Net: a user-level network interface for parallel and distributed computing, *Proceedings of the 15th ACM Symposium on Operating Systems Principles*, December 1995.
19. T. Eicken, D. Culler, S. Goldstein, and K. Schauser, Active messages: a mechanism for integrated communication and computation, *Proceedings of the 19th International Symposium on Computer Architecture*, pp. 256–266, May 1992.
20. E. Felton, R. Alpert, A. Bilas, M. Blumrich, D. Clark, S. Damianakis, C. Dubnicki, L. Iftode, and K. Li, Early experience with message-passing on the SHRIMP multicomputer, *Proceedings of the 23rd International Symposium on Computer Architecture*, pp. 296–307, May 1996.
21. A. Ferrari and V. Sunderam, TPVM: distributed concurrent computing with lightweight processes, *Proceedings of the 4th IEEE International Symposium on High Performance Distributed Computing*, pp. 211–218, August 1995.
22. M. Fischler, The Fermilab lattice supercomputing project, *Nuclear Physics*, Vol. 9, pp. 571–576, 1989.
23. I. Foster, C. Kesselman, and S. Tuecke, The Nexus approach to integrating multithreading and communication, *Journal of Parallel and Distributed Computing*, 1996.
24. I. Foster, J. Geisler, C. Kesselman, and S. Tuecke, Managing multiple communication methods in high-performance networked computing systems, *Journal of Parallel and Distributed Computing*, Vol. 40, pp. 35–48, 1997.
25. D. Culler et al., *Generic Active Message Interface Specification*, Technical Report, Department of Computer Science, University of California, Berkeley, CA, 1995.
26. G. Ciaccio, Optimal communication performance on fast ethernet with GAMMA, *Proceedings of the Workshop PCNOW, IPPS/SPDP'98*, LNCS 1388, pp. 534–548, Orlando, FL, April 1998, Springer-Verlag, New York, 1998.
27. G. Geist, A. Beguelin, J. Dongarra, W. Jiang, R. Mancheck, and V. Sunderam, *PVM—Parallel Virtual Machine: A User's Guide and Tutorial for Networked Parallel Computing*, MIT Press, Cambridge, MA, 1994.
28. B. Gropp, R. Lusk, T. Skjellum, and N. Doss, *Portable MPI Model Implementation*, Argonne National Laboratory, Angonne, IL, July 1994.
29. D. K. Gifford, Weighed voting for replicated data, *Proceedings of the 7th ACM Symposium on Operating System*, pp. 150–162, December 1979.
30. M. Haines, D. Cronk, and P. Mehrotra, On the design of Chant: a talking threads package, *Proceedings of Supercomputing '94*, pp. 350–359, November 1994.
31. R. Harrison, Portable tools and applications for parallel computers, *International Journal of Quantum Chemistry*, Vol. 40, pp. 847–863, February 1990.
32. IBM Corporation, *8260 Nways Multiprotocol Switching Hub*, White Paper 997, IBM, Armonk, NY, 1997.
33. IBM Corporation, *IBM 8285 Nways ATM Workgroup Switch: Installation and User'd Guide*, IBM Publication SA-33-0381-01, IBM, Armonk, NY, June 1996.

34. L. Kleinrock, The latency/bandwidth tradeoff in gigabit networks, *IEEE Communication*, Vol. 30, No. 4, pp. 36–40, April 1992.
35. H. Burkhardt et al., *Overview of the KSR1 Computer System*, Technical Report KSR-TR-9202001, Kendall Square Research, Boston, February 1992.
36. M. Laubach, *Classical IP and ARP over ATM*, Internet RFC-1577, January 1994.
37. M. Lauria and A. Chien, MPI-FM: high performance MPI on workstation clusters, *Journal of Parallel and Distributed Computing*, February 1997.
38. J. Lawton, J. Bronsnan, M. Doyle, S. Riordain, and T. Reddin, Building a high-performance message-passing system for Memory Channel clusters, *Digital Technical Journal*, Vol. 8, No. 2, pp. 96–116, 1996.
39. B. Lewis and D. Berg, *Threads Primer: A Guide to Multithreaded Programming*, SunSoft Press/Prentice Hall, Upper Saddle River, NJ, 1996.
40. R. Martin, HPAM: an active message layer for network of HP workstations, *Proceedings of Hot Interconnects II*, August 1994.
41. L. Bougé, J. Méhaut, and R. Namyst, Efficient communications in multithreaded runtime systems, *Proceedings of the 3rd Workshop on Runtime Systems for Parallel Programming (RTSPP '99)*, Lecture Notes in Computer Science, No. 1586, pp. 468–482, San Juan, Puerto Rico, April 1999.
42. O. Aumage, L. Bouge, and R. Namyst, A portable and adaptive multi-protocol communication library for multithreaded runtime systems, *Proceedings of the 4th Workshop on Runtime Systems for Parallel Programming (RTSPP '00)*, Lecture Notes in Computer Science, No. 1800, pp. 1136–1143, Cancun, Mexico, May 2000.
43. B. D. Fleisch and G. J. Popek, Mirage: A coherent distributed shared memory design, *Proceedings of the 12th ACM Symposium on Operating Systems Principles (SOSP'89)*, pp. 211–223, December 1989.
44. M. Kraimer, T. Coleman, and J. Sullivan, Message passing facility industry pack support, http://www.aps.anl.gov/asd/control/epics/EpicsDocumentation/HardwareManuals/mpf/mpf.html, Argonne National Laboratory, Argonne, IL, April 1999.
45. L. Moser, P. Melliar-Smith, D. Agarwal, R. Budhia, and C. Lingley-Papadopoulos, Totem: a fault-tolerant multicast group communication system, *Communications of the ACM*, Vol. 39, No. 4, pp. 54–63, 1996.
46. MPI Forum, MPI: a message passing interface. *Proceedings of Supercomputing '93*, pp. 878–883, November 1993.
47. F. Mueller, A Library Implementation of POSIX Threads under UNIX, *Proceedings of USENIX Conference Winter '93*, pp. 29–41, January 1993.
48. R. D. Russel and P. J. Hatcher, Efficient kernel support for reliable communication, *Proceedings of 1998 ACM Symposium on Applied Computing*, Atlanta, GA, February 1998.
49. B. Nelson, Remote procedure call, Ph.D dissertation, Carnegie-Mellon University, Pittsburgh, PA, CMU-CS-81-119, 1981.
50. J. M. Squyres, B. V. McCandless, and A. Lumsdaine, Object oriented MPI: a class library for the message passing interface, *Proceedings of the '96 Parallel Object-Oriented Methods and Applications Conference*, Santa Fe, NM, February 1996.
51. P. Marenzoni, G. Rimassa, M. Vignail, M. Bertozzi, G. Conte, and P. Rossi, An operating system support to low-overhead communications in NOW clusters, *Proceed-*

ings of the First International CANPC, LNCS 1199, Springer-Verlag, New York, pp. 130–143, February 1997.

52. S. Pakin, M. Lauria, and A. Chien, High performance messaging on workstations: Illinois fast messages (FM) for Myrinet, *Proceedings of Supercomputing '95*, December 1995.

53. S. Park, S. Hariri, Y. Kim, J. Harris, and R. Yadav, NYNET communication system (NCS): a multithreaded message passing tool over ATM network, *Proceedings of the 5th International Symposium on High Performance Distributed Computing*, pp. 460–469, August 1996.

54. P. Pierce, *The NX/2 Operating System*.

55. R. Renesse, T. Hickey, and K. Birman, *Design and Performance of Horus: A Light-weight Group Communications System*, Technical Report TR94-1442, Cornell University, Sthaca, NY, 1994.

56. A. Reuter, U. Geuder, M. Hdrdtner, B. Wvrner, and R. Zink, GRIDS: a parallel programming system for Grid-based algorithms, *Computer Journal*, Vol. 36, No. 8, 1993.

57. S. Rodrigues, T. Anderson, and D. Culler, High-performance local area communication with fast sockets, *Proceedings of USENIX Conference '97*, 1997.

58. T. Ruhl, H. Bal, and G. Benson, Experience with a portability layer for implementing parallel programming systems, *Proceedings of the International Conference on Parallel and Distributed Processing Techniques and Applications*, pp. 1477–1488, 1996.

59. D. C. Schmit, The adaptive communication environment, *Proceedings of the 11th and 12th Sun User Group Conference*, San Francisco, June 1993.

60. D. Schmidt and T. Suda, Transport system architecture services for high-performance communication systems, *IEEE Journal on Selected Areas in Communications*, Vol. 11, No. 4, pp. 489–506, May 1993.

61. H. Helwagner and A. Reinefeld, eds., *SCI: Scalable Coherent Interface*, Springer-Verlag, New York, 1999.

62. E. Simon, *Distributed Information Systems*, McGraw-Hill, New York, 1996.

63. W. Stevens, *UNIX Network Programming*, Prentice Hall, Upper Saddle River, NJ, 1998.

64. V. Sunderam, PVM: a framework for parallel distributed computing, *Concurrency: Practice and Experience*, Vol. 2, No. 4, pp. 315–340, December 1990.

65. Thinking Machine Corporation, *CMMD Reference Manual*, TMC, May 1993.

66. C. Thekkath, H. M. Levy, and E. D. Lazowska, Separating data and control transfer in distributed operating systems, *Proceedings of ASPLOS*, 1994.

67. C. Amza, A. L. Cox, S. Dwarkadas, P. Keleher, H. Lu, R. Rajamony, W. Yu, and W. Zwaenepoel, TreadMarks: shared memory computing on networks of workstations, *IEEE Computer*, Vol. 29, No. 2, pp. 18–28, February 1996.

68. D. Dunning, G. Regnier, G. McAlpine, D. Cameron, B. Shubert, F. Berry, A.-M. Merritt, E. Gronke, and C. Dodd, The virtual interface architecture, *IEEE Micro*, pp. 66–75, March–April 1998.

69. T. Warschko, J. Blum, and W. Tichy, The ParaStation Project: using workstations as building blocks for parallel computing, *Proceedings of the International Conference*

on Parallel and Distributed Processing, Techniques and Applications (PDPTA'96), pp. 375–386, August 1996.

70. R. Whaley, *Basic Linear Algebra Communication Subprograms: Analysis and Implementation Across Multiple Parallel Architectures*, LAPACK Working Note 73, Technical Report, University of Tennessee, Knoxville, TN, 1994.

71. H. Zhou and A. Geist, LPVM: a step towards multithread PVM, *http://www.epm.ornl.gov/zhou/ltpvm/ltpvm.html*.

CHAPTER 3

Distributed Shared Memory Tools

M. PARASHAR and S. CHANDRA

Department of Electrical and Computer Engineering, Rutgers University, Piscataway, NJ

3.1 INTRODUCTION

Distributed shared memory (DSM) is a software abstraction of shared memory on a distributed memory multiprocessor or cluster of workstations. The DSM approach provides the illusion of a global shared address space by implementing a layer of shared memory abstraction on a physically distributed memory system. DSM systems represent a successful hybrid of two parallel computer classes: shared memory multiprocessors and distributed computer systems. They provide the shared memory abstraction in systems with physically distributed memories, and consequently, combine the advantages of both approaches. DSM expands the notion of virtual memory to different nodes. DSM facility permits processes running at separate hosts on a network to share virtual memory in a transparent fashion, as if the processes were actually running on a single processor.

Two major issues dominate the performance of DSM systems: communication overhead and computation overhead. Communication overhead is incurred in order to access data from remote memory modules and to keep the DSM-managed data consistent. Computation overhead comes in a variety of forms in different systems, including:

- Page fault and signal handling
- System call overheads to protect and unprotect memory
- Thread/context switching overheads

Tools and Environments for Parallel and Distributed Computing, Edited by Salim Hariri and Manish Parashar
ISBN 0-471-33288-7 Copyright © 2004 John Wiley & Sons, Inc.

58 DISTRIBUTED SHARED MEMORY TOOLS

- Copying data to/from communication buffers
- Time spent on blocked synchronous I/Os

The various DSM systems available today, both commercially and academically, can be broadly classified as shown in Figure 3.1.

The effectiveness of DSM systems in providing parallel and distributed systems as a cost-effective option for high-performance computation is qualified by four key properties: simplicity, portability, efficiency, and scalability.

- *Simplicity*. DSM systems provide a relatively easy to use and uniform model for accessing all shared data, whether local or remote. Beyond such uniformity and ease of use, shared memory systems should provide simple programming interfaces that allow them to be platform and language independent.
- *Portability*. Portability of the distributed shared memory programming environment across a wide range of platforms and programming environments is important, as it obviates the labor of having to rewrite large, complex application codes. In addition to being portable across space, however, good DSM systems should also be portable across time (able to run on future systems), as it enables stability.
- *Efficiency*. For DSM systems to achieve widespread acceptance, they should be capable of providing high efficiency over a wide range of applications, especially challenging applications with irregular and/or unpre-

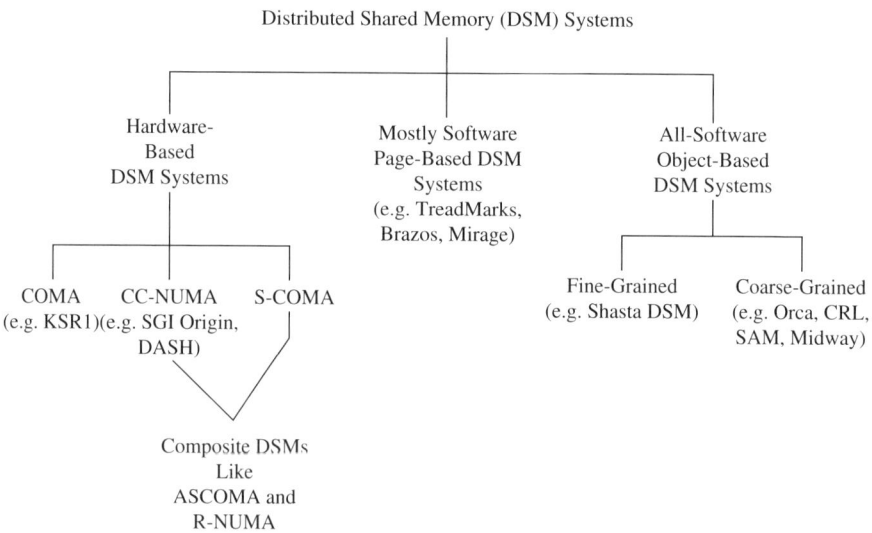

Fig. 3.1 Taxonomy of DSM systems.

dictable communication patterns, without requiring much programming effort.
- *Scalability.* To provide a preferable option for high-performance computing, good DSM systems today should be able to run efficiently on systems with hundreds (or potentially thousands) of processors. Shared memory systems that scale well to large systems offer end users yet another form of stability—knowing that applications running on small to medium-scale platforms could run unchanged and still deliver good performance on large-scale platforms.

3.2 CACHE COHERENCE

DSM systems facilitate global access to remote data in a straightforward manner from a programmer's point of view. However, the difference in access times (latencies) of local and remote memories in some of these architectures is significant (could differ by a factor of 10 or higher). Uniprocessors hide these long main memory access times by the use of local caches at each processor. Implementing (multiple) caches in a multiprocessor environment presents a challenging problem of maintaining cached data coherent with the main memory (possibly remote), that is, *cache coherence* (Figure 3.2).

3.2.1 Directory-Based Cache Coherence

The directory-based cache coherence protocols use a directory to keep track of the caches that share the same cache line. The individual caches are inserted and deleted from the directory to reflect the use or rollout of shared cache lines. This directory is also used to purge (invalidate) a cached line that is necessitated by a remote write to a shared cache line.

Time	Processor P1	Processor P2
↓	$x = 0$ $x = a$ ⋮ $y = c$	$y = 0$ $y = b$ ⋮ $x = d$

Fig. 3.2 Coherence problem when shared data are cached by multiple processors. Suppose that initially $x = y = 0$ and both P1 and P2 have cached copies of x and y. If coherence is not maintained, P1 does not get the changed value of y and P2 does not get the changed value of x.

The directory can either be centralized, or distributed among the local nodes in a scalable shared memory machine. Generally, a centralized directory is implemented as a bit map of the individual caches, where each bit set represents a shared copy of a particular cache line. The advantage of this type of implementation is that the entire sharing list can be found simply by examining the appropriate bit map. However, the centralization of the directory also forces each potential reader and writer to access the directory, which becomes an instant bottleneck. Additionally, the reliability of such a scheme is an issue, as a fault in the bit map would result in an incorrect sharing list.

The bottleneck presented by the centralized structure is avoided by distributing the directory. This approach also increases the reliability of the scheme. The *distributed directory scheme* (also called the *distributed pointer protocol*) implements the sharing list as a distributed linked list. In this implementation, each directory entry (being that of a cache line) points to the next member of the sharing list. The caches are inserted and deleted from the linked list as necessary. This avoids having an entry for every node in the directory.

3.3 SHARED MEMORY CONSISTENCY MODELS

In addition to the use of caches, scalable shared memory systems migrate or replicate data to local processors. Most scalable systems choose to replicate (rather than migrate) data, as this gives the best performance for a wide range of application parameters of interest. With replicated data, the provision of *memory consistency* becomes an important issue. The shared memory scheme (in hardware or software) must control replication in a manner that preserves the abstraction of a single address-space shared memory.

The shared memory consistency model refers to how local updates to shared memory are communicated to the processors in the system. The most intuitive model of shared memory is that a read should always return the last value written. However, the idea of the last value written is not well defined, and its different interpretations have given rise to a variety of memory consistency models: namely, sequential consistency, processor consistency, release consistency, entry consistency, scope consistency, and variations of these.

Sequential consistency implies that the shared memory appears to all processes as if they were executing on a single multiprogrammed processor. In a sequentially consistent system, one processor's update to a shared data value is reflected in every other processor's memory before the updating processor is able to issue another memory access. The simplicity of this model, however, exacts a high price, since sequentially consistent memory systems preclude many optimizations, such as reordering, batching, or coalescing. These optimizations reduce the performance impact of having distributed memories and have led to a class of weakly consistent models.

A weaker memory consistency model offers fewer guarantees about memory consistency, but it ensures that a well-behaved program executes as though it were running on a sequentially consistent memory system. Again, the definition of *well behaved* varies according to the model. For example, in *processor-consistent systems*, a load or store is globally performed when it is performed with respect to all processors. A load is performed with respect to a processor when no write by that processor can change the value returned by the load. A store is performed with respect to a processor when a load by that processor will return the value of the store. Thus, the programmer may not assume that all memory operations are performed in the same order at all processors.

Memory consistency requirements can be relaxed by exploiting the fact that most parallel programs define their own high-level consistency requirements. In many programs, this is done by means of explicit synchronization operations on synchronization objects such as lock acquisition and barrier entry. These operations impose an ordering on access to data within the program. In the absence of such operations, a program is in effect relinquishing all control over the order and atomicity of memory operations to the underlying memory system. In a *release consistency model*, the processor issuing a *releasing synchronization operation* guarantees that its previous updates will be performed at other processors. Similarly, a processor *acquiring synchronization operation* guarantees that other processors' updates have been performed locally. A releasing synchronization operation signals other processes that shared data are available, while an acquiring operation signals that shared data are needed. In an *entry consistency model*, data are guarded to be consistent only after an *acquiring synchronization operation* and only the data known to be guarded by the acquired object are guaranteed to be consistent. Thus, a processor must not access a shared item until it has performed a synchronization operation on the items associated with the synchronization object.

Programs with good behavior do not assume a stronger consistency guarantee from the memory system than is actually provided. For each model, the definition of good behavior places demands on the programmer to ensure that a program's access to the shared data conforms to that model's consistency rules. These rules add an additional dimension of complexity to the already difficult task of writing new parallel programs and porting old ones. But the additional programming complexity provides greater control over communication and may result in higher performance. For example, with entry consistency, communication between processors occurs only when a processor acquires a synchronization object. A large variety of DSM system models have been proposed over the years with one or multiple consistency models, different granularities of shared data (e.g., object, virtual memory page), and a variety of underlying hardware.

3.4 DISTRIBUTED MEMORY ARCHITECTURES

The structure of a typical distributed memory multiprocessor system is shown in Figure 3.3. This architecture enables scalability by distributing the memory throughout the machine, using a scalable interconnect to enable processors to

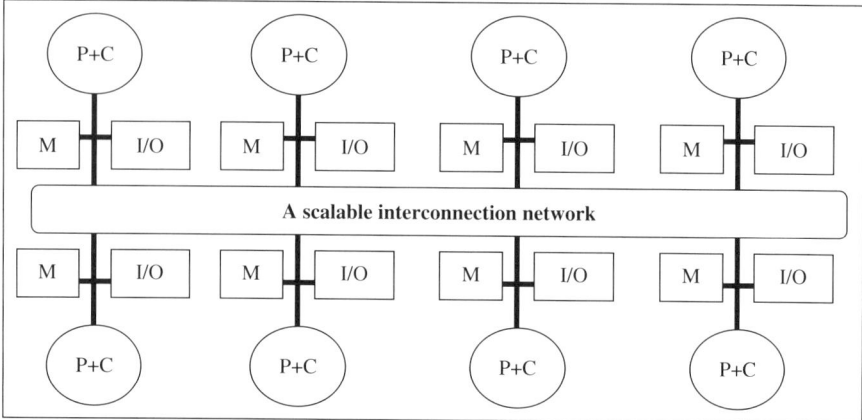

Fig. 3.3 Distributed memory multiprocessors (P+C, processor + cache; M, memory). Message-passing systems and DSM systems have the same basic organization. The key distinction is that the DSMs implement a single shared address space, whereas message-passing architectures have distributed address space.

communicate with the memory modules. Based on the communication mechanism provided, these architectures are classified as:

- Multicomputer/message-passing architectures
- DSM architectures

The multicomputers use a software (*message-passing*) layer to communicate among themselves and hence are called *message-passing architectures*. In these systems, programmers are required explicitly to send messages to request/send remote data. As these systems connect multiple computing nodes, sharing only the scalable interconnect, they are also referred to as *multicomputers*. DSM machines logically implement a single global address space although the memory is physically distributed. The memory access times in these systems depended on the physical location of the processors and are no longer uniform. As a result, these systems are also termed *nonuniform memory access* (NUMA) *systems*.

3.5 CLASSIFICATION OF DISTRIBUTED SHARED MEMORY SYSTEMS

Providing DSM functionality on physically distributed memory requires the implementation of three basic mechanisms:

- *Processor-side hit/miss check*. This operation, on the processor side, is used to determine whether or not a particular data request is satisfied in the processor's local cache. A *hit* is a data request satisfied in the local cache; a *miss* requires the data to be fetched from main memory or the cache of another processor.
- *Processor-side request send*. This operation is used on the processor side in response to a miss, to send a request to another processor or main memory for the latest copy of the relevant data item and waits for eventual response.
- *Memory-side operations*. These operations enable the memory to receive a request from a processor, perform any necessary coherence actions, and send its response, typically in the form of the data requested.

Depending on how these mechanisms are implemented in hardware or software helps classify the various DSM systems as follows:

- *Hardware-based DSM systems*. In these systems, all processor-side mechanisms are implemented in hardware, while some part of memory-side support may be handled in software. Hardware-based DSM systems include SGI Origin [14], HP/Convex Exemplar [16], MIT Alewife [2], and Stanford FLASH [1].
- *Mostly software page-based DSM systems*. These DSM systems implement hit/miss check in hardware by making use of virtual memory protection mechanisms to provide access control. All other support is implemented in software. Coherence units in such systems are the size of virtual memory pages. Mostly software page-based DSM systems include TreadMarks [5], Brazos [6], and Mirage+ [7].
- *Software/Object-based DSM systems*. In this class of DSM systems, all three mechanisms mentioned above are implemented entirely in software. Software/object-based DSM systems include Orca [8], SAM [10], CRL [9], Midway [11], and Shasta [17].

Almost all DSM models employ a directory-based cache coherence mechanism, implemented either in hardware or software. DSM systems have demonstrated the potential to meet the objectives of scalability, ease of programming, and cost-effectiveness. Directory-based coherence makes these systems highly scalable. The globally addressable memory model is retained in these systems, although the memory access times depend on the location of the processor and are no longer uniform. In general, hardware DSM systems allow programmers to realize excellent performance without sacrificing programmability. Software DSM systems typically provide a similar level of programmability. These systems, however, trade off somewhat lower performance for reduced hardware complexity and cost.

3.5.1 Hardware-Based DSM Systems

Hardware-based DSM systems implement the coherence and consistency mechanisms in hardware, making them faster but more complex. Clusters of symmetric multiprocessors (SMPs) with hardware support for shared memory have emerged as a promising approach to building large-scale DSM parallel machines. Each node in these systems is an SMP with multiple processors. The relatively high volumes of these small-scale parallel servers make them extremely cost-effective as building blocks. The software compatibility is preserved through a directory-based cache coherence protocol. This also helps support a shared memory abstraction despite having memory physically distributed across the nodes. A number of different cache coherence protocols have been proposed for these systems. These include: (1) cache-coherent nonuniform memory access (CC-NUMA), (2) cache-only memory access (COMA), (3) simple cache-only memory access (S-COMA), (4) reactive NUMA, and (5) adaptive S-COMA. Figure 3.4 illustrates the processor memory hierarchies in CC-NUMA, COMA, and S-COMA architectures.

Cache-Coherent Nonuniform Memory Access (CC-NUMA) Figure 3.4(*a*) shows the processor memory hierarchy in a CC-NUMA system. In this system, a per-node cluster cache lies next to the processor cache in the hierarchy. Remote data may be cached in a processor's cache or in the per-node cluster cache. Memory references not satisfied by these hardware caches must be sent to the referenced page's home node to obtain the data requested and to perform necessary coherence actions. The first processor to access a remote page within each node results in a software page fault. The operating system's page fault handler maps the page to a CC-NUMA global physical address and updates the node's page table. The Stanford DASH and SGI Origin systems implement the CC-NUMA protocol.

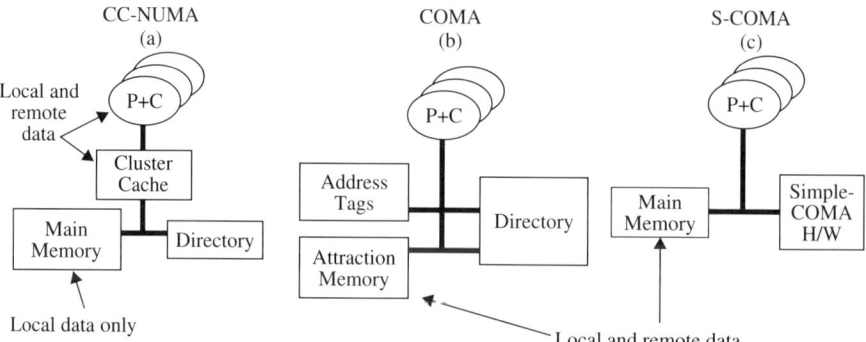

Fig. 3.4 Processor memory hierarchies in CC-NUMA, COMA, and S-COMA (P+C, processor + cache; H/W, hardware).

Cache-Only Memory Access (COMA) The key idea in COMA architecture is to use the memory within each node of the multiprocessor as a giant cache (also termed an *attraction memory*) as shown in Figure 3.4(*b*). Data migration and replication are done just as in caches. The advantage of this scheme is the ability to capture the remote capacity misses as hits in the local memory; that is, if a data item is initially allocated in a remote memory and is frequently used by a processor, it can be replicated in the local memory of the node where it is being referenced frequently. The attraction memory maintains both the address tags and the state of data. The COMA implementation requires customized hardware and hence has not become a popular design choice. The Kendall Square Research KSR1 [18] machine implemented COMA architecture.

Simple Cache-Only Memory Access (S-COMA) An S-COMA system, shown in Figure 3.4(*c*), uses the same coherence protocol as CC-NUMA, but allocates part of the local node's main memory to act as a large cache for remote pages. S-COMA is much cheaper and simpler to implement than COMA, as it can be built with off-the-shelf hardware building blocks. It also uses standard address translation hardware. On a first reference to a remote page from any node, a software page fault occurs which is handled by the operating system. It initializes the page table and maps the page in the part of main memory being used as cache. The essential extra hardware required in S-COMA is a set of fine-grain access control bits (one or two per block) and an auxiliary translation table. The S-COMA page cache, being part of main memory, is much larger than the CC-NUMA cluster cache. As a result, S-COMA can outperform CC-NUMA for many applications. However, S-COMA incurs substantial page overhead, as it invokes the operating system for local address translation. Additionally, programs with large sparse data sets suffer from severe internal fragmentation, resulting in a thrashing[1] of the S-COMA page cache. In such applications, CC-NUMA may perform better. Since S-COMA requires only incrementally more hardware than CC-NUMA, some systems have proposed providing support for both protocols. For example, the S3.mp [19] project at Sun Microsystems supports both S-COMA and CC-NUMA protocols.

Hybrid Schemes Given these diverse application requirements, hybrid schemes such as reactive NUMA (R-NUMA) [3] and adaptive S-COMA (ASCOMA) [4] have been proposed. These techniques combine CC-NUMA and S-COMA to get the best of both with incrementally more hardware. These schemes have not yet been implemented in commercial systems.

Reactive Nonuniform Memory Access (R-NUMA) R-NUMA dynamically reacts to program and system behavior to switch between CC-NUMA

---

[1] *Thrashing*: if a process does not have "enough" pages, the page-fault rate is very high. This leads to low CPU utilization as a process is busy swapping pages in and out.

and S-COMA. The algorithm initially allocates all remote pages as CC-NUMA but maintains a per-node, per-page count of the number of times that a block is re-fetched as a result of conflict[2] or capacity[3] miss. When the re-fetch count exceeds a threshold, the operating system intervenes and reallocates the page in the S-COMA page cache. Thus, based on the number of re-fetches, R-NUMA classifies the remote pages as reuse pages and communication pages and maps them as CC-NUMA and S-COMA, respectively. A CC-NUMA page is upgraded to be an S-COMA page if the re-fetch count exceeds a threshold figure.

Adaptive Simple Cache-Only Memory Access (ASCOMA) The ASCOMA scheme proposes a page allocation algorithm that prefers S-COMA pages at low memory pressures and a page replacement algorithm that dynamically backs off the rate of page remappings between CC-NUMA and S-COMA mode at high memory pressures.

ASCOMA initially maps pages in S-COMA mode. Thus, when memory pressure is low, S-COMA neither suffers any remote conflict or capacity misses, nor does it pay the high cost of remapping. ASCOMA reacts to an increase in memory pressure by evicting cold pages (i.e., pages not accessed for a long time) from and remapping hot pages (i.e., pages that are frequently accessed) to the local page cache. It adapts to differing memory pressures to fully utilize large page cache at low memory pressures and avoids thrashing at high memory pressures. The adaptivity is implemented by dynamically adjusting the re-fetch threshold that triggers remapping, increasing it when memory pressure is high.

The DSM architecture provides global addressability of all memory in a system. While the two processors on a node share the same bus, they do not function as a snoopy cluster. Instead, they operate as two separate processors multiplexed over a single physical bus. This is unlike in many other CC-NUMA systems, where the node is a SMP cluster. Such an architecture helps reduce both local and remote latencies and increases memory bandwidth. Thus both the absolute memory latency and the ratio of remote to local memory latencies is kept to a minimum.

Other CC-NUMA features provided in the Origin system include combinations of hardware and software support for page migration and replication. These include per-page hardware memory reference counters, a block-copy engine that copies data at near-peak memory speeds, mechanisms for reducing the cost of TLB updates, and a high-performance local and global interconnect design. Furthermore, the cache coherence protocol minimizes latency and bandwidth per access with a rich set of synchronization primitives.

---

[2] *Conflict miss*: a miss in cache due to mutually exclusive data access requests.
[3] *Capacity miss*: a miss in cache due to insufficient capacity of the cache.

MIT Alewife Machine The MIT Alewife machine [2] is an example of a CC-NUMA shared memory programming environment on a scalable hardware base. Figure 3.5 shows an overview of the MIT Alewife architecture. Each node consists of a processor, a floating-point unit, 64 kB of direct-mapped cache, 8 MB of DRAM, a network router, and a custom-designed communication and memory management unit (CMMU). The nodes can communicate using either shared memory or message passing via the single-chip CMMU. The CMMU is the heart of an Alewife node and is responsible for coordinating message-passing and shared memory communication. It implements a scalable cache-coherence protocol and provides the processor with a low-latency network interface.

Shared memory is distributed in the sense that the shared address space is physically partitioned among nodes. Cache lines in Alewife are 16 bytes in size and are kept coherent through software extended directory protocol. Each of

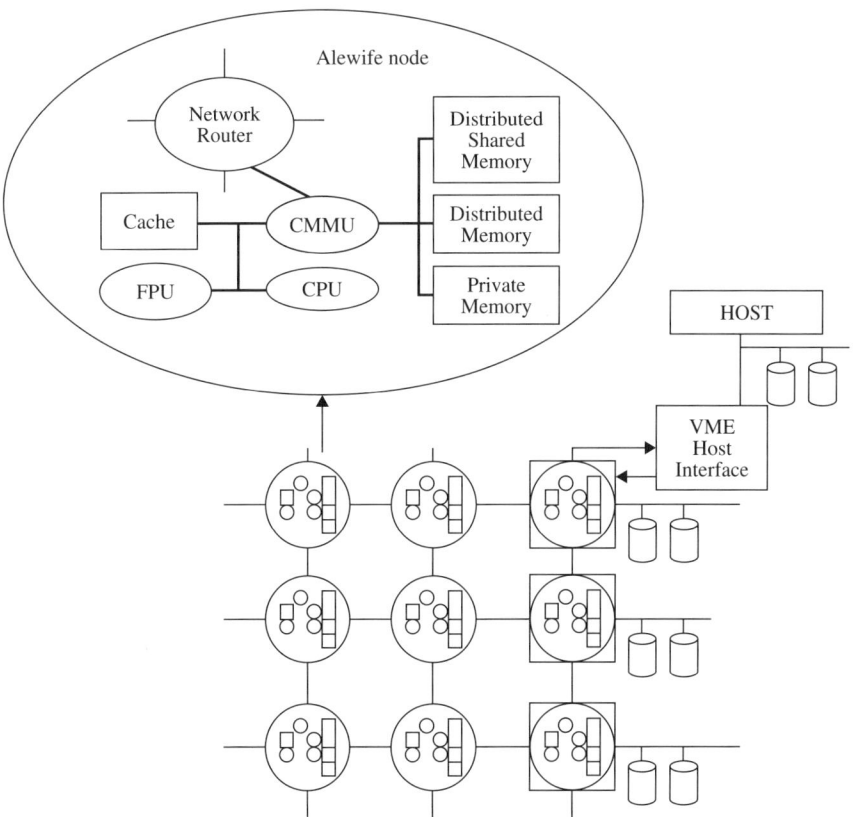

Fig. 3.5 Alewife architecture (CMMU, communication and memory management unit; FPU, floating-point unit).

the 16-byte memory lines has a home node that contains storage for its data and coherence directory. All coherence operations for given memory line, whether handled by hardware or software, are coordinated by its home node. Each node contains the data and coherence directories for a 4-MB portion of shared memory.

Alewife provides four classes of architectural mechanisms that implement an automatic locality management strategy which seeks to maximize the amount of local communication by consolidating related blocks of computation and data, and attempts to minimize the effects of nonlocal communication when it is unavoidable. The four classes are:

- *Coherent caches for shared memory.* Although the system's physical memory is statically distributed over the nodes in the machine, Alewife provides the abstraction of globally shared memory to programmers. The memory hardware helps manage locality by caching both private and shared data on each node.
- *Fine-grained computation.* Alewife supports fine-grained computation by including fast user-level messages.
- *Integrated message passing.* Although the programmer sees a shared memory-programming model, for performance reasons much of the underlying software is implemented using message passing. The hardware supports a seamless interface.
- *Latency tolerance.* The mechanisms of block multithreading and pre-fetching attempt to tolerate the latency of interprocessor communication when it cannot be avoided. These mechanisms require caches that continue to supply instructions and data while waiting for the pre-fetched data or during miss (called *lockup-free caches*).

The MIT Alewife machine implements a complete programming environment consisting of hardware, compiler, and operating system, all combined to achieve the goal of programmability by solving problems such as scheduling computation, and moving data between processing elements. Features of this environment include globally shared address space, a compiler that automatically partitions regular programs with loops, a library of efficient synchronization and communication routines, distributed garbage collection, and a parallel debugger.

Stanford FLASH Multiprocessor Like Alewife, the Stanford FLASH multiprocessor [1] emphasizes efficient integration of both cache-coherent shared memory and low-overhead user-level message passing. FLASH, shown in Figure 3.6, is a single-address-space machine consisting of a large number of processing nodes connected by a low-latency high-bandwidth interconnection network. Every node is identical, containing a high-performance off-the-shelf microprocessor and its caches. These caches form a portion of the machine's

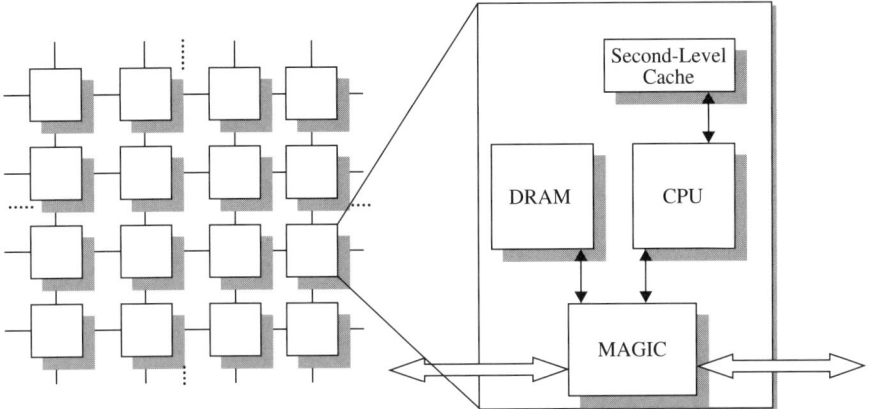

Fig. 3.6 FLASH system architecture. (From J. Kuskin et al. [1].)

distributed memory and a node controller chip MAGIC (memory and general interconnect controller). The MAGIC chip forms the heart of the node, integrating a memory controller, I/O controller, network interface, and programmable protocol processor. This integration allows for low hardware overhead while supporting both cache coherence and message-passing protocols in a scalable and cohesive fashion. The MAGIC includes a programmable protocol processor that offers flexibility. The hardwired data movement logic achieves low latency and high bandwidth by supporting highly pipelined data transfers without extra-copying within the chip. MAGIC separates data movement logic from protocol state manipulation logic, which ensures that it does not become a latency or bandwidth bottleneck.

FLASH's base cache coherence protocol is directory based and has two components: a scalable directory data structure and a set of handlers. For a scalable directory structure, FLASH uses dynamic pointer allocation, wherein each cache line-sized block (128 bytes) of main memory is associated with an 8-byte state word called *directory header*. This header is stored in a contiguous section of main memory devoted solely to the cache coherence protocol. A significant advantage of dynamic pointer allocation is that the directory storage requirements are scalable. Overall, the directory occupies 7 to 9 percent of main memory, depending on system configuration.

3.5.2 Mostly Software Page-Based DSM Systems

An alternative approach, making use of software to implement, has seen the evolution of quite a number of page-based DSM systems. These techniques make use of the virtual memory hardware in the underlying system, to implement the shared memory consistency models in software to resolve the conflicting memory accesses (memory accesses to the same location by different processors, at least one of which is a write access). Examples of mostly software page-based DSM systems include TreadMarks [5], Brazos [6], and Mirage+ [7].

The advantage of page-based DSM systems is that they eliminate the shared memory hardware requirement, making them inexpensive and readily implementable. These systems are found to work well for dense matrix codes. As the coherence policy is implemented in software, it can be optimized to make use of the operating system to implement coherence mechanisms. The use of operating system, however, makes them slow compared to hardware coherence mechanisms. Additionally, the coarse sharing granularity (i.e., large page size) results into false sharing and relatively higher communication time per page. One solution is to have multigrain systems; using fine-grained shared memory within an SMP and page-based distributed shared memory across the SMPs.

A key issue in page-based DSM systems is *write protocols*.

- *Write-update and write-invalidate protocols*. There are two approaches to maintaining the memory coherence requirement. One approach is to ensure that a processor has exclusive access to a data item before it writes that item. This type of protocol is called a *write-invalidate protocol* because it invalidates all other copies on a write. This is by far the most common protocol. The other alternative is to update all the cached copies of a data item when it is written. This type of protocol is called a *write-update protocol*.

- *Single- and multiple-writer protocols*. Most hardware cache and DSM systems use *single-writer protocols*. These protocols allow multiple readers to access a given page simultaneously, but a writer is required to have sole access to a page before performing modifications. Single-writer protocols are easy to implement because all copies of a given page are always identical, and page fault can always be satisfied by retrieving a copy of the page from any other processor that currently has a valid copy. This simplicity often comes at the expense of high message traffic. Before a page can be written, all other copies must be invalidated. These invalidations can then cause subsequent access misses if the processors whose pages have been invalidated are still accessing the page's data. *False sharing* occurs when two or more unrelated data objects are located on the same page and are written concurrently by separate processors. Since the consistency unit (usually, a virtual memory page) is large in size, false sharing is a potentially serious problem and causes the performance of single-writer protocol to deteriorate further, due to interference between un-related accesses. *Multiple-writer protocols* allow multiple processors to have a writable copy of the page at the same time.

TreadMarks TreadMarks [5] supports parallel computing on networks of workstations (NOWs) by providing the application with a shared memory abstraction. The TreadMarks application programming interface (API) provides facilities for process creation and destruction, synchronization, and shared memory allocation. *Synchronization*, a way for the programmer to express ordering constraints between the shared memory accesses of different processes, is implemented with *critical sections*. TreadMarks provides two synchronization primitives: barriers and exclusive locks. *Barriers* are global in the sense that calling the barrier process is stalled until all the processes in the system have arrived at that barrier. In the case of *locks*, a lock-acquire call acquires a lock for the calling process and a lock-release call releases it.

TreadMarks uses multiple-writer protocol. The shared page is initially write-protected. When a write occurs in a processor (say P1), TreadMarks creates a copy of the page, or a *twin*, and saves it as a part of TreadMarks' data structure on P1. It then un-protects the page in the user's address space so that further writes to that page occur without software intervention. Later, P1 arrives at a barrier; there is an unmodified *twin* and a modified copy in the user's address space. By making a *word-by-word* comparison of the two, a run-length encoding of the modifications of the page, called a *diff*, is created. Once the diff is created, it is sent to all the processors sharing that page. These processors then modify the page, discarding the twin. The same sequence of events takes place on every other processor. Once the diff is received, the entire sequence of events is local to each processor and does not require message exchanges, unlike in single-writer protocols.

Brazos Brazos [6] is a page-based DSM that makes use of relaxed consistency models and multithreading on a network of multiprocessor computers. It executes on x86 multiprocessor workstations running Windows NT 4.0. Brazos is based on selective multicast in a time-multiplexed network environment such as Ethernet. Selective multicast is used in Brazos to reduce the number of consistency-related messages and to efficiently implement its version of scope consistency. One disadvantage with multicast is the potential harmful effect of unused indirect diff (i.e., run-length encoding of the modifications of a page). Although receiving multicast diffs for inactive pages does not increase network traffic, it does cause processors to be interrupted frequently to process incoming multicast messages. These messages and subsequent changes are not accessed before the next time that page is invalidated; thus, they detract user-code computation time. The dynamic copyset reduction mechanism ameliorates this effect by allowing processes to drop out of the copyset for a particular page. This causes them to be excluded from multicast messages, providing diffs for the page.

Brazos uses multithreading at both user level and DSM system level. Multiple user-level threads allow applications to take advantage of SMP servers by using all available processors for computation. The Brazos runtime system has two threads. One thread is responsible for responding quickly to asynchronous requests for data from other processes and runs at the highest possible priority. The other thread handles replies to requests sent previously by the process.

Brazos implements a version of a *scope consistency model*, which is a bridge between a release consistency model and an entry consistency model. The scope consistency model seeks to reduce the false sharing present in page-based DSM systems. False sharing occurs when two or more threads modify different parts of the same page of data but do not actually share the same data element. This leads to unnecessary network traffic. Scope consistency divides the execution of a program into global and local scopes, and only data modified within a single scope is guaranteed to be cohered at the end of that scope. Brazos implements software-only scope consistency that requires no additional hardware support.

Mirage+ Mirage+ [7], developed at University of California, Riverside, allocates a time window during which processors at a node possess a page. At the end of the time window, the node may be interrupted to relinquish the page. During the time window, processes at the site(s) having read-only access may read, or processes at the site having write access may read or write the page. The page may also be unused during the time window. Thus, the time window provides some degree of control over processor locality (i.e., the number of references to a given page that a processor will make before another processor is allowed to reference that page). Mirage+ is a write-invalidate coherent system (i.e., a store requires that all read-only copies of a page be invalidated before storing to the page with the referenced location).

Mirage+ defines one distinguished site called the *library site*. Requests for pages are sent to the library site, queried, and processed sequentially. All pages must be checked out from the library. Another distinguished site is the clock site. It is the site that has the most recent copy of a page. The library site records which site is acting as a clock site. The process of converting a reader to a writer when a page fault occurs is called an *upgrade*. The process of converting a writer to a reader is called a *downgrade*.

Mirage makes use of performance improvement techniques in a networked environment such as *high-level packet blasting* and *compression*. High-level packet blasting eliminates the overhead of explicitly handshaking each packet, thus improving the total time for a remote page significantly. Compression works by reducing the number of packets that the system must transmit at each page fault.

3.5.3 All-Software/Object-Based DSM Systems

In the all-software (object-based) approach, shared memory support is entirely supported in software. Orca, SAM, Midway, CRL, and Shasta are examples of this approach. Shasta is unique in that it uses a fine-grained approach.

Orca Orca [8] defines an object- and language-based DSM model. It encapsulates shared data in objects and allows programmers to define operations on these objects using abstract data types. This model is supported by the Orca language, designed specifically for parallel programming on DSM systems. Orca integrates synchronization and data accesses giving an advantage that programmers, while developing parallel programs, do not have to use explicit synchronization primitives.

Orca migrates and replicates shared data (objects) and supports an update coherence protocol for implementing write operations. Objects are updated using function shipping (i.e., the operation and its parameters are sent to all machines containing a copy of the object to be updated). The operation is then applied to the local copies. To ensure that the replicated copies are updated in a coherent manner, the operation is sent using totally ordered group communication. All updates are executed in the same order at all machines (i.e., sequential consistency is guaranteed). Orca is implemented entirely in software and requires the operating system (or hardware) to provide only basic communication primitives. This flexibility of being an all-software system is exploited to implement several important optimizations.

Portability is achieved in Orca by using a layered approach. The system contains three layers, and the machine-specific parts are isolated in the lowest layer. This layer (called *Panda*) implements a virtual machine that provides the communication and multitasking primitives needed by a runtime. Portability of Orca requires only portability of Panda.

SAM Stanford SAM [10] is a shared-object system for distributed shared memory machines. SAM has been implemented as a C library. It is a portable runtime system that provides a global name space and automatic caching of shared data. SAM allows communication of data at the level of user-defined data types, thus allowing user control over communication in a DSM machine. The basic principle underlying SAM is to require the programmer to designate the way in which data are to be accessed. There are two kinds of data relationships (hence synchronization) in parallel programs: *values* with single assignment constraints, and *accumulators*, which allow mutually exclusive accesses to the requesting processors.

Values make it simple to express producer–consumer relationships or precedence constraints; any read of a value must wait for the creation of the value. *Accumulators* allow automatic migration of data to the requesting processors, making sure that the data accesses are mutually exclusive.

SAM incorporates mechanisms to address the problems of high communication overheads; these mechanisms include tying synchronization to data access, chaotic access to data, pre-fetching of data, and pushing of data to remote processors. SAM deals only with management and communication of shared data; data that are completely local to a processor can be managed by any appropriate method. The creator of a value or accumulator should specify the type of the new data. With the help of a preprocessor, SAM uses this type of information to allocate space for the messages, to pack them, unpack them, and to free the storage of the data. The preprocessor can handle complex C data types.

An important mechanism for tolerating communication latency is to support for asynchronous access. SAM provides the capability to fetch values and accumulators asynchronously. An asynchronous fetch succeeds immediately if a copy of the value is available on the local processor. If the value is not available immediately, the fetch operation returns an indication of non-availability, and the requesting process can proceed with other access or computation. The requesting process is notified when the value becomes available on the local processor. For asynchronous access to an accumulator, the process is notified when the accumulator has been fetched to the local processor and mutual exclusion has been obtained.

Midway Midway [11], at Carnegie Mellon University, is also an object-based DSM programming system supporting multiple consistency models within a single parallel program. Midway contains data that may be processor consistent, release consistent, or entry consistent. Midway programs are written in C and the association between synchronization objects and data must be made with explicit annotations. Midway requires a small amount of compile time support to implement its consistency protocols (e.g., whenever the compiler generates its code to store a new value into a shared data item, it also generates code that marks the item as "dirty" in an auxiliary data structure). Distributed synchronization management, implemented in Midway, enables processors to acquire synchronization objects not presently held in their local memories. Two types of synchronization objects are supported: locks and barriers. Locks are acquired in either exclusive or nonexclusive mode by locating the lock's owner using a distributed queuing algorithm. Distributed cache management ensures that a processor never enters a critical section without having received all updates to the shared data guarded by that synchronization object (a lock or a barrier). Midway implements entry consistency with an update-based protocol, thereby requiring interprocessor communication only during acquisition of synchronization objects. Entry consistency guarantees that shared data become consistent at a processor when the processor acquires a synchronization object known to guard the data.

CRL: C Region Library CRL [9] is an all-software DSM model that is system and language independent. It is portable and employs a region-based approach. Each region is an arbitrarily sized contiguous area of memory identified by a unique region identifier. CRL is implemented entirely as a library. CRL requires no functionality from the underlying hardware, compiler, or operating system beyond that necessary to send and receive messages. CRL considers entire operations on regions of data as individual units and provides sequential consistency for the read and write operations. In terms of individual loads and stores, CRL provides memory coherence through entry or release consistency. CRL employs a fixed-home directory-based write-invalidate protocol.

CRL is able to use part of main memory as a large secondary cache instead of relying only on hardware caches, which are typically small. Regions, chosen to correspond to user-defined data structures, assist coherence actions to transfer exactly the data required by the application.

Fine-Grained Shasta DSM Fine-grained sharing is an alternative all-software approach proposed to overcome both the false sharing and unnecessary transmission. Shasta [17] is a fine-grained all-software DSM developed at Western Research Laboratory. It supports coherence at fine-granularity and thus alleviates the need for complex mechanisms for dealing with false sharing typically present in software page-based DSM systems. To reduce the high overheads associated with software message handling, the cache coherence protocol is designed to minimize extraneous coherence messages. It also includes optimizations such as nonblocking stores, detection of migratory data sharing, issuing multiple load misses in a batch, merging of load, sharing misses to the same line, and support for pre-fetching and home-placement directives.

Shared data in Shasta has three basic states:

- *Invalid*. The data are not valid on this processor.
- *Shared*. The data are valid on this processor and other processors have copies of it.
- *Exclusive*. The data are valid on this processor and no other processor has a copy of it.

Communication is required if a processor attempts to read data that are in an invalid or shared state. This is called a *shared miss*.

The shared address space in Shasta is divided into ranges of memory called *blocks*. The block size can be different for different ranges of the shared address space (i.e., for different program data). The line size is configurable at compile time and is typically set to 64 or 128 bytes. The size of each block must be a multiple of the fixed line size. Coherence is maintained using a directory-based invalidation protocol, which supports three types of requests: *read*, *read exclusive*, and *exclusive* (or upgrade). Supporting exclusive requests is an important optimization since it reduces message latency and overhead if the requesting processor has the line in shared state. Shasta supports three types of synchronization primitives: locks, barriers, and event flags.

A home processor is associated with each virtual page of shared data, and each processor maintains directory information for the shared data pages assigned to it. The protocol maintains the notion of an *owner processor* for each line which corresponds to the last processor that maintained an exclusive copy of the line. Directory information consists of two components: a pointer to the current owner processor and a full-bit vector of the processor that are sharing the data. The protocol supports dirty sharing, which allows the data to be shared without requiring the home node to have an up-to-date copy. A request coming to the home node is forwarded to the current owner as an optimization; this forwarding is avoided if the home processor has a copy of the data.

To avoid the high cost of handling messages via interrupts, messages from other processors are serviced through a polling mechanism. Polls are also inserted at every loop back-edge to ensure reasonable response times. The protocol aggressively exploits the release consistency model by emulating the behavior of a processor with nonblocking stores and lockup-free caches.

REFERENCES

1. J. Kuskin, D. Ofelt, M. Heinrich, J. Heinlein, R. Simoni, K. Gharachorloo, J. Chapin, D. Nakahira, J. Baxter, M. Horowitz, A. Gupta, M. Roseblum, and J. Henessy, The Stanford FLASH multiprocessor, *Proceedings of the 21st International Symposium on Computer Architecture*, April 1994.
2. A. Agarwal, R. Bianchini, D. Chaiken, K. L. Johnson, D. Krauz, J. Kubiatowicz, B. Lim, K. Mackenzie and D. Yeung, The MIT Alewife machine: architecture and performance, *Proceedings of the 22nd International Symposium on Computer Architecture* (ISCA), June 1995.
3. B. Falsafi and D. A. Wood, Reactive NUMA: a design for unifying S-COMA and CC-NUMA, *Proceedings of the 24th International Symposium on Computer Architecture* (ISCA), 1997.
4. C. Kuo, J. Carter, R. Kumarkote, and M. Swanson, ASCOMA: an adaptive hybrid shared memory architecture, *International Conference on Parallel Processing* (ICPPË98), August 1998.
5. C. Amza, A. Cox, S. Dwarakadas, P. Keleher, H. Lu, R. Rajamony, W. Yu, and W. Zwaenepoel, TreadMarks: shared memory computing on networks of workstations, *IEEE Computer*, Vol. 29, No. 2, pp. 18–28, 1996.
6. E. Speight and J. K. Bennett, Brazos: a third generation DSM system, *Proceedings of the 1997 USENIX Windows NT Workshop*, August 1997.
7. B. D. Fleisch, R. L. Hyde, and N. Christian, Mirage+: a kernel implementation of distributed shared memory for a network of personal computers, *Software Practice and Experience*, Vol. 24, No. 10, pp. 887–909, October 1994.
8. H. E. Bal, R. Bhoedjang, R. Hofman, C. Jacobs, K. Langendoen, and T. Ruhl, Performance evaluation of the Orca shared object system, *ACM Transactions on Computer Systems*, Vol. 16, No. 1, pp. 1–40, 1998.
9. K. L. Johnson, M. Kaashoek, and D. Wallach, CRL: high-performance all-software distributed shared memory, *Proceedings of the 15th ACM Symposium on Operating Systems Principles* (SOSP '95), 1995.
10. D. J. Scales and M. S. Lam, The design and evaluation of a shared object system for distributed memory machines, *Proceedings of the First Symposium on Operating Systems Design and Implementation*, November 1994.

11. B. Bershad, M. Zekauskas, and W. Swadon, The Midway distributed shared memory system, *IEEE International Compute Conference* (COMPCON), 1993.
12. E. Hagersten, A. Saulsbury, and A. Landin, Simple COMA node implementations, *Proceedings of the 27th Hawaii International Conference on System Sciences* (HICSS-27), Vol. I, pp. 522–533, January 1994.
13. B. Verghese, S. Devine, A. Gupta, and M. Rosenblum, Operating system support for improving data locality on CC-NUMA computer servers, *Proceedings of the 7th Symposium on Architectural Support for Programming Languages and Operating Systems (ASPOLS VII)*, 1996.
14. J. Laudon and D. Lenoski, The SGI Origin: a ccNUMA highly scalable server, *http://www-europe.sgi.com/origin/tech_info.html*.
15. A. Charlesworth, STARFIRE: extending the SMP envelope, *IEEE MICRO*, January–February 1998.
16. T. Brewer and G. Astfalk, The evolution of HP/convex exemplar, *Proceedings of the IEEE Computer Conference (COMPCON), Spring*, February 1997.
17. D. J. Scales, K. Gharachorloo, and A. Aggarwal, *Fine-Grain Software Distributed Shared Memory on SMP Clusters*, Research Report 97/3, February 1997.
18. H. Burkhardt III, S. Frank, B. Knobe, and J. Rothnie, *Overview of the KSR1 Computer System*, Technical Report KSR-TR-9202001, Kendall Square Research, Boston, February 1992.
19. A. Saulsbury and A. Nowatzyk, Simple COMA on S3.MP, *Proceedings of the 1995 International Symposium on Computer Architecture Shared Memory Workshop*, Portofino, Italy, June 1995.

CHAPTER 4

Distributed-Object Computing Tools

R. RAJE, A. KALYANARAMAN, and N. NAYANI

Department of Computer and Information Science, Indiana University Purdue University, Indianapolis, IN

4.1 INTRODUCTION

Distributed computing systems are omnipresent in today's world. The rapid progress in the semiconductor and networking infrastructures have blurred the differentiation between parallel and distributed computing systems and made distributed computing a workable alternative to high-performance parallel architectures.

However attractive distributed computing may be, developing software for such systems is hardly a trivial task. Many different models and technologies have been proposed by academia and industry for developing robust distributed software systems. Despite a large number of such systems, one fact is clear that the software for distributed computing can be written efficiently using the principles of distributed-object computing. The concept of objects residing in different address spaces and communicating via messages over a network meshes well with the principles of distributed computation. Out of the existing alternatives, Java-RMI (Remote Method Invocation) from Sun Microsystems, CORBA (Common Object Request Broker Architecture) from Object Management Group, and DCOM (Distributed Component Object Model) from Microsoft are the most popular distributed-object models among researchers and practitioners. This chapter provides a brief overview of these three popular approaches. As each of these models is fairly comprehensive, a detailed treatment of them in one chapter is not feasible. However, the chapter provides information about the basic model of each approach, followed by three actual examples, chosen from different domains, each having a different flavor with code segments, followed by a comparison and experimental eval-

---

Tools and Environments for Parallel and Distributed Computing, Edited by Salim Hariri and Manish Parashar
ISBN 0-471-33288-7 Copyright © 2004 John Wiley & Sons, Inc.

uation of these approaches. A brief discussion on a proposed Unified Meta-Object Model is presented at the end of the chapter.

4.2 BASIC MODEL

4.2.1 RMI

Java Remote Method Invocation [2] allows the implementation of distributed objects in Java. It allows a client running on any Java virtual machine to access a Java object hosted on a remote virtual machine. RMI follows the language-centric model [16]. This fact is two-faceted. First, the clients and servers need to be implemented in Java. This gives them an inherent object-oriented appearance and allows objects to interact with all the features of Java, such as JNI and JDBC. It also means that a server object can be run and accessed from any virtual machine, thus achieving platform independency. Second, the model is tied to Java, and hence objects cannot be implemented using any other language, thereby prohibiting interactions between heterogeneous (i.e., implemented in different languages) objects.

Basic Model The basic model of RMI consists of a client program, which intends to access a remote object, and a server program, which hosts the remote object [2]. For a client to connect to a remote object requires a reference to the object hosted by the server program [4]. A client can locate the remote server object in two ways. These two ways differ in the manner in which the client obtains the remote reference. These are described below.

1. *Explicitly obtaining a remote reference.* RMI provides a nonpersistent registry called RMIREGISTRY, which should be deployed on the server machine. The server object when instantiated should register itself to the local RMIREGISTRY. This action is achieved by calling *Naming.bind()*. When trying to connect to a remote object, the client looks up a named instance registered at the RMIREGISTRY. Figure 4.1 explains the architecture and the sequence of events in a typical RMI application.
2. *Implicitly obtaining a remote reference.* A reference to a remote object can also be obtained as a parameter or return value in a method call. This, too, can serve as a means of accessing a remote object from a client. It is assumed that a RMI client knows which server machine the remote object is currently hosted on for it to connect so that a lookup for that object can be performed on that server machine for obtaining a reference.

Irrespective of the approach used, once a remote reference is available to the client it achieves the remote method invocation using stubs and skeletons. The client-side stub acts as the proxy for the server. The server-side skeleton

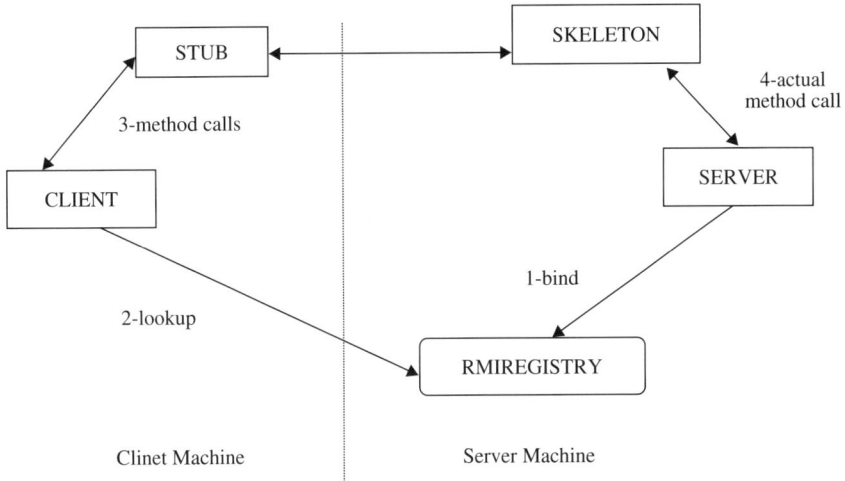

Fig. 4.1 RMI architecture and sequence of events.

handles the method invocations done by all the remote stubs to the local server object. When a client invokes a method on the object reference, the call is first received by the stub. Marshaling is done by the stub and the data are sent to the server. The server-side skeleton unmarshals the method call and routes it to the actual server object. Upon completion of method execution the skeleton receives the return parameters, marshals the contents, and sends it back to the client stub, which would then unmarshal it. This entire process is transparent to the client and the method invocation looks like a local method call. The serialization ability of Java is used for the marshaling/unmarshaling of arguments and return values.

4.2.2 CORBA

CORBA (Common Object Request Broker Architecture) [13] is a distributed object architecture that provides a communication infrastructure for a heterogeneous and distributed collection of collaborating objects [18]. These remote or local collaborating objects can interoperate across networks regardless of the language in which they are written or the platform on which they are deployed.

CORBA is a suite of specifications issued by the Object Management Group (OMG) [13]. The OMG is a nonprofit consortium comprising about 1000 computer companies. It was formed in 1989 with the purpose of promoting the theory and practice of object technology in distributed computing systems. OMG realizes its goals through creating standards which allow interoperability and portability of distributed object-oriented applications [17]. The CORBA standards for interoperability in heterogeneous computing environments, promoted by the OMG, lay down guidelines for developing distributed applications whose components collaborate transparently, scalably, reliably, and efficiently [18].

Basic Model: CORBA Architecture The Object Management Architecture (OMA), defined by the OMG, is a high-level design of a complete distributed environment. OMA provides the conceptual infrastructure and forms the basis for all OMG specifications, including the object model and the reference model. The object model underlies the CORBA architecture and defines common object semantics for specifying an object and its visible characteristics in a heterogeneous environment, and the reference model defines object interactions. The OMA comprises of four main components: object request brokers and object services (system-oriented components) and application objects and common facilities (application-oriented components) [17]. The object request broker (ORB) is the middleware that handles the communication details between the objects. Figure 4.2 shows the main components of the CORBA architecture and their interconnections. Below, a brief explanation of each of the components is provided. This explanation is a condensed form of [14,16,21].

A CORBA *object* is a virtual entity that consists of an *identity* (the object reference that helps to identify, locate, and address a CORBA object), an *inter-*

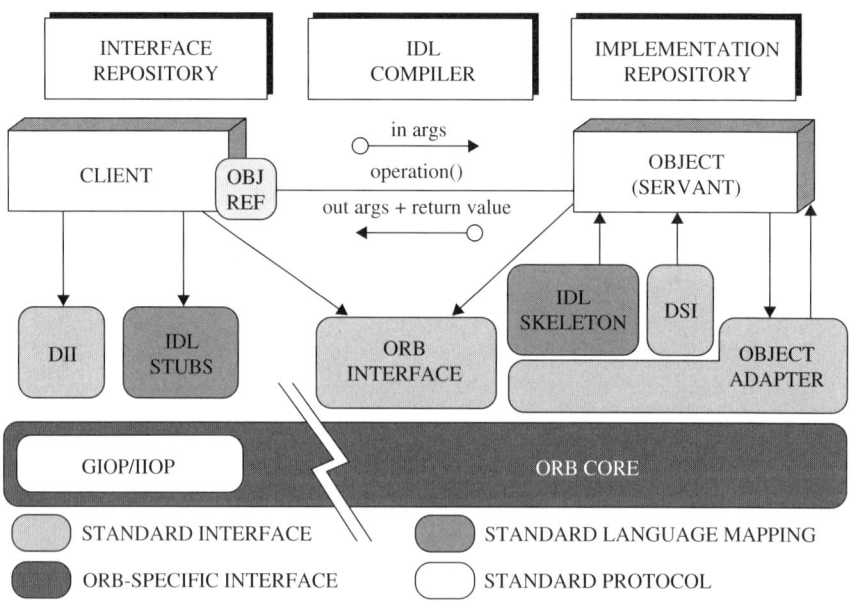

Fig. 4.2 CORBA architecture. (From Schmidt [14].)

face, and an *implementation*. The object implementation is known as a *servant*. Every CORBA object maps to a servant.

A *servant* is a programming language entity that implements the operations that are defined in the CORBA object's Interface Definition Language (IDL) interface. Servants can be implemented in various languages, such as C, C++, Java, Smalltalk, and Ada. The servants exist in the context of a server and are located and invoked by the ORB and the object adapter (OA) with the help of the object references.

A *client* application is a program entity that invokes an operation on a remote object by maintaining a reference to the object. A client can obtain a reference to a remote server object by binding to the CORBA naming or trader service.

The *object request broker* (ORB) is the middleware that provides a communication channel for routing client requests to target object implementations transparently. A client can access the services of an object implementation only through the ORB. The ORB is responsible for finding the object implementation, activating it if necessary, delivering the request to the object, and returning any response to the calling object. CORBA 2.0 specifies that each ORB must support a standard adapter called the *basic object adapter* (BOA). Servers may support more than one object adapter. CORBA 3.0 introduces a portable version of BOA called the *portable object adapter* (POA). The BOA and POA are responsible for the transparent activation of objects. POA provides a more flexible architecture that allows the ORB implementations to be designed such that the CORBA servers can fit a variety of application needs. The POA also introduces some additional features, such as providing the option of using a *servant manager* for each implementation of an object reference. These servant managers, also called *callback objects* or *instance managers*, assist the POA in the management of server-side objects [16].

The *ORB interface* is an abstract interface defined in the CORBA specification, containing various helper functions for *stringification* (converting object references to strings), *destringification* (reverse of stringification), and creating argument lists for requests made through the *dynamic invocation interface* (DII). This logical ORB entity can be implemented in various ways by different vendors.

A *CORBA IDL stub* serves as a connection between the client applications and the ORB. The IDL compiler generates the client-side stubs and the server-side skeletons.

A *skeleton* is a programming language entity that serves as a connection between the OA and the servant and allows the OA to dispatch requests to the servant.

The *dynamic invocation interface* (DII) allows a client application to invoke a request on a server object directly by using the underlying request mechanisms provided by an ORB without having to go through the IDL interface-specific stubs. The DII allows clients to make both nonblocking *deferred synchronous* and *one-way* calls [14].

The *dynamic skeleton interface* (DSI) is the server-side counterpart of the DII. The DSI allows an ORB to deliver requests to an object implementation that does not have IDL-based compiled skeletons or stubs.

The *object adapter* acts as an intermediary between the ORB and the object implementation. The object adapter is responsible for associating object implementations with the ORB, activating/deactivating the objects and delivering requests to the objects. Object implementations can support multiple object adapters.

For various objects of different ORBs to be able to communicate seamlessly with one another, the CORBA 2.0 specification provides a methodology known as the ORB Interoperability Architecture or the General Inter-ORB Protocol (GIOP). The GIOP [13] is a collection of message requests that ORBs can make over a network. GIOP maps ORB requests to different network transports. The Internet Inter-ORB Protocol (IIOP) [13], which maps GIOP messages to TCP/IP, is a GIOP implementation but a standardized version that all ORBs must be able to use. An Environment Specific Inter-ORB Protocol (ESIOP) is the complement of GIOP. ESIOPs let GIOP type messages be mapped to a proprietary network protocol such as the Open Software Foundation's (OSF's) Distributed Computing Environment (DCE). Any 2.0 ORB based on an ESIOP must include a half bridge to IIOP so that IIOP requests can also be made on it [15].

IDL (Interface Definition Language) The Interface Definition Language (IDL), defined by the OMG, is used to describe object interfaces in a standard manner. IDL [5] is a declarative language and its grammar is an extension of a subset of the ANSI C++ standard. The IDL interfaces are similar to the interfaces in Java and abstract classes in C++. OMG provides mappings from IDL to different implementation languages such as Java and C++ [13]. The IDL compiler generates the client-side stubs and server-side skeletons.

CORBA Object Services CORBA object services are a set of interfaces and objects used for handling the invoking and implementation of objects. Currently, CORBA provides about 15 object services. The prominent ones are:

- *Naming service:* helps clients find object implementations based on their name.
- *Trading service:* allows objects to advertise their services and bid for contracts.
- *Event service:* provides for an event-channel interface that distributes events among components.

Other services are *persistent object service, life-cycle service, time service, transaction service, relationship service, externalization service, concurrency control service, query service, licensing service, property service, security service,* and *collection service.*

4.2.3 DCOM

DCOM [8] is the distributed extension of COM (component object model) that allows components distributed across networks to communicate directly in a secure and reliable manner. It sits on the DCERPC layer and builds its object remote procedure calls [6]. It is a binary standard, which allows it to be implemented in any language that generates a binary code compatible to this standard [7]. The main feature of DCOM is that the operating system acts as the central registry repository for maintaining object references.

Basic Model DCOM supports two types of object activation, in-process and out-of-process activations. In *in-process activation* the server object instance is created and run in the client's address space. In *out-of-process activation* the server object is hosted in a separate process address space. This can either be, *local*, where it is on the same machine as the client, or *remote*, where it is on a different machine altogether. Depending on the requirement of the application on object-sharing constraints, object visibility to clients and deployment feasibility, the developer can choose between in-process or out-of-process implementation of the server object. If each client requires a separate instance of server implementation, an in-process activation might be chosen. If a separate server instance is required to be running independently catering to requests from clients on the fly, out-of-process activation is the choice.

DCOM clients can locate objects in more than one way. The server object interface ID could be registered on the client machine's system registry as a fixed configuration. The other option is to allow the client to specify explicitly the location of the server object (*CoCreateInstanceEx()*). The third option is to specify a name that uniquely identifies a COM object in a directory namespace. This unique name given to an object instance is also referred to as a *moniker* [9].

Each COM component exposes a set of functionally related methods through a COM interface. *Object classes* are those that implement one or more of these interfaces. Each COM interface and object class has a global identifier to be uniquely identified. Each COM server instantiates object instances of the object classes. Figure 4.3 depicts all components involved in the COM architecture [6].

The COM-SCM (service control manager) provides a set of methods for a client to perform a remote activation on the server object. This layer receives calls from the OLE32 and routes them to its server machine counterpart. A new server object instance is created on the server if this is the first request for the server object. The call returns the interface pointer to the client, and the client henceforth can invoke methods on the remote object. On subsequent requests for the same object instance, the same interface pointer is returned. The client can interact with the server object with only those methods described in the interface. COM interfaces are defined using *Microsoft Interface Definition Language* (MIDL).

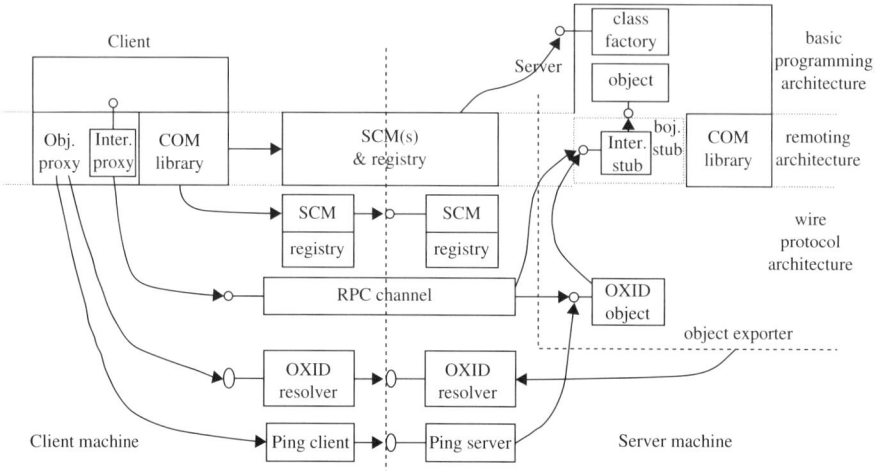

Fig. 4.3 DCOM architecture. (From Chung et al. [6].)

Any COM interface should derive from a standard base interface called *IUnknown*, directly or indirectly. *IUnknown* is an interface that exposes three methods: *AddRef*, *QueryInterface*, and *Release*. It forces implementation of these three methods by the implementation class object. Each time a client connects, the reference count for the object instance is incremented by one, and when the client disconnects, the count is decremented. This is done by the invocation of *AddRef* and *Release* methods, respectively. DCOM provides robust connection management through this mechanism. At any point of time, if the reference count is greater than zero, the server object instance resides in the memory, as it means that at least one client is connected to this object. When the reference count hits zero, the server object instance is unloaded from memory. The *QueryInterface* method takes in an interface ID and returns the requested COM interface on the same object [10]. A COM component supports a list of interfaces and is represented in MIDL through a *coclass*.

Once a client receives an object pointer, it invokes methods as it would on any of its local objects. On any method invocation on the object, marshaling is done, by reading the stack and writing into a flat memory buffer which holds data over the RPC network. On the client side this is done by the client-side stub called *Proxy*. The buffer is received by the server-side skeleton called *Stub*, which recreates the stack on the server side and invokes the method.

4.3 EXAMPLES

In an attempt to give a general idea on the implementation techniques and to arrive at a comparative study of the three distributed technologies—RMI,

CORBA, and DCOM—three experiments are depicted here. The first experiment is a ping experiment, the objective for which is to measure performance by response time. To detail a typical way of implementing a concurrency problem using these technologies, a producer–consumer problem is shown as the second experiment. A matrix-by-vector multiplication experiment shows the implementation of a numerical computation problem in a distributed environment. For sake of brevity, all implementation details are not indicated. However, all the important features are highlighted in the examples, which will enable the reader to write their applications using these three methodologies.

4.3.1 Experimental Setup

All the experiments were conducted on Pentium MMX (Model 4, CPU family 5, CPU MHz 200.456) machines connected by 10-Mbps Ethernet. The operating system used was Red Hat Linux. Java (JDK 1.3) was used as the programming language, for the obvious reason that RMI is one of the technologies. The CORBA implementations were done using Visibroker for Java 4.1 [19], which is fully compliant with the CORBA 2.3 specification. Deviating from the conventional approach, a tool that implements DCOM on UNIX platforms was chosen. This was done to make sure that all three experiments using all three paradigms were conducted under the same environment, so that a true comparative study could be made. The tool used was J-Integra Pure Java-COM bridge [26]. It offers a platform-independent implementation of COM libraries and hence suits the Java-DCOM implementation on UNIX platforms.

4.3.2 Developing Applications under RMI, CORBA, and DCOM

Steps Involved in Design and Implementation of RMI Applications The steps to be followed in developing a RMI server and a client are described below.

Server Side

1. Design the remote interface. As a rule, the remote interface should extend *java.rmi.Remote* directly or indirectly. In addition, each remote method should throw *java.rmi.RemoteException*, which gets thrown for any problem on the server side or network during the span of the remote method call.
2. Implement the remote interface. The implementation class must provide an implementation for every method listed in the interface. The implementation class needs to extend from *RemoteObject*, typically through *UnicastRemoteObject*.
3. Implement the RMI server. This involves creating and installing the remote object. The setup procedure is:

a. Create and install *RMISecurityManager*. This step is strongly recommended, although optional. This protects the access to system resources from any untrusted code downloaded from the remote virtual machine [2].
b. Create instances of the server object.
c. Bind or register the server object(s) with the RMI remote object registry (*rmiregistry*) or other naming service. If *rmiregistry* is being used as the naming service, it needs to be deployed on the server machine before the RMI server program runs.

Client Side

1. Create and install *RMISecurityManager*.
2. Lookup for the server object. A bind string that contains the remote server name where the object is hosted and the name bound with that object instance is supplied to the *lookup()* method on the *java.rmi.Naming* class. This method returns the object reference of the remote object.
3. Invoke methods on the object reference thus obtained.

Steps Involved in Design and Implementation of CORBA Applications

The steps involved in developing a typical CORBA application are:

1. Write a specification that describes the interfaces of the object or objects to be implemented using the IDL.
2. Compile the IDL specification using the IDL compiler provided by the particular ORB and for a particular target implementation language. This produces the client stub code and server skeleton code.
3. Identify the interfaces and classes generated by the IDL compiler that would be used or specialized to invoke or implement operations.
4. Write the server object code.
5. To implement the server object code derived from the POA classes, provide implementations of the interface's methods and implement the server's main routine.
6. Write the client program code.
7. For the client implementation code, initialize the ORB and obtain the references to any CORBA objects that we have created by doing a bind. Invoke methods on these objects.
8. Compile all the code generated and our application code with the target language compiler.
9. Start the ORB on the host.
10. Run the distributed application.

Steps Involved in Design and Implementation of DCOM Applications

The steps shown below provide a general set of procedures involved in the design and implementation of a typical DCOM client–server application. Although there are some idiosyncrasies of developing a DCOM application under the UNIX environment based on the tool used, they are not shown here, to avoid confusion.

Server Side

1. Create the MIDL specification. As a rule, each interface should extend *IUnknown* directly or indirectly. If the interface derives from *IDispatch* (which is itself derived from *IUnknown*), it means that the DCOM object supports late binding on remote method calls. In this case, each method call is routed through *IDispatch::Invoke()*. This feature of the server object is described as *Automation* [11]. Each interface should be contained in at least one *coclass*. A *coclass* represents a server component and specifies a listing of all supported interfaces for that component object. Each *coclass* is represented by a unique 128-bit number called CLSID. The list of all *coclasses* is embedded in a *library*, which contains all information that the MIDL compiler uses to generate a *type library*. A *type library* is a binary file that contains information similar to that contained in a header file.
2. Implement the *coclass*. The implementation class provides an implementation for every method listed in each component's contained *interface*. As more than one *interface* can be a part of one *coclass*, the same implementation class can be used to implement many interfaces. Also, as the same *interface* can be a part of more than one *coclass*, one *interface* can have more than one implementation.
3. Register the component. This step could vary depending on the access method the component's clients would follow. For instance, if the Windows system registry is used by the clients for lookup, a program (*regsvr32*) to register the CLSID and IID of the components is run. This program can be executed by a user, who has rights to create/modify entries in the system registry. If the clients use monikers, a separate server program is run, which instantiates a new server object. After instantiation, this program stores the named instance (*moniker*) in a file, which would then be read by any client program for binding purposes. The second approach was used for our experimentation purposes.

Client Side

1. Locate the server object. This again depends on the access method used. If monikers are used, the moniker file has to be read to get the name of the named interface object reference running on the server for binding.

90 DISTRIBUTED-OBJECT COMPUTING TOOLS

In a normal case, a typical Java-DCOM client creates a local reference to the remote interface object as though it is a local class object. The calls to the COM-SCM (like *coCreateInstance()*) are internally handled once the JVM knows that it is a remote object activation.

2. Invoke methods. The client then starts invoking methods on the object reference as if it were a local object.

4.3.3 Experiment 1: Ping

The objective of this experiment is to assess the performance of the distributed technologies, RMI, CORBA, and DCOM. The server object implements an interface, that takes in a floating-point array from the client and returns a reversed array back to the client. The client program first obtains a reference to this remote server object. It then creates a local float array and invokes a remote method on the object. This remote method reverses the float-array object and returns back the resultant array. This method invocation is done repeatedly on the object, and the average time for one method call is calculated. It is to be noted that for getting a realistic measurement of time, a Java native call for obtaining the system time is used in place of a call on the Java virtual machine. As a locally created object is passed from the client and got back from the server, this gives a good measurement strategy for assessing performance of these three technologies under the same environment. Although the load on the network is a variant that is not taken into consideration, the ping experiment (for RMI, CORBA, and DCOM) was carried out when no other user processes were deployed on the machines or using the network.

RMI

Step 1: Create the Interface File—PingRMI.java

```
public interface PingRMI extends java.rmi.Remote
{
float[]   doReverse(float[]   inputVect)   throws   java.rmi.RemoteException;
}// end of PingRMI
```

Step 2: Create the Ping Implementation Class—PingRMIImpl.java

```
import java.rmi.*;
import java.rmi.server.UnicastRemoteObject;
public class PingRMIImpl extends UnicastRemoteObject
         implements PingRMI
{
private String m_sName;
```

```
public PingRMIImpl(String sName) throws RemoteException
    {
        // constructor implementation
}// end of PingRMIImpl constructor

public    float[]   doReverse(float[]   inputVect)   throws
RemoteException
    {
    // reverse the input vector onto a temporary vector
    and
          // return the temporary vector
 }// end of doReverse
}// end of PingRMIImpl
```

Step 3: Implement the Server Class—PingRMIServer.java

```
import java.rmi.*;
import java.rmi.server.*;
public class PingRMIServer
{
    public static void main(String[] args)
    {
        // creates the security manager for RMI
         // this is done to make sure access to system
         resources is restricted
        System.setSecurityManager(new RMISecurityManager());
        try
        {
            // instantiates an instance of the server object
            PingRMIImpl pingObject = new PingRMIImpl
            ("PingServer");
            System.out.println("RMI Object Created");
            // binds the created object instance to the
            rmiregistry
            Naming.rebind("PingServer",pingObject);
            System.out.println("Binding Done");
        }
        catch (Exception e)
        {
System.out.println("Exception in PingRMIServer main: " +
e.getMessage());
    e.printStackTrace();
        }
    }// end of main
}// end of PingRMIServer
```

Step 4: Define the Ping Client—PingRMIClient.java

```java
//This is a client-side activity.
import java.rmi.*;
import java.rmi.registry.*;
import java.rmi.server.*;
public class PingRMIClient
{
public static void main(String[] args)
{
        // creates the security manager for RMI
        // this is done to make sure access to system
        // resources is restricted
        System.setSecurityManager(new RMISecurityManager());
        try
        {
           // looksup for the remote object and obtains
           // a local reference
           PingRMI myPingObject = (PingRMI)
            Naming.lookup("rmi://"+args[0]+"/
            PingServer");

                // initialize and populate the input
                // vector inputVect
        // initialize the output return vector
        // create a timer object
           TimeWrap oTimer = new TimeWrap();
           // start the timer this will be a native
           // interface call
           String sStartTime = oTimer.getFromTimer();

    // loop around to perform repeated reversals through
    // remote call
              for(int i=0;i<iLoop;i++)
              {
                outVect = myPingObject.doReverse(inputVect);
         }

              // stop the timer
           String sEndTime = oTimer.getFromTimer();
              // print the input and return vector con-
              tents for verification

    // calculate the total time taken on an average for
    // each method call
        lTimeDiff = (endTime-startTime) / iLoop;
```

EXAMPLES

```
    // display the ping results
            System.out.print("\nTime Taken for one RMI
            call on an average
                    (in MicroSec)= ");
            System.out.println(lTimeDiff);

    }
    catch(Exception e)
    {
        System.out.println("Exception    in    Client=
        "+e.getMessage());
        e.printStackTrace();
    }
} // end of main
} // end of PingRMIClinent
```

The underlying assumption above is that a timer is already implemented using JNI for getting a more realistic value for the start and end times.

Step 5: Define the Makefile
Makefile:

```
all :
    @echo "You must specify a taret"
java :
    \$(MAKE) -f Makefile.java
clean_java :
    \$(MAKE) -f Makefile.java clean
```

Makefile.java:

```
default:
    javac PingRMI.java
    javac PingRMIImpl.java
    rmic PingRMIImpl
    javac PingRMIServer.java
    javac PingRMIClient.jave

clean:
    rm -f *.lass
```

Step 6: Define the Security Policy Files As RMI requires the implementation of security manager on both the server and the client sides, it is required to specify the rights that need to be granted explicitly, for launching the server and client programs. This is done through a policy file. A sample of both server and client policy files is shown here.

Server.policy:

```
grant
{
permission java.net.SocketPermission
           ''*:1024-65535'',''accept,listen,connect,
           resolve'' ;
}
```

The server program needs *connect, resolve* rights to connect to the *RMIREGISTRY* and *accept, listen* rights to accept a new connection from a client. The *Server.policy* file grants these rights on any ports specified in the range.

Client.policy:

```
grant
{
    permission java.net.SocketPermission
           ''*:1024-65535'',''connect,resolve'';
}
```

The client program needs *connect, resolve* rights to connect to the remote server's *RMIREGISTRY*. The *client.policy* file grants these rights on any ports specified in the range.

Step 7: Execute the Programs The steps to be followed on the server side are:

```
Prompt> rmiregistry &
Prompt>  java  -Djava.security.policy=Server.policy
PingRMIServer &
```

The first step brings up the *rmiregistry*, and the second step launches the RMI ping server object.

The client program is launched the following way:

```
Prompt>  java  -Djava.security.policy=client.policy
PingRMIClient Pegasus
```

The machine on which the RMI server has been launched is specified as the argument to the client program. In the sample case shown, it is *Pegasus*.

CORBA

Step 1: Create the IDL File—Ping.idl

```
//Ping.idl
module Ping
{
  //unbounded sequence of floats.
typedef sequence<float> oneDimArray;
//Specify the interface for PingCorbaClass
interface PingCorba
{
            oneDimArray doReverse(in oneDimArray X);
    };
};
```

The CORBA IDL type *module* maps to a Java *Package* with the same name as the IDL module. The IDL type *interface* maps to a Java *interface* with the same name. A *sequence* is a variable-sized one-dimensional array of elements, where the element can be of any IDL-defined type. The sequence must be named using an IDL *typedef* before it can be used as an IDL type. A CORBA IDL *sequence* maps to a Java *array* with the same name. A CORBA *sequence* can be either bounded to a maximum length or unbounded [16]. In the ping example here an unbounded sequence has been used so that no restrictions are imposed on the maximum number of elements in the sequence.

Step 2: Use the IDL Compiler to Generate Client Stubs and Server Servants
Compile the .idl file using the command: idl2java Ping.idl -no_tie. The -no_tie option declares that *ties* which are meant for delegation-based implementations for non-OO languages [16], are not used. The idl2java compiler creates a separate directory called Ping and puts all the generated files in this directory. This is because the IDL specification *module* maps to a java equivalent of *package*. In this case since the module is named *Ping*, the generated Java files will be part of the package *Ping*.

Step 3: Provide an Implementation for the PingCorba Object—PingCorbaImpl.java The PingCorbaImpl class should extend from the PingCorbaPOA class, which is a part of the package Ping [20].

```
// PingCorbaImpl.java
public class PingCorbaImpl extends Ping.PingCorbaPOA
{
     PingCorbaImpl Constructor
            ...
public float[] doReverse (float [] X)
```

```
{
        // reverse the input array and return it.
                    ...
} //end of doReverse
} //end of PingCorbaImpl
```

Step 4: Implement the Server Program—PingCorbaServer.java The server program does the following: initializes the ORB, creates a portable object adapter (POA) with the required policies—in this case with a *LifespanPolicy* value of *PERSISTENT*, creates the PingServant object, activates the servant object, activates the POA manager (and the POA), and then waits for incoming requests. The lifespan policy specifies the lifespan of the object and can have the values *TRANSIENT* (default) or *PERSISTENT*. A transient object activated by a POA cannot outlive the POA that created it, whereas a persistent object activated by a POA can outlive the process in which it was first created. Requests invoked on a persistent object may result in the implicit activation of a process, a POA, and the servant that implements the object [20].

```
// PingCorbaServer.java
import org.omg.PortableServer.*;
public class PingCorbaServer
{
public static void main(String[] args)
{
        try
{
            // Initialize the ORB.
            org.omg.CORBA.ORB orb = org.omg.CORBA.ORB.
            init(args,null);

            // get a reference to the root POA
POA rootPOA =
            POAHelper.narrow(orb.resolve_initial_refer-
            ences ("RootPOA"));

            // Create policies for our persistent POA
org.omg.CORBA.Policy[] policies = {
rootPOA.create_lifespan_policy(LifespanPolicyValue.
PERSISTENT)
};

// Create myPOA with the right policies
POA myPOA =
rootPOA.create_POA( "PingCorba_poa", rootPOA.the_POAMan-
ager(), policies );
```

```
// Create the servant
PingCorbaImpl PingServant = new PingCorbaImpl();

// Decide on the ID for the servant
byte[] PingId = "Ping".getBytes();

// Activate the servant with the ID on myPOA
myPOA.activate_object_with_id(PingId, PingServant);

// Activate the POA manager
rootPOA.the_POAManager().activate();

System.out.println(myPOA.servant_to_reference(PingServant)
                   + " is ready. ");

// Wait for incoming requests
orb.run();
}
catch (Exception e)
{
          e.printStackTrace();
}
}//end of main
}//end of PingCorbaServer
```

Step 5: Implement the Client—PingCorbaClient.java

```
// PingCorbaClient.java
public class PingCorbaClient
{
public static void main(String[] args)
{
// Initialize the ORB.
org.omg.CORBA.ORB    orb    =    org.omg.CORBA.ORB.init
(args,null);

// Get the Id
byte[] PingId = "Ping".getBytes();

// Locate a PingCorba object reference. Give the full
// POA name and the servant ID.
Ping.PingCorba myPingObj =
Ping.PingCorbaHelper.bind(orb, "/PingCorba_poa", PingId);
```

```
//Create a float array (inputArray) of length N and
// populate it.
                          ...
//Create a float array (outputArray) of same length as
//inputArray.
                          ...

 // Create a timer object
 TimeWrap oTimer = new TimeWrap();

// Start the timer—this will be a native interface call
String sStartTime = oTimer.getFromTimer();
// Loop around to perform repeated reversals through
// remote call
 for(int i=0;i<iLoop;i++)
 {
                outputArray  =  myPingObj.doReverse
                (inputArray);
 }
 // Stop the timer
 String sEndTime = oTimer.getFromTimer();

       // print the input and return vector contents
       for verification
                      ...

// calculate the total time taken on an average for each
// method call
       lTimeDiff = (endTime-startTime) / iLoop;

// display the ping results
 System.out.print("\nTime Taken for one call on an
 average (in MicroSec)= ");
 System.out.println(lTimeDiff);
} //end of main
} //end of class PingCorbaClinent
```

Step 6: Create the Makefile to Compile all the Java files The Makefile for this application is shown here. This Makefile should be used in conjunction with Makefile.java shown below. To run the makefile, issue the following command: *Prompt> make java.*

Makefile:

```
all :
    @echo "You must specify a target"
```

```
java :
    \$(MAKE) -f Makefile.java
clean_java :
    \$(MAKE) -f Makefile.java clean
```

Makefile.java:

```
.SUFFIXES: .java .class .idl .module

.java.class:
    vbjc \$<
.idl.module:
    idl2java \$<
    touch \$@
default: all
clean:
    rm -rf Ping
    rm -f *.class *.tmp *.module *~
IDLS = \
    Ping.idl
MODULES = \$(IDLS: .idl = .module)
SRCS = \
    PingCorbaImpl.java \
    PingCorbaClient.java \
    PingCorbaServer.java
CLASSES = \$(SRCS: .java=.class
all:    \$(MODULES) \$(CLASSES)
```

Step 7: Launch the Application Before running the client programs or server applications, you must start the Visibroker Smart Agent [20] on at least one host in your local network. Launch the application as follows:

- Start the Smart Agent: *Prompt> osagent*
- Start the server: *Prompt> vbj PingCorbaServer*
- Run the client: *Prompt> vbj PingCorbaClient*

DCOM

Step 1: Create the .idl file—PingDCOM.idl

```
[
    // A unique 128-bit identifier for the PingDCOM
    // library
    // This can be generated by using utilities like
    // guidgen, provided by Microsoft
```

```
    uuid(5f648dc9-00e2-1000-5000-86448cae0000),
    version(1.0),
    helpstring("PingDCOM library definition. ")
]

library PingDCOM
{
// import the standard OLE library. This gives access
// to the standard OLE types
importlib("STDOLE2.TLB");
// Forward declare all types defined in this IDL file
interface IPingServerDCOM;
coclass PingServerDCOM;
[
  odl,
  uuid(5f651112-00e2-1000-5002-86448cae0000),
  helpstring("Interface for Java class PingServerDCOM "),
  dual,
  oleautomation
]
interface IPingServerDCOM : IDispatch
{
[id(0x1), helpstring("Java method: public float[] PingServerDCOM.doReverse(float[])")]
HRESULT doReverse([in] VARIANT p1, [out, retval] VARIANT *retVal);
};
[
  uuid(5f651112-00e2-1000-5001-86448cae0000),
  helpstring("Java class PingServerDCOM ")
]
coclass PingServerDCOM
{
    interface IPingServerDCOM;
};
}
```

HRESULT is the accepted form of return parameter for any DCOM method invocation. It defines a set of possible return values based on the success of the remote operation. *S_OK, E_FAIL, E_POINTER,* and *E_UNEXPECTED* are some of the common return values.

Step 2: Run MIDL on the idl File   The PingDCOM.idl file is compiled using Microsoft's MIDL compiler. This is done by: midl PingDCOM.idl. This generates PingDCOM.tlb, which is the type library that will be used by the client. A type library is a binary representation of the component [5].

Step 3: Register the .tlb File   The command *javatlb PingDCOM.tlb* is run next. This creates the .class files for the type library that have enough knowledge of how to convert the Java bytecode to COM-compatible calls. The tlb file, once registered, makes an entry into the system registry, which could be verified by running *regedit*.

Step 4: Implement the PingDCOM Interface

```
import java.io.*;
import java.util.*;
import com.ms.com.*;
public class PingServerDCOM implements IPingServerDCOM
{
public float [] doReverse (float[] inputVect)
{
        // reverse the input vector onto a temporary
        // vector and
// return the temporary vector
} // end of doReverse
} // end of PingServerDCOM
```

The implementation above is now compiled and the class file is placed in the <windows>\Java\Lib directory.

Step 5: Register the Class File   The implementation class file is registered using *javareg/register/class PingServerD-COM.class/clsid:5f651112-00e2-1000-5001-86448cae0000/surrogate*. Javareg [22] is a command line tool provided by Microsoft SDK for Java that allows registering of Java classes as COM components in the Windows system registry. Surrogate suggests that this class server, when brought up, would associate itself with a surrogate process address space.

Step 6: Set up DCOMCNFG   The level and security and access are defined by DCOMCNFG for each registered class. Each registered class is treated as an application and the details pertaining to the location of where the application can be hosted and *endpoints* are furnished at this level. Machine-level access and launch rights are also set using this utility. The following steps are to be done at the client side.

Step 7: Register the Type Library   *Javatlb PingDCOM.tlb* is run on the client machine too, to register the interface IID on to the client's registry.

Step 8: Register the Object Class CLSID Javareg /register /class: PingServerDCOM.class /clsid:5f651112-00e2-1000-5001-86448cae0000. This command registers the remote object class id on to the local client machine.

Step 9: Set up DCOMCNFG to Specify Location The server machine where the remote object is required to be hosted is specified using DCOMCNFG location tab.

Step 10: Define Client Implementation

```
import java.io.*;
import java.util.*;
public class PingDCOMClient
{
public static void main(String[] args)
{
        try
        {
           // create the Ping Object - if the server
           // is not already running, this
           // would launch the server object
            IPingServerDCOM       myPingObject    =
            (IPingServerDCOM)
                 new PingServerDCOM();
        // initialize and populate the input vector
        // inputVect
             // initialize the output return vector
        // create a timer object
              TimeWrap oTimer = new TimeWrap();
           // start the timer - this will be a native
           // interface call
          String sStartTime = oTimer.getFromTimer();
  // loop around to perform repeated reversals through
  // remote call
           for(int i=0;i<iLoop;i++)
{
              outVect = myPingObject.doReverse(inputVect);
           }
           // stop the timer
           String sEndTime = oTimer.getFromTimer();

// print the input and return vector contents for
// verification
// calculate the total time taken on an average for each
// method call
```

```
lTimeDiff = (endTime-startTime) / iLoop;

// display the ping results
        System.out.print("\nTime Taken for one DCOM call
        on an average (in MicroSec)= ");
        System.out.println(lTimeDiff);
}
    catch(Exception e)
    {
System.out.println("Exception   in   Client="+e.getMes-
sage());
            e.printStackTrace();
}
} // end of main
}// end of PingDCOMClient
```

All the steps above outline the list of activities involved in implementing a DCOM server and client under a Windows environment. However, as the objective of this experiment was to measure the performance of DCOM and compare it with RMI and CORBA, the DCOM application was run on UNIX using a Pure Java-COM bridge [23]. Only the salient idiosyncrasies pertaining to that tool are outlined in brief as follows:

- All COM-related libraries are implemented in the package *com.linar.jintegra.**.
- As UNIX-based systems do not have a system registry like-Windows, registration of the COM components are done through *monikers*. When a server object is instantiated, the object moniker (named instance) is written down as a string into a moniker file. When a client requests for that server object reference, this moniker file is read and the string is converted back to an interface pointer pointing to the server object. This conversion is done internally at the time of binding to the server object after obtaining the moniker string.
- The tool provides command line utilities, which allow the programmer to introduce COM-related specifics in a plain Java code. The command *java2com* converts a Java server implementation code to the corresponding COM IDL. The command *com2java* allows us to convert a *type library (.tlb)* into a Java package.

4.3.4 Experiment 2: Producer–Consumer Problem

This problem gives an overview of how concurrency control can be achieved in a distributed environment using the three technologies RMI, CORBA, and DCOM. In this implementation the server object hosts a synchronized buffer. The client has a *producer* and a *consumer*, each running concurrently in its own thread and accessing the shared buffer on the server. The producer thread

104 DISTRIBUTED-OBJECT COMPUTING TOOLS

generates a float value which it writes onto the shared buffer, and the consumer thread reads this value.

RMI

Interface Definition of the Buffer: SyncBufferRMI.java

```
public interface SyncBufferRMI extends java.rmi.Remote
{
    public void deposit(float fInputData) throws
    java.rmi.RemoteException;
    public float consume() throws java.rmi.RemoteException;
} // end of SyncBufferRMI
```

This is the base interface, which represents the buffer, on to which the producer deposits new data and from which the consumer reads the next available data.

Interface Definition of the Buffer Manager: SyncBufferManagerRMI.java

```
public interface SyncBufferManagerRMI extends java.rmi.
Remote
{
        SyncBufferRMI   createNewSyncBuffer(int   iSize)
        throws java.rmi.RemoteException;
} // end of SyncBufferManagerRMI
```

This is the interface that provides a new buffer to a client. This is required to make sure that each client creates and acts on a new synchronized buffer.

Implementation of the Buffer: SyncBufferRMIImpl.java

```
import java.rmi.*;
import java.rmi.server.UnicastRemoteObject;
public class SyncBufferRMIImpl extends UnicastRemoteObject
implements SyncBufferRMI
{
private int m_iCapacity;
private int m_iCount;
private int m_iFront;
private int m_iRear;
private float[] m_data;
```

```java
// this will be called by createNewSyncBuffer of the
// SyncBufferManagerRMIImpl
public  SyncBufferRMIImpl(int   iSize)    throws  RemoteException
{
        super();
        // initialise the matrix with the size provided
} // end of constructor

// deposit is called by the client directly by the pro
// ducer thread
public synchronized void deposit(float inputData) throws RemoteException
    {
        try
        {
        while(m_iCount==m_iCapacity) // means its full
        {
                wait();
        }
// write the new data into the next buffer position and
// notify all
        notifyAll();
      }
    catch(InterruptedException e)
        {
            System.out.println("Interrupted Exception in
            deposit()");
            e.printStackTrace();
        }
    } // end of deposit

    // consume is called by the client directly by the
    // consumer thread
    public synchronized float consume() throws RemoteException
    {
try
    {
            while(m_iCount==0)
            {
// means buff is empty and hence nothing to consume
            wait();
            }
    }
```

106 DISTRIBUTED-OBJECT COMPUTING TOOLS

```
            catch(InterruptedException e)
    {
    e.printStackTrace();
            throw new RemoteException();
    }
// store the next available data into retValue and notify
// all saying done
    notifyAll();
    return retValue;
  } // end of consume
} // end of SyncBufferRMIImpl
```

Implementation of the Buffer Manager: SyncBufferManagerRMIImpl.java

```
import java.rmi.*;
import java.rmi.server.UnicastRemoteObject;
public class SyncBufferManagerRMIImpl extends Unicast-
RemoteObject implements SyncBufferManagerRMI
{
private String m_sName;

// this is called by RMIServer code
public   SyncBufferManagerRMIImpl(String   sName)   throws
RemoteException
{
        super();
        m_sName = sName;
} // end of constructor
// this is called by the client directly and acts as a
// new buffer provider
public   SyncBufferRMI   createNewSyncBuffer(int   iSize)
throws RemoteException
    {
        return new SyncBufferRMIImpl(iSize);
} // end of createNewSyncBuffer
} // end of SyncBufferManagerRMIImpl
```

Implementation of the Buffer Server: SyncBufferRMIServer.java

```
import java.rmi.*;
import java.rmi.server.*;
public class SyncBufferRMIServer
{
    public static void main(String[] args)
    {
        System.setSecurityManager(new RMISecurityManager());
```

```
        try
        {
            SyncBufferManagerRMIImpl syncBufferManager =
            new SyncBufferManagerRMIImpl("SyncBufferMan-
            ager");
                System.out.println("RMI Object Created");
                Naming.rebind("SyncBufferManager",sync-
                BufferManager);
                System.out.println("Binding Done");
        }
        catch (Exception e)
        {
            System.out.println("Exception in SyncBuffer-
            RMIServer main: " +
                                        e.getMessage());
            e.printStackTrace();
        }
    } // end of main
} // end of SyncBufferRMIServer
```

Implementation of the Buffer Client: SyncBufferRMIClient.java

```
import java.rmi.*;
import java.rmi.registry.*;
import java.rmi.server.*;
public class SyncBufferRMIClient
{
public static void main(String[] args)
{
System.setSecurityManager(new RMISecurityManager());
        try
        {

        SyncBufferManagerRMI    mySyncBufferManager    =
        (SyncBufferManagerRMI)
        Naming.lookup("rmi://"+args[0]+"/SyncBufferManager");

   // initialize buffer size
            SyncBufferRMI mySyncBuffer =
                        mySyncBufferManager.create-
                        NewSyncBuffer (iBufSize);

            int iLoop=100;
            // create new producer and consumer threads
```

```
                Producer   myProducer  =  new   Producer
                (mySyncBuffer,iLoop);
                Consumer   myConsumer  =  new   Consumer
                (mySyncBuffer,iLoop);
                // the producer thread when started would
                // keep writing onto the syncbuffer
                // iLoop times
                myProducer.start();
    // the consumer thread when started would keep reading
    // from the sync buffer
                // the data written by the producer, iLoop
                // times
                myConsumer.start();

                // Main Thread of client waiting for
                // the producer and consumer threads to
                // terminate
       }
       catch(Exception e)
       {
          System.out.println("Exception   in   Client="+e.
          getMessage());
          e.printStackTrace();
       }
} // end of main
} // end of SyncBufferRMIClient
```

The implementation of the producer and consumer threads is not shown here.

Makefile: Makefile.java

```
default:
    javac SyncBufferRMI.java
    javac SyncBufferRMIImpl.java
    rmic SyncBufferRMIImpl
    javac SyncBufferManagerRMI.java
    javac SyncBufferManagerRMIImpl.java
    rmic SyncBufferManagerRMIImpl
    javac SyncBufferRMIServer.java
    javac SyncBufferRMIClient.java

clean:
    rm -f *.class
```

CORBA

IDL: ProducerConsumer.idl

```
// ProducerConsumer.idl
module ProducerConsumer
{

    //Interface for SyncBufferCorba class
 interface SyncBufferCorba
{
 //Methods of the class that this interface exposes.
 void deposit(in float value);
 float consume();
 };

 //Interface for SyncBufferCorbaManager class
  interface SyncBufferCorbaManager
{
        //Method of the class that this interface exposes.
        SyncBufferCorba createNewSyncBuffer();
 };
};
```

Implementation of the SyncBufferCorba Object: SyncBufferCorbaImpl.java

```
// SyncBufferCorbaImpl.java
public class SyncBufferCorbaImpl extends ProducerCon-
sumer.SyncBufferCorbaPOA
{
    private int bufferCount = 10;
    private int availableCount = 0;
    private float[] buffer;

    //Constructor
                ...

public synchronized void deposit(float value)
    {
        while(availableCount >= bufferCount )
        {
try
{
```

110 DISTRIBUTED-OBJECT COMPUTING TOOLS

```
                //Wait for Consumer to get Value
                wait();
}catch(InterruptedException ie)
{
System.out.println(ie);
}
}//end of while

//Add the value to the buffer and increment available count.
                    ...
//Notify Consumer that buffer has been set.
notifyAll();

}//end of deposit

public synchronized float consume()
{
        while(availableCount <= 0)
{
try
{
//wait for Producer to put value
wait();

}catch(InterruptedException ie){
System.out.println(ie);
}
}//end of while

//Retrieve value from buffer and decrement available
//count.
                                    ...
//Notify Producer that value has been retrieved from
buffer.
notifyAll();

return value;
}//end of consume
} //end of SyncBufferCorbaImpl
```

Implementation of the SyncBufferCorbaManager Object: SyncBufferCorbaManagerImpl.java

```
// SyncBufferCorbaManagerImpl.java
import org.omg.PortableServer.*;
```

```java
public class SyncBufferCorbaManagerImpl extends Producer-
Consumer.SyncBufferCorba{
public   synchronized   ProducerConsumer.SyncBufferCorba
createNewSyncBuffer()
{
SyncBufferCorbaImpl   SyncBufferCorbaServant   =   new
SyncBufferCorbaImpl();
ProducerConsumer.SyncBufferCorba syncBuffer = null;
try
{
// Activate it on the default POA which is root POA for
this servant
syncBuffer  =  ProducerConsumer.SyncBufferCorbaHelper.
narrow(
}
        catch (Exception e)
{
e.printStackTrace();
}
// Return the syncBuffer reference.
return syncBuffer;

}//end of createNewSyncBuffer
}//end of SyncBufferCorbaManagerImpl
```

Implementation of the Server Program: SyncCorbaServer.java

```java
// SyncCorbaServer.java
import org.omg.PortableServer.*;
public class SyncCorbaServer
{
 public static void main(String[] args)
{
        try
{

           // Initialize the ORB.
org.omg.CORBA.ORB orb = org.omg.CORBA.ORB.init(args, null);

// get a reference to the root POA
POA   rootPOA   =   POAHelper.narrow(orb.resolve_initial_
references("RootPOA"));

// Create policies for our persistent POA
org.omg.CORBA.Policy[] policies = {
```

112 DISTRIBUTED-OBJECT COMPUTING TOOLS

```java
rootPOA.create_lifespan_policy(LifespanPolicyValue.
PERSISTENT)
};

// Create myPOA with the right policies
POA myPOA = rootPOA.create_POA( "SyncBuffer_poa",
rootPOA.the_POAManager(), policies );

// Create the servant
SyncBufferCorbaManagerImpl SyncBufferManagerServant =
new SyncBufferCorbaManagerImpl();

// Decide on the ID for the servant
byte[] bufferManagerId = "SyncBuffer".getBytes();

// Activate the servant with the ID on myPOA
myPOA.activate_object_with_id(bufferManagerId,
SyncBufferManagerServant);

// Activate the POA manager
rootPOA.the_POAManager().activate();

System.out.println(myPOA.servant_to_reference(Sync-
                   BufferManagerServant) + " is
                   ready.");

// Wait for incoming requests
orb.run();
        }
catch (Exception e)
        {
e.printStackTrace();
        }
    }//end of main
}//end SyncCorbaServer
```

Implementation of the Client: SyncCorbaClient.java

```java
// SyncCorbaClient.java
public class SyncCorbaClient implements Runnable
{
private org.omg.CORBA.ORB orb;
private ProducerConsumer.SyncBufferCorbaManager syncBuffer
Manager;
private ProducerConsumer.SyncBufferCorba syncBuffer;
```

```java
public SyncCorbaClient(String[] args)
{

// Initialize the ORB.
        orb = org.omg.CORBA.ORB.init(args,null);

 // Get the Id
 byte[] bufferManagerId = "SyncBuffer".getBytes();

 // Locate the SyncBufferCorbaManager reference.
 //Give the full POA name and the servant ID.
 syncBufferManager =
 ProducerConsumer.SyncBufferCorbaManagerHelper.
 bind(orb, "/SyncBuffer_poa", bufferManagerId);

 //Get a SyncBufferCorba reference.
 syncBuffer = syncBufferManager.createNewSyncBuffer();

 Consumer consumer = new Consumer();
 Thread consumerThread = new Thread(consumer);
 //Start the Consumer Thread.
 consumerThread.start();

//Start the Producer Thread.
run();

}//end of SyncCorbaClient

public void run()
{
//Producer thread implementation to call the deposit
//method on the
//syncBuffer object and deposit values into the syn-
//chronous buffer.
        ...
} //end of ProducerRun

//Define the inner class Consumer implementing Runnable
//which calls the consume
//method on the syncBuffer object to consume values from
//the synchronous buffer.
        ...

public static void main(String[] args)
{
```

```
SyncCorbaClient myClient = new SyncCorbaClient(args);
}//end of main

}//end of SyncCorbaClient
```

Makefile.java for this Application   To be used in conjunction with the file Makefile provided in the ping example.

```
.SUFFIXES: .java .class .idl .module
.java.class:
    vbjc \$<
.idl.module:
    idl2java \$<
    touch \$@
default: all
clean:
    rm -rf ProducerConsumer
    rm -f χlass τmp μodule *~
IDLS = \
    ProducerConsumer.idl
MODULES = \$(IDLS:.idl=.module)
SRCS = \
    SyncBufferCorbaImpl.java \
    SyncBufferCorbaManagerImpl.java \
    SyncCorbaClient.java \
    SyncCorbaServer.java
CLASSES = \$(SRCS:.java=.class)
all:    \$(MODULES) \$(CLASSES)
```

DCOM

Interface Definition of the Buffer and Buffer Manager: ISyncBufferManagerDCOM.idl

```
[
    uuid(3ebf6888-00e2-1000-5000-7f0000010000),
    version(1.0),
    helpstring("SyncBufferManager    generated    from
    SyncBufferManagerDCOM")
]
library SyncBufferManager
{
importlib("STDOLE2.TLB");

// Forward declare all types defined in this IDL file
interface ISyncBufferDCOM;
```

```
interface ISyncBufferManagerDCOM;
coclass SyncBufferManagerDCOM;
[
  odl,
  uuid(3ec03fde-00e2-1000-5006-7f0000010000),
  helpstring("Interface for Java class SyncBufferDCOM "),
  dual,
  oleautomation
]
interface ISyncBufferDCOM : IDispatch
{
[id(0x1), helpstring("Java method: public synchronized
float                      SyncBufferDCOM.consume()")]
HRESULT consume([out, retval] float *retVal);
        [id(0x2), helpstring("Java method: public syn-
        chronized void
                            SyncBufferDCOM.deposit(float)")]
        HRESULT deposit([in] float p1);
};
[
odl,
    uuid(3ec03f07-00e2-1000-5002-7f0000010000),
        helpstring("Interface for Java class SyncBuffer-
        ManagerDCOM "),
        dual,
        oleautomation
]
interface ISyncBufferManagerDCOM : IDispatch
{
        [id(0x2), helpstring("Java method: public
        SyncBufferDCOM
            SyncBufferManagerDCOM.createNewSyncBuffer
            (int)")]
        HRESULT createNewSyncBuffer([in] long p1,
            [out, retval] SyncBufferDCOM* *retVal);
};
[
        uuid(3ec03f06-00e2-1000-5001-7f0000010000),
        helpstring("Java class SyncBufferManagerDCOM ")
]
coclass SyncBufferManagerDCOM
{
            interface ISyncBufferManagerDCOM;
};
}
```

Note that there are two interfaces defined in the same .idl file. *ISyncBuffer-DCOM* is the main buffer interface that is used by the client. *ISyncBuffer-ManagerDCOM* is the manager interface, which is again used just to provide a newly created buffer to a client program. The *coclass* above comprises only the manager interface, as that is what will be used first directly by the client. Also note that the interface derives from *IDispatch*, indicating that it is an automation server.

Implementation of the Buffer Object: SyncBufferDCOM.java This provides implementation for the ISyncBufferDCOM interface.

```
public class SyncBufferDCOM implements ISyncBufferDCOM
{
private int m_iCapacity;
private int m_iCount;
private int m_iFront;
private int m_iRear;
private float[] m_data;

public SyncBufferDCOM(int iSize)
     {
// initialise the buffer
}
// deposit is called by the client directly
public synchronized void deposit(float inputData)
{
try
        {
while(m_iCount==m_iCapacity)    // means its full
{
wait();
             }
// write the new data into the next buffer position and
// notify all notifyAll();
}
    catch(InterruptedException e)
    {
            System.out.println("Interrupted Exception in
            deposit()");
            e.printStackTrace();
    }
  } // end of deposit

    // this can be called by the client directly
    public synchronized float consume()
    {
```

```
        try
        {
        while(m_iCount==0)
{
// means buff is empty and hence nothing to consume
        wait();
        }
    }
    catch(InterruptedException e)
    {
        System.out.println("Interrupted   Exception   in
        deposit()");
        e.printStackTrace();
    }

    // store the next available data into retValue and
    // notify all
notifyAll();
    return retValue;
  } // end of consume
} // end of SyncBufferDCOM
```

Implementation of the Buffer Manager Object: SyncBufferManagerDCOM.java

```
public    class    SyncBufferManagerDCOM    implements
ISyncBufferManagerDCOM
{
// this will be called by the client directory to obtain
// a new SyncBufferDCOM object
// reference
public SyncBufferDCOM createNewSyncBuffer(int iSize)
    {
        return new SyncBufferDCOM(iSize);
} // end of createNewSyncBuffer
} // end of SyncBufferManagerDCOM
```

Implementation of the Buffer Client: SyncBufferDCOMClient.java

```
public class SyncBufferDCOMClient
{
   public static void main(String[] args)
   {
        try
        {
```

```
ISyncBufferManagerDCOM mySyncBufferManager =
            (ISyncBufferManagerDCOM) new SyncBuffer-
            ManagerDCOM();
// init buffer size and loop variables like iLoop
  // create new sync buffer
            ISyncBufferDCOM    mySyncBuffer         =
            (ISyncBufferDCOM)
                mySyncBufferProvider.createNew-
                SyncBuffer (iBufSize);

            Producer      myProducer     =      new
            Producer(mySyncBuffer, iLoop);
            Consumer    myConsumer   =   new   Consumer
            (mySyncBuffer, iLoop);
// start producer and consumer threads
            myProducer.start();
            myConsumer.start();

                // Main Thread of client waiting for the
                producer and consumer threads to
                // terminate
}
        catch(Exception e)
        {
            System.out.println("Exception          in
            Client="+e.getMessage());
            e.printStackTrace();
        }
} // end of main
} // end of SyncBufferDCOMClient
```

4.3.5 Experiment 3: Numerical Computation

The objective of this experiment is to indicate an implementation of a numerical algorithm in a distributed fashion. The problem that is taken for this purpose is a matrix-by-vector multiplication, which uses the algorithm given in [12]. Given an $m * n$ matrix, A, and an $n * 1$ vector, u, it is required to compute the $m * 1$ product vector, v. This is done using a linear array of m processors, $P_1, P_2, \ldots, P_m$, in a parallel fashion. Assume that v_i corresponds to the ith row in the final vector v. Initially, v_i is 0. The strategy is to compute v_i in P_i cumulatively. Figure 4.4 shows a modified version of the pictorial representation of the algorithm described in [12]. In this figure, the value of m is 2. a_{ij} indicates the element in the ith row and jth column of matrix A. u_i indicates the ith value in the vector u.

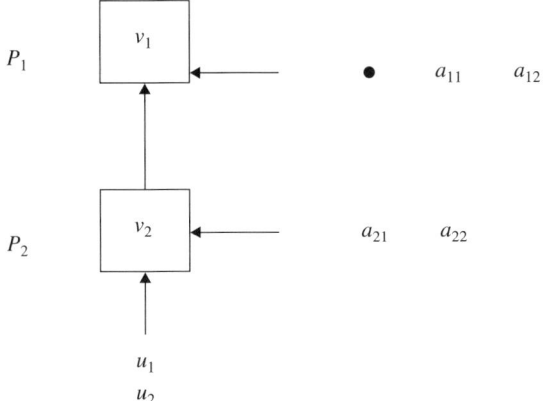

Fig. 4.4 Matrix-by-vector multiplication.

There are two server objects for this experiment. The first server object represents a processor object, which merely supports a *product* method to calculate the product of two float numbers and stores the resultant sum cumulatively in a member variable. The second server object acts as the central arbitrator, which actually implements the method *doMultiply*, taking in a matrix and a vector. The client sends the input matrix and vector to this central server object. The central server object, in turn, creates two processor objects locally and passes them to two child threads. Each child thread then does a parallel computation for each resultant matrix row by invoking the *doProduct* method on the processor object. The results are compiled and sent back to the client by the central server object. This suggests a possible approach to tackle a numerical parallel computation problem using all three distributed technologies.

RMI

Interface Definition of the Matrix: MatixRMI.java

```
public interface MatrixRMI extends java.rmi.Remote
{
     int getRows() throws java.rmi.RemoteException;
     int getCols()  throws java.rmi.RemoteException;
     float  getElement(int   iRows,   int   iCols)   throws
     java.rmi.RemoteException;
     void setElement(int iRows, int iCols, float value)
     throws java.rmi.RemoteException;
     void populateMatrix() throws java.rmi.RemoteException;
} // end of MatrixRMI
```

Interface Definition of the Matrix Manager: MatrixManagerRMI.java

```java
public   interface   MatrixManagerRMI   extends   java.rmi.
Remote
{
MatrixRMI createNewMatrix(int iRows,int iCols) throws
                                java.rmi.RemoteException;
  MatrixRMI  doMultiply(MatrixRMI  matA,  MatrixRMI  matB)
  throws java.rmi.RemoteException;
} // end of MatrixManagerRMI
```

Interface Definition of the Processor: ProcessorRMI.java

```java
public interface ProcessorRMI extends java.rmi.Remote
{
void   doProduct(float    value1,   float    value2)    throws
java.rmi.RemoteException;
      float getResult() throws java.rmi.RemoteException;
} // end of ProcessorRMI
```

Implementation of the Matrix Object: MatrixRMIImpl.java

```java
import java.rmi.*;
import java.rmi.server.UnicastRemoteObject;
public class MatrixRMIImpl extends UnicastRemoteObject
         implements MatrixRMI
{
private int m_iRows;
private int m_iCols;
private float[][] m_data;

// constructors
...
// functions for accessing the matrix elements
...
// functions for initializing and populating the matrix
...
} // end of MatrixRMIImpl
```

Implementation of the Processor Object: ProcessorRMIImpl.java

```java
import java.rmi.*;
import java.rmi.server.UnicastRemoteObject;
```

EXAMPLES

```java
// this class does a product of two floats and stores the
// cumulative sum
public class ProcessorRMIImpl extends UnicastRemoteObject
        implements ProcessorRMI
{
private float m_fSum;
private String m_sName;

public ProcessorRMIImpl(String sName) throws RemoteException
    {
       super();
       m_fSum=0;
    } // end of constructor

// this is called by the RowMultiplier Threads of Matrix
// Manager
    public void doProduct(float value1, float value2)
    throws RemoteException
{
       m_fSum = m_fSum + (value1 * value2);
} // end of doProduct

public float getResult() throws RemoteException
{
float retSum;
        retSum = m_fSum;   // once returned the sum is
        // re-initialized to 0
        m_fSum = 0;
        return retSum;
} // end of getResult
} // end of ProcessorRMIImpl
```

Implementation of the Matrix Manager Object: MatrixManagerRMIImpl.java

```java
import java.rmi.*;
import java.rmi.server.UnicastRemoteObject;
public class MatrixManagerRMIImpl extends UnicastRemoteObject implements MatrixManagerRMI
{
private String m_sName;
private int m_iNoOfRows;

public MatrixManagerRMIImpl(String sName) throws RemoteException
```

```
    {
        super();
// initialize the internal variables like the number of
// rows of the matrix
// this can handle
} // end of constructor
    public   MatrixRMI  createNewMatrix(int    iRows,int
    iCols) throws RemoteException
    {
        return new MatrixRMIImpl(iRows,iCols);
} // end of createNewMatrix

public  MatrixRMI  doMultiply(MatrixRMI  matA,  MatrixRMI
vectorB) throws
                      RemoteException
    {
        try
        {
                // create proc1 and proc2 object refer
                // ences for the two processors running
    // in two different machines
            ProcessorRMI proc1 = (ProcessorRMI)
                Naming.lookup("rmi://pegasus/Multiplier-
                Processor");
             ProcessorRMI proc2 = (ProcessorRMI)
                Naming.lookup("rmi://reliant/Multiplier-
                Processor");
    // perform checks on the number of rows and columns
    // initialize the result matrix
    MatrixRMI resultMatrix ;
    resultMatrix = new MatrixRMIImpl(rowsA,colsB);
    // A shared buffer which is synchronized is used for
    // this purpose
    Buffer syncBuf = new Buffer(vectorB);
    // have two threads for computing each of the two
    // rows of the result matrix
    // these threads will invoke doProduct methods of
    // the processor object
    RowMultiplier1             t1           =          new
    RowMultiplier1(proc1,syncBuf, row2,resultMatrix);
    RowMultiplier2             t2           =          new
    RowMultiplier2(proc2,syncBuf, row1,resultMatrix);

    t1.start();
    t2.start();
```

```
    while(t1.isAlive() || t2.isAlive())
    {
    // do nothing wait
    }
    // results are already in resultMatrix
    // return the merged matrix/vector
       return resultMatrix;
     }
     catch(Exception e)
     {
        System.out.println("Exception                in
        Client="+e.getMessage());
        e.printStackTrace();
            throw new RemoteException();
     }
} // end of doMultiply
} // end of MatrixManagerRMIImpl
```

The implementation for the RowMultiplier and buffer are not shown here.

Implementation of the Matrix Server: MatrixRMIServer.java

```
import java.rmi.*;
import java.rmi.server.*;
public class MatrixRMIServer
{
    public static void main(String[] args)
    {
        System.setSecurityManager(new RMISecurityManager());
        try
        {
        MatrixManagerRMIImpl matMgrObject =
        new MatrixManagerRMIImpl("MatrixManager");
            System.out.println("RMI Object Created");
            Naming.rebind("MatrixManager",matMgrObject);
            System.out.println("Binding Done");
        }
        catch (Exception e)
        {
            System.out.println("Exception in MatrixRMIS-
            erver main: " + e.getMessage());
        e.printStackTrace();
        }
    } // end of main
} // end of MatrixRMIServer
```

Implementation of the Processor Server: ProcessorRMIServer.java

```java
import java.rmi.*;
import java.rmi.server.*;
public class ProcessorRMIServer
{
    public static void main(String[] args)
    {
        System.setSecurityManager(new RMISecurityManager());
        try
        {
        ProcessorRMIImpl procObject =
        new ProcessorRMIImpl("MultiplierProcessor");
        System.out.println("RMI Object Created");
        Naming.rebind("MultiplierProcessor",procObject);
        System.out.println("Binding Done");
        }
        catch (Exception e)
        {
           System.out.println("Exception  in  ProcessorRMI-
           Server main: " + e.getMessage());
           e.printStackTrace();
        }
    }// end of main
}// end of ProcessorRMIServer
```

Implementation of the Matrix Client: MatrixRMIClient.java

```java
import java.rmi.*;
import java.rmi.registry.*;
import java.rmi.server.*;
public class MatrixRMIClient
{
    public static void main(String[] args)
    {
        System.setSecurityManager(new RMISecurityManager());
        try
        {
        MatrixManagerRMI myMatManager = (MatrixManagerRMI)
        Naming.lookup("rmi://"+args[0]+"/MatrixManager");

               // init rows and columns for the matrix
               MatrixRMI MatA  = myMatManager.createNew-
               Matrix (iRowsA,iColsA);
```

```
      // init rows and columns for the vector
      MatrixRMI MatB   = myMatManager.createNewMatrix
      (iRowsB,iColsB);
      MatA.populateMatrix();
      MatB.populateMatrix();
// initialize the output matrix
         MatrixRMI MatC  = myMatManager.createNewMa-
         trix(iRowsC, iColsC);
         // start timer
         String sStartTime = oTimer.getFromTimer();
         for(int i=0;i<iLoop;i++)
         {
            MatC = myMatManager.doMultiply(MatA,MatB);
      }
        // end timer
      String sEndTime = oTimer.getFromTimer();
        // print the input and return vector contents
        // for verification
      // calculate the total time taken on an average
      // for each method call
      lTimeDiff =   (endTime-startTime) / iLoop;
        System.out.print("\nTime Taken for one RMI call
        on an average
           (in MicroSec)= ");
        System.out.println(lTimeDiff);
   }
     catch(Exception e)
     {
           System.out.println("Exception in Client="+
           e.getMessage());
           e.printStackTrace();
        }
   } // end of main
} // end of MatrixRMIClient
```

Makefile: Makefile.java

```
default:
    javac ProcessorRMI.java
    javac ProcessorRMIImpl.java
    rmic ProcessorRMIImpl
    javac MatrixRMI.java
    javac MatrixManagerRMI.java
    javac MatrixRMIImpl.java
    javac MatrixManagerRMIImpl.java
```

```
      rmic MatrixRMIImpl
      rmic MatrixManagerRMIImpl
      javac MatrixRMIServer.java
      javac ProcessorRMIServer.java
      javac SyncBufferRMIClient.java

clean:
      rm -f    x.lass
```

CORBA

IDL: MatMult.idl

```
// MatMult.idl
module MatMult
{
interface MatrixCorba
{
short getRows();
short getCols();
void populateMatrix();
float getElement(in short row,in short col);
void setElement(in short row,in short col,in float val);
};

interface MatrixCorbaManager
     {
MatrixCorba createNewMatrix(in short row,in short col);
MatrixCorba doMultiply(in MatrixCorba A,in MatrixCorba B);
};

interface ProcessorCorbaManager
{
void doProduct(in float U,in float A);
float getResult();
};
};
```

Implementation of the MatrixCorba Object: MatrixCorbaImpl.java

```
// MatrixCorbaImpl.java
public class MatrixCorbaImpl extends MatMult.MatrixCorbaPOA
{
    private short rows;
```

```
    private short cols;
    private float[][] matrix;

    //Constructor
            ...

    //Functions for getting the number of rows and columns.
            ...

    //Functions for accessing the elements of the matrix
            ...
    //Function for populating the Matrix
            ...
} //end of MatrixCorbaImpl
```

Implementation of the MatrixCorbaManager Object:
MatrixCorbaManagerImpl.java

```
// MatrixCorbaManagerImpl.java
import org.omg.PortableServer.*;
public class MatrixCorbaManagerImpl extends MatMult.
MatrixCorbaManagerPOA
{
public synchronized MatMult.MatrixCorba createNewMatrix
(short row,short col)
{
MatrixCorbaImpl matrixServant = new MatrixCorbaImpl(row,
col);
MatMult.MatrixCorba matrix = null;

try
{
 // Activate it on the default POA which is root POA
 // for this servant
 matrix = MatMult.MatrixCorbaHelper.narrow(
  _default_POA().servant_to_reference(matrixServant));
 }
 catch (Exception e)
{
 e.printStackTrace();
 }

 // Return the matrix.
 return matrix;
}//end of createNewMatrix
```

```
public synchronized MatMult.MatrixCorba
doMultiply(MatMult.MatrixCorba A,MatMult.MatrixCorba B)
{

String[] args = null;

// Initialize the ORB.
org.omg.CORBA.ORB orb = org.omg.CORBA.ORB.init (args,
null);

//Steps to get the object reference for processor2 which
//is running on
// on a different machine:

// Step 1) Get the Processor Id
byte[] processor2Id = "Processor2".getBytes();
// Step 2) Locate the ProcessorCorbaManager object
reference .
MatMult.ProcessorCorbaManager processor2 =
MatMult.ProcessorCorbaManagerHelper.bind(orb, "/Proces-
sor2_poa", processor2Id);

//Initialize the resultMatrix which is a MatrixCorbaImpl
//object.
MatrixCorbaImpl resultMatrix = null;

//Initialize matrix which is a MatrixCorba object.
MatMult.MatrixCorba matrix = null;

//Get the number of rows and columns in A and B by
//calling getRows() and
//getCols on matrix references A and B passed to this
//method.
                ...
//Perform checks on number of rows and columns in matri-
//ces A and B.
       ...
//buffer is a synchronized shared Buffer object which
//will be accessed by the two
//processor objects.
Buffer buffer = new Buffer();

//Instantiate the resultMatrix .
resultMatrix = new MatrixCorbaImpl(rowsA,colsB);
```

```
//Do a narrow on the resultMatrix to obtain a MatrixCorba
//object reference.
try
{
// Activate it on the default POA which is root POA for
// this servant
matrix = MatMult.MatrixCorbaHelper.narrow(
 _default_POA().servant_to_reference(resultMatrix));

}
 catch (Exception e)
{
e.printStackTrace();
}

//rowMultiply is the thread which will compute the result
//for the first row of the
//matrix by invoking the doProduct() method on proces
//sor1 object.
RowMultiplier rowMultiply = new RowMultiplier(buffer,A,
matrix,0);
rowMultiply.start();

//Here the  currentThread performs computations to get
//the result for the second
//row of the matrix by invoking the doProduct() method
//on the processor2 object
//whose object reference we had obtained earlier.
        ...

//Iteratively pick each element from  row 2 of Matrix A
//and the column of Vector B
// and invoke doProduct() on processor2 by passing these
// coefficients.
        ...
processor2.doProduct(coeffU,coeffA);

//Set the synchronized buffer with the coefficient from
//Vector B which will be read
//by the rowMultiply thread and used in the result cal-
//culations for row 1.
buffer.setBuffer(coeffU);

//Get the computed result for this row and set the element
//in the resultant matrix.
```

```
float result = processor2.getResult();
matrix.setElement((short)rowNum,(short)0,result);

//Wait in a no-op loop for the rowMultiply thread to
//complete.
        ...
//Returning the result matrix
return matrix;
}//end of doMultiply
}//end of MatrixCorbaManagerImpl
```

Implementation of the RowMultiplier Thread Object: RowMultiplier.java

```
class RowMultiplier extends Thread
{
private int arrayLen;
private int rowNum;
private MatMult.MatrixCorba matrixA;
private MatMult.MatrixCorba resultMatrix;
private Buffer bufferObj;

//RowMultiplier Constructor which initializes all its
//data members.
public void run()
    {
String[] args = null;

// Initialize the ORB.
org.omg.CORBA.ORB orb = org.omg.CORBA.ORB.init(args,
null);

//Steps to get the object reference for processor1 which
//is running on
// on a different machine:
// Step 1) Get the Processor Id
byte[] processor1Id = "Processor1".getBytes();
//Step 2) Locate the ProcessorCorbaManager object ref-
//erence .
MatMult.ProcessorCorbaManager processor1 =
MatMult.ProcessorCorbaManagerHelper.bind(orb, "/Proces-
sor1_poa", processor1Id);

//The computations performed by this thread are similar
//to those performed by
// doMultiply(..) thread. The result for the first row
// of the matrix is obtained
```

```
// invoking the doProduct() method on the processor1
// object.
            ...
}//end of run
}//end of class RowMultiplier
```

Implementation of the ProcessorCorbaManager Object: ProcessorCorbaManagerImpl.java

```
// ProcessorCorbaManagerImpl.java
import org.omg.PortableServer.*;
public    class    ProcessorCorbaManagerImpl    extends
MatMult.ProcessorCorbaManagerPOA
private float result;

//Constructor for ProcessorCorbaManagerImpl
            ...
//void doProduct(float,float) implementation: Multiply
//input parameters and store result.
            ...
// float getResult() implementation: Return the computed
// result.
            ...
}//end of ProcessorCorbaManagerImpl
```

Implementation of the MatrixCorbaClient Class: MatrixCorbaClient.java

```
// MatrixCorbaClient.java
public class MatrixCorbaClient
{
public static void main(String[] args)
{

// Initialize the ORB.
org.omg.CORBA.ORB  orb  =  org.omg.CORBA.ORB.init(args,
null);

// Get the Id
byte[] MatrixManagerId = "Multiplier".getBytes();

// Locate a matrix manager. Give the full POA name and
// the servant ID.
MatMult.MatrixCorbaManager manager =
MatMult.MatrixCorbaManagerHelper.bind(orb, "/matrix_agent_
poa", MatrixManagerId);
```

132   DISTRIBUTED-OBJECT COMPUTING TOOLS

```
//Create matrix A with 2 rows and N columns and Vector
//B with N rows and 1 column.
MatMult.MatrixCorba   matrixA  =  manager.createNewMatrix
(rowsA,colsA);
MatMult.MatrixCorba   matrixB  =  manager.createNewMatrix
(rowsB,colsB);

//Populate matrices A and B.
matrixA.populateMatrix();
matrixB.populateMatrix();

//Create the output matrix - matrixC
MatMult.MatrixCorba   matrixC  =  manager.createNewMatrix
(rowsA,colsB);

//Instantiate the Timer object.
TimeWrap oTimer = new TimeWrap();
//Starting the timer
String sStartTime = oTimer.getFromTimer();

  for(int i=0;i<iLoop;i++)
{
        matrixC = manager.doMultiply(matrixA,matrixB);
}
  //Stopping the timer.
  String sEndTime = oTimer.getFromTimer();

//Printing the input and resultant matrix contents for
verification.
            ...

//Calculate the total time taken on an average for each
//method call.
lTimeDiff = (endTime - startTime)/iLoop;

System.out.print("\nTime Taken for one call on an average
(in MicroSec)= ");
System.out.println(lTimeDiff);

} //end of main
} //end of MatrixCorbaClient
```

Implementation of the MatrixCorbaServer Object: MatrixCorbaServer.java

```
// MatrixCorbaServer.java
import org.omg.PortableServer.*;
```

```java
public class MatrixCorbaServer
{
public static void main(String[] args)
{
  try
{
// Initialize the ORB.
org.omg.CORBA.ORB     orb     =     org.omg.CORBA.ORB.init
(args,null);

// get a reference to the root POA
POA    rootPOA    =    POAHelper.narrow(orb.resolve_initial_
references("RootPOA"));

// Create policies for our persistent POA
org.omg.CORBA.Policy[] policies = {
rootPOA.create_lifespan_policy(LifespanPolicyValue.
PERSISTENT)
};

// Create myPOA with the right policies
POA myPOA =     rootPOA.create_POA( "matrix_agent_poa",

// Create the servant
MatrixCorbaManagerImpl managerServant = new MatrixCorba-
ManagerImpl();

// Decide on the ID for the servant
byte[] matrixId = "Multiplier".getBytes();

// Activate the servant with the ID on myPOA
myPOA.activate_object_with_id(matrixId, managerServant);

// Activate the POA manager
rootPOA.the_POAManager().activate();

System.out.println(myPOA.servant_to_reference
(managerServant) + " is ready.");

// Wait for incoming requests
orb.run();
}
catch (Exception e)
{
e.printStackTrace();
```

}
}//end of main
}//end of MatrixCorbaServer

Implementation of the First ProcessorCorbaServer:
ProcessorCorbaServer1.java

```
// ProcessorCorbaServer1.java
import org.omg.PortableServer.*;
public class ProcessorCorbaServer1
{
public static void main(String[] args)
{
try
{
 // Initialize the ORB.
org.omg.CORBA.ORB orb = org.omg.CORBA.ORB.init(args,null);

// get a reference to the root POA
POA   rootPOA  =   POAHelper.narrow(orb.resolve_initial_
references("RootPOA"));

// Create policies for our persistent POA
org.omg.CORBA.Policy[] policies = {
rootPOA.create_lifespan_policy(LifespanPolicyValue.
PERSISTENT)
};

// Create myPOA with the right policies
POA   myPOA   =   rootPOA.create_POA(   "Processor1_poa",
rootPOA.the_POAManager(),
policies );

// Create the servant
ProcessorCorbaManagerImpl processor1Servant =
new ProcessorCorbaManagerImpl();

// Decide on the ID for the servant
byte[] processId = "Processor1".getBytes();

// Activate the servant with the ID on myPOA
myPOA.activate_object_with_id(processId, processor1Servant);

// Activate the POA manager
```

```
rootPOA.the_POAManager().activate();
System.out.println(myPOA.servant_to_reference(proces-
sor1Servant) + " is ready.");

// Wait for incoming requests
orb.run();
}
catch (Exception e)
{
e.printStackTrace();
}
}//end of main
}//end of ProcessorCorbaServer1
```

Implementation of the ProcessorCorbaServer2 is similar to Processor CorbaServer1 and hence it is not shown here. Implementation of the Buffer object is also not shown.

Makefile.java for this Example This makefile is to be used in conjunction with the file Makefile provided in the ping example.

```
.SUFFIXES: .java .class .idl .module
.java.class:
    vbjc \$<

.idl.module:
    idl2java \$<
    touch \$@
default: all
clean:
    rm -rf MatMult
    rm -f *.class *.tmp *.module *~
IDLS = \
    MatMult.idl
MODULES = \$(IDLS:.idl=.module)
SRCS = \
    MatrixCorbaImpl.java \
    MatrixCorbaManagerImpl.java \
    ProcessorCorbaManagerImpl.java\
    Buffer.java\
    MatrixCorbaServer.java\
    ProcessorCorbaServer1.java\
    ProcessorCorbaServer2.java\
    RowMultiplier.java\
    MatrixCorbaClient.java
```

```
CLASSES = \$(SRCS:.java=.class)
all: \$(MODULES) \$(CLASSES)
```

DCOM

Interface Definition of the Matrix and Matrix Manager: MatrixManager.idl

```
[
    uuid(49fbcf3f-00e2-1000-5000-7f0000010000),
    version(1.0),
    helpstring("MatrixManager generated from MatrixMan-
    agerDCOM ")
]
library MatrixManager
{
importlib("STDOLE2.TLB");
// Forward declare all types defined in this IDL file
interface IMatrixManagerDCOM;
coclass MatrixManagerDCOM;
interface IMatrixDCOM;
[
  odl,
  uuid(49fc4a47-00e2-1000-5002-7f0000010000),
  helpstring("Interface for Java class MatrixManagerDCOM "),
  dual,
  oleautomation
]
interface IMatrixManagerDCOM : IDispatch
{
[id(0x2), helpstring("Java method: doMultiply")]
      HRESULT doMultiply([in] IMatrixDCOM* p1, [in] IMa-
      trixDCOM* p2, [in] BSTR p3, [in] BSTR p4, [out,
      retval] IMatrixDCOM* *retVal);
      [id(0x3), helpstring("Java method: public IMa-
      trixDCOM
         MatrixManagerDCOM.createNewMatrix(int,int)")]
      HRESULT createNewMatrix([in] long p1,
                      [in] long p2,
           [out, retval] IMatrixDCOM* *retVal);
};
[
      uuid(49fc4a46-00e2-1000-5001-7f0000010000),
      helpstring("Java class MatrixManagerDCOM ")
]
```

```
coclass MatrixManagerDCOM
{
            interface IMatrixManagerDCOM;
};
[
        odl,
        uuid(49fc4b87-00e2-1000-5006-7f0000010000),
        helpstring("Interface for Java class IMatrixDCOM "),
        dual,
        oleautomation
]
interface IMatrixDCOM : IDispatch
{
        [id(0x1), helpstring("Java method: public int
        IMatrixDCOM.getRows()")]
        HRESULT getRows([out, retval] long *retVal);
        [id(0x2), helpstring("Java method: public int
        IMatrixDCOM.getCols()")]
        HRESULT getCols([out, retval] long *retVal);
        [id(0x3), helpstring("Java method: public float
            IMatrixDCOM.getElement(int,int)")]
HRESULT getElement([in] long p1, [in] long p2,[out,
retval] float *retVal);
        [id(0x4), helpstring("Java method: public void
            MatrixDCOM.setElement(int,int,float)")]
        HRESULT setElement([in] long p1, [in] long p2,
        [in] float p3);
        [id(0x5), helpstring("Java method: public void
        IMatrixDCOM.populate()")]
        HRESULT populateMatrix();
}; // end of IMatrixDCOM
} // end of MatrixManager library
```

Interface Definition of the Processor: Processor.idl

```
[
    uuid(49f8de44-00e2-1000-5000-7f0000010000),
    version(1.0),
    helpstring("Processor generated from ProcessorDCOM
    (J-Integra)")
]
library Processor
{
importlib("STDOLE2.TLB");
// Forward declare all types defined in this IDL file
```

```
interface IProcessorDCOM;
coclass ProcessorDCOM;
[
  odl,
  uuid(49f9502c-00e2-1000-5002-7f0000010000),
  helpstring("Interface for Java class ProcessorDCOM "),
  dual,
  oleautomation
]
interface IProcessorDCOM : IDispatch
{
[id(0x1), helpstring("Java method: public void
        ProcessorDCOM.doProduct(float,float)")]
      HRESULT doProduct([in] float p1,[in] float p2);
      [id(0x3), helpstring("Java method: public float
      ProcessorDCOM.getResult()")]
      HRESULT getResult([out, retval] float *retVal);
};
[
      uuid(49f9502c-00e2-1000-5001-7f0000010000),
      helpstring("Java class ProcessorDCOM ")
]
coclass ProcessorDCOM
{
          interface IProcessorDCOM;
}; // end of ProcessorDCOM
} // end of Processor library
```

Implementation of the Matrix Object: MatrixDCOM.java

```
public class MatrixDCOM implements IMatrixDCOM
{
private int m_iRows;
private int m_iCols;
private float[][] m_data;

// constructors
...
// functions for accessing the matrix elements
...
// functions for initializing and populating the matrix
...
} // end of MatrixDCOM
```

Implementation of the Processor Object: ProcessorDCOM.java

```java
public class ProcessorDCOM implements IProcessorDCOM
{
private float m_fSum;

// constructors
// this can be called by the MatrixManager Server Object
// directly
public void doProduct(float value1, float value2)
{
        m_fSum = m_fSum + (value1 * value2);
} // end of doProduct

public float getResult()
{
        // assumes that the result is being retrieved
        // ..so initialise back the variable
// return cumulative sum and initialize it to zero
} // end of getResult
}
```

Implementation of the Matrix Manager Object: MatrixManagerDCOM.java

```java
public class MatrixManagerDCOM implements IMatrix-
ManagerDCOM
{
// constructor
// this method returns reference to a new matrix
public IMatrixDCOM createNewMatrix(int iRows,int iCols)
{
        return new MatrixDCOM(iRows,iCols);
} // end of createNewMatrix

public IMatrixDCOM doMultiply(IMatrixDCOM matA, IMa-
trixDCOM vectorB)
    {
try
{
    // create proc1 and proc2 object references for the
    // two processors running
    // in two different machines
        IProcessorDCOM proc1 = (IProcessorDCOM) new
        ProcessorDCOM();
```

```
            IProcessorDCOM   proc2  =  (IProcessorDCOM)   new
            ProcessorDCOM();
    // perform checks on the number of rows and columns
    // initialize the result matrix
    IMatrixDCOM resultMatrix ;
    resultMatrix = (IMatrixDCOM) new MatrixDCOM(rowsA,
    colsB);
    // A shared buffer which is synchronized is used for
    // this purpose
    Buffer  syncBuf = new Buffer(vectorB);
    // have two threads for computing each of the two
    // rows of the result matrix
    // these threads will invoke doProduct methods of
    the processor object
    RowMultiplier1              t1            =          new
    RowMultiplier1(proc1,syncBuf, row2,resultMatrix);
    RowMultiplier2              t2            =          new
    RowMultiplier2(proc2,syncBuf, row1,resultMatrix);
    t1.start();
    t2.start();
    while(t1.isAlive() || t2.isAlive())
    {
     // do nothing wait
    }
    // results are already in resultMatrix
    // return the merged matrix/vector
    return resultMatrix;
     }
     catch(Exception e)
        {
System.out.println("Exception   in   Client="+e.getMes-
sage());
e.printStackTrace();
throw new RemoteException();
}
} // end of doMultiply
} // end of MatrixManagerDCOM
```

The implementation for RowMultiplier and the synchronized buffer is not shown.

Implementation of the Matrix DCOM Client: MatrixDCOMClient.java

```
import java.io.*;
import java.util.*;
public class MatrixDCOMClient
```

```java
{
public static void main(String[] args)
    {
try
        {
// create the MatrixManager Object - if the server is
// not already running, this
  // would launch the server object
            IMatrixManagerDCOM myMatManager = (IMatrix-
            ManagerDCOM)
            new MatrixManagerDCOM();

            // init rows and columns for the matrix
             IMatrixDCOM MatA  = myMatManager.createNew-
             Matrix(iRowsA,iColsA);
            // init rows and columns for the vector
             IMatrixDCOM MatB  = myMatManager.createNew-
             Matrix(iRowsB,iColsB);
            MatA.populateMatrix();
            MatB.populateMatrix();
// initialize the output matrix
IMatrixDCOM MatC  = myMatManager.createNewMatrix(iRowsC,
iColsC);
            // start timer
            String sStartTime = oTimer.getFromTimer();
            for(int i=0;i<iLoop;i++)
            {
               MatC = myMatManager.doMultiply(MatA,MatB);
            }
            // end timer
        String sEndTime = oTimer.getFromTimer();
            // print the input and return vector con-
            // tents for verification
        // calculate the total time taken on an average
        // for each method call
          lTimeDiff = (endTime-startTime) / iLoop;
            System.out.print("\nTime Taken for one DCOM
            call on an average
               (in MicroSec)= ");
            System.out.println(lTimeDiff);
          }
          catch(Exception e)
          {
             System.out.println("Exception           in
             Client="+e. getMessage());
             e.printStackTrace();
```

```
        }
    } // end of main
} // end of MatrixDCOMClient
```

4.4 COMPARISON OF THE THREE PARADIGMS

A comparison of the three paradigms based on the listed factors follows.

4.4.1 Dependency Issues

Issues related to language and platform dependency are discussed in Table 4.1.

4.4.2 Implementation Details

A comparative study is done of the manner in which the three paradigms allow implementation of distributed applications, shown in Table 4.2. Factors considered include IDL specifications, location transparency (client's knowledge of the server location), object registration (manner in which the server object is registered), and mode of obtaining an object reference (manner in which a server object reference is obtained by the client).

4.4.3 Architecture Details

The communication protocols used by the three paradigms and system resources involved are noted in Table 4.3.

TABLE 4.1 Comparison Based on Language and Platform Dependencies

RMI	CORBA	DCOM
Can only be implemented using Java.	Since CORBA is a specification, implementation is possible in all languages which provide support to ORB libraries and language mappings.	DCOM is a binary standard. Hence it can be implemented in any language, which could generate the required binary code.
Can run on all platforms for which a Java virtual machine implementation is available.	Can run on all platforms (UNIX, mainframe, Windows, etc.) for which ORB implementation is available.	Can run on all platforms for which COM service implementation is available. However, DCOM is strongly integrated to Windowsbased systems.

TABLE 4.2 Comparison Based on Implementation Specifics

RMI	CORBA	DCOM
IDL supports multiple inheritance.	IDL supports multiple inheritance.	MIDL does not support multiple inheritance. Instead multiple interfaces can be embedded into a single *coclass* and navigation across interfaces is enabled using *Aggregation* and *Containment* techniques.
Allows exceptions to be specified at IDL level.	Allows exceptions to be specified at IDL level.	Does not allow exceptions to be specified at the IDL level.
Client stub is called *Stub* and the server stub is called *Skeleton*.	Client stub is called *Stub* and the server stub is called *Skeleton*.	Client stub is called *Proxy* and the server stub is called *Stub*.
The interface name uniquely identifies an interface. The implementation of the server object is mapped to a unique name in the RMIREGISTRY.	The interface name uniquely identifies an interface. The implementation of the server object is mapped to a unique name in the Implementation Repository.	Each interface has a unique Interface Identifier (IID). Each object implementation class has a unique Class ID (CLSID). Both these are stored in the system registry.
A client can obtain a reference to a remote server object by performing a *lookup()* on the remote server machine.	A client can obtain a reference to a remote server object by invoking the *bind()* method or by binding to the Naming or Trader service.	A client can obtain a remote interface pointer by invoking *CoCreateInstance()*. However in a Java-COM client, type casting to interface internally invokes these COM methods.
A client code has to know the remote machine on which the server object is hosted to obtain a reference.	A client code need not know where the server object is hosted.	A client code need not know where the server object is hosted.
Dynamic invocation of methods [24] on objects is possible via *Reflection*.	Run time type information of a remote interface is stored in *Interface Repository*, on which the client can query to invoke a method using *Dynamic Invocation Interface*.	To support dynamic invocation, an interface should derive from *IDispatch*. This is a *dual interface* which queries the *type library* to retrieve the run time information of the object.

TABLE 4.3 Comparison Based on Architecture

RMI	CORBA	DCOM
Uses Java Remote Method Protocol (JRMP) as the communication protocol.	Uses Internet Inter-ORB Protocol (IIOP) as the communication protocol.	Uses Object Remote Procedure Call (ORPC) as the communication protocol.
JVM is responsible for locating Vand activating an object implementation [24].	The Basic Object Adapter (BOA) or the Portable Object Adapter (POA) are responsible for object activation, while the ORB is responsible for locating objects.	The DCOM-Service Control Manager is responsible for both locating and activating objects.

4.4.4 Support for Additional Features

A comparison if the security features, garbage collection mechanisms, and callback mechanisms in each of the three paradigms is provided in Table 4.4.

4.4.5 Performance Comparison

The performance comparison is based on the results of ping and matrix-by-vector multiplication examples. In the ping example, a 100-element float array was passed-by-value to the remote server object, and a reversed array was passed back to the client. The average time computed for 10 such method invocations is shown in Table 4.5 for each paradigm. In the matrix-by-vector multiplication, a 2×100 matrix was multiplied by a 100×1 vector. The references to these two input objects were passed to the server object, and a reference to the product matrix was returned back to the client. The average time computed for 10 such multiplications is shown in Table 4.5 for each paradigm.

Time measurement was done through a native system call using JNI. Use of the Java system call for getting time was avoided because a more realistic time could be obtained through a native call than from the Java virtual machine. From the results it can be observed that time taken for computation was the least while using RMI for the ping experiment, where the parameter was passed-by-value. A possible reason could be the efficiency of object serialization in RMI. From the results of matrix-by-vector multiplication, it could be observed that CORBA requires the least time for computation. A possible reason could be that objects pass-by-reference is strongly supported in CORBA by the process of *stringification* and *destringification*. The computation time using DCOM for passing parameter-by-reference is found high. This could be the result of two factors. First, the DCOM used for the experiments was a customized implementation of a third-party tool, which could explain a

Table 4.4 Comparison Based on Support for Additional Features

RMI	CORBA	DCOM
Enforces the creation of a *RMISecurityManager* object. This ensures that downloaded class code for any object passed to the client does not access the system resources.	The CORBA Security Service supports the identification, authentication, authorization, and access control of the principles. It also provides security auditing.	DCOM supports robust security by allowing users to specify user-level authentication and access-level rights (through access control list) over objects.
Distributed garbage collection is handled by the Java virtual machine.	Distributed garbage collection is not specified.	Distributed garbage collection is activated by a pinging mechanism by which the server object detects whether clients are connected.
Asynchronous call-back routines are supported where in a server can call back a method on any of its clients.	Deferred synchronous calls allow clients to poll on a delayed response from the server. Event service allows consumers to either request events or be notified of events.	Call-back interfaces are supported in DCOM.

TABLE 4.5 Comparison Based on Performance

Experiment	Parameter Passing	RMI (ms)	CORBA (ms)	DCOM (ms)
Ping	By value	25.792	163.823	135.545
Matrix-by-vector multiplication	By reference	6781.155	1546.716	123,305.330

part of the overhead. Second, the DCOM implementation uses the concept of *moniker* for obtaining object reference. This is achieved by converting the *moniker* into a string and writing the string into a *moniker file*, which could later be read by the client program to obtain the reference.

In the case of matrix-by-vector multiplication, the client passes the matrix and vector objects by references to the central server. The central server then looks up the available processor objects by reading the *moniker file* corresponding to the processor object and then performs the computation. This reading of the *moniker file* is an I/O activity, which very much stands as rationale for the slow performance of DCOM in the matrix-by-vector multiplication experiment. However, in the ping experiment, as the *moniker file* was read before the object was passed-by-value, the result shows a reasonably lower computation time.

4.5 CONCLUSIONS

As evident from Section 4.4, each model has strengths and weaknesses. Each performs better under some conditions, while the performance degrades in some other situations. Hence the question "Which approach is better?" does not have a unique answer. Instead, the open nature of the future distributed systems will need the creation of a comprehensive metaobject model, which will seamlessly encompass the objects adhering to different models, thereby promoting a conglomeration of heterogeneous objects. UMM (the Unified Meta-object Model) [25] is one such proposed metamodel being developed for providing solutions to the software development of future open systems. UMM is based on an amalgamation of three concepts: objects, service, and collaboration. More details about UMM are available in [25].

REFERENCES

1. Sun Microsystems, Inc., Java remote method invocation: distributed computing for Java, *http://java.sun.com/marketing/collateral/javarmi.html*.
2. Sun Microsystems, Inc., An overview of RMI applications, *http://java.sun.com/docs/ books/tutorial/rmi/overview/html*.
3. Sun Microsystems, Inc., RMI and Java™ distributed computing, *http://java.sun. com/features/1997/nov/rmi.html*.
4. Sun Microsystems, Inc., Distributed object applications, *http://java.sum.com/products/jdk/1.2/docs/guide/rmi/spec/rmi-objmode.doc1.html*.
5. R. Buyya, *High Performance Cluster Computing*, Prentice Hall, Upper Saddle River, NJ, 1999.
6. P. E. Chung, Yennun Huang, Shalini Yajnik, Deron Liang, J. C. Shih, Chung-Yih Wang, and Yi-Min Wang, DCOM and CORBA side by side, step by step, and layer by layer, *http://research.microsoft.com/~ymwang/papers/C++R97CR.htm*.
7. G. S. Raj, The component object model, *http://www.execpc.com/~gopalan/com/com_ravings.html*.
8. Microsoft Corporation, Microsoft COM technologies: DCOM, *http://www.microsoft.com/com/tech/dcom.asp*.
9. M. Horstmann and M. Kirtland, DCOM architecture, *http://msdn.microsoft.com/library/default.asp?URL=/library/backgrnd/htmlmsdn_dcomarch.htm*.
10. C. Goswell, *The COM Programmer's Cookbook*, Microsoft Office Product Unit, *http://msdn.microsoft.com/library/default.asp?url=/library/en-us/dncomg/html/msdn_com_co.asp*.

11. K. Brockschmidt, *Inside OLe (Microsoft Programming)*, Microsoft Press, Redmond, WA, 1995.
12. S. G. Akl, *Parallel Computation: Models and Methods*, Prentice Hall, Upper Saddle River, NJ, 1997.
13. Object Management Group, OMG formal documentation, *http://www.omg.org/technology/documents/new_formal/index.htm*.
14. D. C. Schmidt, Overview of Corba, *http://www.cs.wustl.edu/~schmidt/corba-overview.html*.
15. G. Minton, IIOP specification: a closer look, *http://www.blackmagic.com/people/gabe/iiop.html*.
16. R. Orfali and D. Harkey, *Client/Server Programming with JAVA and CORBA*, Wiley, New York, 1998.
17. K. Keahey, A brief tutorial on Corba, *http://www.cs.indiana.edu/hyplan/kksiazek/tuto.html*.
18. D. C. Schmidt, Developing distributed object computing applications with CORBA, *http://www.cs.wustl.edu/~schmidt/PDF/corba4.pdf*.
19. Borland Software Corporation, VisiBroker 4, *http://info.borland.com/techpubs/visibroker/visibroker4/*.
20. Borland Software Corporation, Visibroker for Java 4.1: programmers guide, *http://info.borland.com/techpubs/books/vbj/vbj40/framesetindex.html*.
21. CORBA basics, *http://ootips.org/corba-basics.html*.
22. Microsoft Corporation, *http://www.microsoft.com/java*.
23. Linar Ltd., J-Integra, pure Java–COM bridge, *www.linar.com*.
24. G. S. Raj, A detailed comparison of CORBA, DCOM and Java/RMI, *http://www.execpc.com/~gopalan/misc/compare.html*.
25. R. R. Raje, UMM: unified meta-object model for open distributed systems, *Proceedings of the 4th IEEE International Conference on Algorithms and Architecture for Parallel Processing*, Word Scientific Publishing Company, Singapore, 2000.
26. J-Integra, *http://j-integra.intrinsyc.com*.

CHAPTER 5

Gestalt of the Grid

G. VON LASZEWSKI

Argonne National Laboratory, Argonne, IL

P. WAGSTROM

Argonne National Laboratory, Argonne, IL
and Illinois Institute of Technology, Chicago, IL

5.1 INTRODUCTION

The *Grid approach* is an important development in the discipline of computer science and engineering. Rapid progress is being made on several levels, including the definition of terminology, the design of an architecture and framework, the application in the scientific problem-solving process, and the creation of physical instantiations of Grids on a production level. In this chapter we provide an overview of important influences, developments, and technologies that are shaping state-of-the-art Grid computing. In particular, we address the following questions:

- What motivates the Grid approach? (see Section 5.1.1)
- What is a Grid? (see Section 5.2)
- What is the architecture of a Grid? (see Section 5.3)
- Which Grid research activities are performed? (see Section 5.5)
- How do researchers use a Grid? (see Section 5.7.7)
- What will the future bring? (see Section 5.8)

Before we begin our discussion, we start with an observation that leads us to the title of this chapter. A strong overlap between past, current, and future research in other disciplines influences this new area and makes answers to

---

Tools and Environments for Parallel and Distributed Computing, Edited by Salim Hariri and Manish Parashar
ISBN 0-471-33288-7 Copyright © 2004 John Wiley & Sons, Inc.

some of the questions complex. Moreover, although we are able to define the term *Grid approach*, we need to recognize that, similar to the *gestalt approach* in psychology, we face different responses by the community to this evolving field of research. Based on the gestalt approach, which hypothesizes that a person's perception of stimuli has an effect on his response, we will see a variety of stimuli on the Grid approach that influence current and future research directions.

We close this introductory section with a famous picture used in early psychology experiments. If we examine the drawing in detail, it will be rather difficult to decide what the different components represent in each of the interpretations. Although hat, feather, and ear are identifiable in the figure, one's interpretation (Is it an old woman or a young girl?) is based instead on "perceptual evidence." This figure should remind us to be open to individual perceptions about Grids and to be aware of the multifaceted aspects that constitute the *gestalt of the Grid*.

5.1.1 Motivation

To define the term *Grid* we first identify what motivates its development. We provide an example from weather forecasting and modeling that includes a user community with strong influence on the newest trends of computer science over the past several decades. L. F. Richardson [68,72] expressed the first modern vision of numerical weather prediction in 1922. Within two decades, the first prototype of a prediction system had been implemented by von Neumann, Charney, and others on the first generation of computers [70]. With the increased power of computers, numerical weather prediction became a reality in the 1960s and initiated a revolution in the field that we are still experiencing. In contrast to these early weather prediction models, today the scientific community understands that complex chemical processes and their interactions with land, sea, and atmosphere have to be considered.

Several factors make this effort challenging. Massive amounts of data must be gathered worldwide; those data must be incorporated into sophisticated models; the results must be analyzed; feedback must be provided to the modelers; and predictions must be supplied to consumers (Figure 5.1).

Analyzing this process further, we observe that the data needed as input to the models based on observations and measurements of weather and climate variables are still incomplete, and sophisticated sensor networks must be put in place to improve this situation. The complexity of these systems has reached a level where it is no longer possible for a single scientist to manage the entire process; the era of the lonely scientist working in seclusion is coming to an end. Today, accurate weather models are derived by sharing the intellectual property within a community of interdisciplinary researchers.

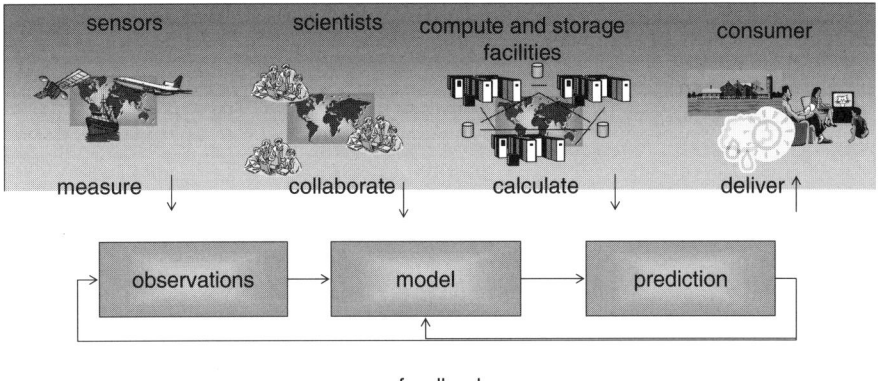

Fig. 5.1 Weather forecasting is a complex process that requires a complex infrastructure.

This increase in the complexity on the numerical methods and amount of data required, along with the factor of community access, requires access to massive amounts of computational and storage resources. Although today's supercomputers offer enormous power, accurate climate and weather modeling requires access to even larger resources that may be integrated from resources at dispersed locations. Therefore, weather prediction promotes more than just a focus on making compute resources available as part of a networked environment. We have identified the need for an infrastructure to be created from a dynamic, dispersed set of sensor, data, compute, collaboration, and delivery networks. Clearly, weather forecasting is a complex process that requires flexible, secure, coordinated sharing of a wide variety of resources.

5.1.2 Enabling Factors

When we look at why it is now possible to develop very sophisticated forecast models, we see an increase in understanding, capacity, capability, and accuracy on all levels of our infrastructure. Clearly, technology has advanced dramatically. Communication satellites and the Internet enable remote access to regional and international databases and sensor networks. Collaborative infrastructures (such as the Access Grid [29]) have moved exchange of information beyond the desktop. These advances have affected and will continue to profoundly affect the way scientists work with each other. Computing power has also increased steadily. Indeed, for more than three decades, computer speed has doubled every 18 months (supporting Moore's law [62]), and this trend is expected to last for at least the next decade. Furthermore, over the past five years, network bandwidth has increased at a much larger rate, leading experts to believe that the network speed doubles every nine months. At the same time, the cost of production for network and computer hardware is decreasing.

We also observe a change in *modality of computer operation*. The first generation of supercomputers comprised high-end mainframes, vector processors, and parallel computers. Access to this expensive infrastructure was provided and controlled as part of a single institution within a single administrative domain. With the advent of network technologies, promoting connectivity between computers, and the creation of the Internet, promoting connectivity between different organizations, a new trend arose, leading away from the centralized computing center to a decentralized environment. As part of this trend, it was natural to collect geographically dispersed and possibly heterogeneous computer resources, typically as networks of workstations or supercomputers. The first connections between high-end computers used to solve a problem in parallel on these machines were termed a *metacomputer*. (The term is believed to have originated as part of a gigabit testbed [60].)

Thus, increases in capacity, capability, and modality are enabling a new way of doing *distributed science*. Additionally, technology once viewed as specialized infrastructure is becoming a commodity technology, making it possible to access resources, for example through the use of the Internet [68], more easily. This vision, which has become clearer over the past few decades, now applies to many other disciplines that will provide commercial viability in the near future. It has had, and will continue to have, a profound impact on several scientific disciplines, including computer science.

5.2 DEFINITIONS

In this section we provide the most elementary definition of the term *Grid* and its use within the community. As we have seen, the Grid approach has been guided by a complex and diverse set of requirements but at the same time provides us with a vision for an infrastructure that promotes sophisticated international scientific and business-oriented collaborations. Much research in this area, some of which is mentioned in this chapter, has been influential in shaping what we now term the *Grid approach*:

Definition: Grid Approach A strategy that promotes a vision for sophisticated international scientific and business-oriented collaborations.

The term *Grid* is an analogy to the electric power grid that allows pervasive access to electric power. In a similar fashion, computational Grids provide access to collections of compute-related resources and services. As early as 1965, the designers of the Multics operating system envisioned and named requirements for a computer facility operating "like a power company or water company" [80], and others envisioned Grid-like scenarios [59]. However, we emphasize that our current understanding of the Grid approach goes far beyond simply sharing compute resources in a distributed fashion. Besides supercomputer and compute pools, Grids include access to information resources (such as large-scale databases) and access to knowledge resources (such as collaborative interactions between colleagues). Essential is that these resources may be at geographically dispersed locations and may be controlled by different organizations. Thus, the following definition for a Grid is appropriate:

Definition: Grid An infrastructure that allows for flexible, secure, coordinated resource sharing among dynamic collections of individuals, resources, and organizations.

So far we have used the term *Grid* rather abstract manner. To distinguish the concept of a Grid from an actual instantiation of a Grid as a real, available infrastructure, we use the term *production Grid*. Such production Grids are typically shared among a set of users. The analogy in the electrical power Grid would be a power company or agglomerate of companies that maintain their own Grid while providing persistent services to the user community. Thus, the following definition is introduced:

Definition: Production Grid An instantiaion of a Grid that manifests itself by including a set of resources to be accessed by Grid users.

Additionally, we expect that multiple production Grids will exist and be supported by multiple organizations. Fundamental to the Grid is the idea of *sharing*. Naturally, it should be possible to connect such Grids with each other so as to share resources. Thus, it is important to define a set of elementary standards that assist to provide interoperability between production Grids.

Some production Grids are created based on the need to support a particular community. Although the resources within such a community are usually controlled in different administrative domains, they can be accessed as part of a *community production Grid*. Examples of production and community production Grids are introduced in Section 5.5.1.

Definition: Community Production Grid A production Grid in which creation and maintenance are performed by a community of users, developers, and administrators.

The management of a community production Grid is usually handled by a *virtual organization* [46], which defines the rules that guide membership and use of resources.

Definition: Virtual Organization An organization that defines rules that guide membership and use of individuals, resources, and institutions within a community production Grid.

A typical Grid will contain a number of high-end resources such as supercomputers or data storage facilities. As these resources can be consumed by users, we term them in analogy to electrical power plants as follows:

Definition: Grid Plane A high-end resource that is integrated in a virtual organization and can be shared by its users.

The user, on the other hand, is able to access these resources through a user-specific device such as a computer, handheld device, or cell phone.

Definition: Grid Appliance A device that can be integrated into a Grid while providing the user with a service that uses resources accessible through the Grid.

Grid appliances provide a portal that enables easy access, utilization, and control of resources available through a Grid by the user. We define the term *Grid* portal in more detail in Section 5.7.

One important concept that was originally not sufficiently addressed within the Grid community was the acknowledgment of sporadic and ad hoc Grids that promote the creation of time-limited services. This concept was first formulated as part of an initial Grid application to conduct structural biology and computed microtomography experiments at Argonne National Laboratory's Advanced Photon Source (APS). In these applications, it was not possible to install, on long-term basis, Grid-related middleware on the resources, because of policy and security considerations. Hence, besides the provision for a pervasive infrastructure, we require Grid middleware to enable sporadic and ad hoc Grids that provide services with limited lifetime. Furthermore, the administrative overhead of installing such services must be small, to allow the installation and maintenance to be conducted by the nonexpert with few system privileges.

5.3 MULTIFACETED GRID ARCHITECTURE

A review of the literature about existing Grid research projects shows that three different architectural representations are commonly used. Each of these architectural views attempts to present a particular aspect of Grids. Thus, we believe it is important recognize that the architecture of the Grid is multifaceted and an architectural abstraction should be chosen that fits best to describe the given aspect of the Grid research. Nevertheless, in each case one needs to consider the distributed nature and unique security aspects. Next we describe these common architectural views in more detail.

System Level   User Level

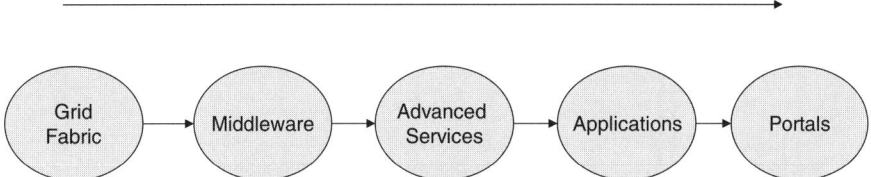

Fig. 5.2 *N*-tiered Grid architecture based on an application user's point of view.

5.3.1 *N*-Tiered Grid Architecture

The *N*-tiered application architecture (Figure 5.2) provides a model for Grid developers to create flexible and reusable Grid applications. Decomposing a Grid application into tiers allows developers to modify or add only to a specific layer rather than to focus on the reimplementation of all parts of the application. *N*-tiered application architectures are common within and are most often represented as part of layer 7 of the OSI model [64]. Many Grid projects provide an *N*-tiered architecture. The advantage of an *N*-tiered architecture is its familiarity and its applicability to many conceptual Grid problems that try to separate issues between the application and the physical layer.

5.3.2 Role-Based Grid Architecture

The secure access to a collectively controlled set of physical resources reused by applications motivates a role-based layered architecture [46,47]. Within this architecture, it is easy to identify fundamental system components, specify the purpose and function of these components, and indicate how these components interact with one another. This architecture classifies protocols, services, application programming interfaces, and software development kits according to their roles in enabling resource sharing. It identifies five layers: fabric, connectivity, resource, collective, and application layer (Figure 5.3). Interoperability is preserved by using a small standard set of protocols assisting in the secure exchange of information and data among single resources. These resources are managed by collective services in order provide the illusion of a single resource to application designers and users.

The layers within the architecture are defined as follows:

- The *fabric layer* contains protocols, application interfaces, and toolkits that allow development of services and components to access locally controlled resources, such as computers, storage resources, networks, and sensors.

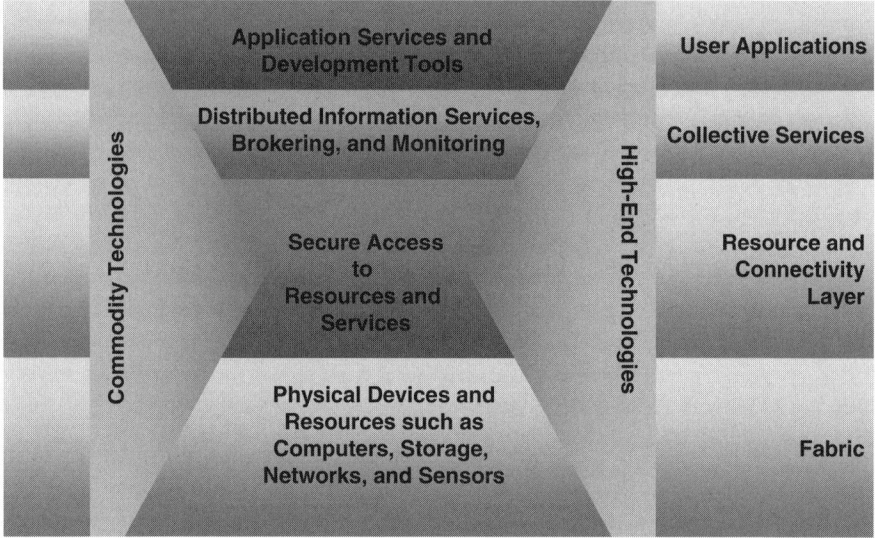

Fig. 5.3 Role-based layered view of Grid architecture.

- The *connectivity layer* includes the necessary Grid-specific core communication and authentication support to perform secure network transactions with the resources within the Grid fabric. This includes protocols and services allowing secure message exchange, authentication, and authorization. It is beneficial to develop a small set of standard protocols and services to provide the means of interoperability.
- The *resource layer* contains protocols that enable secure access and monitoring by collective operations.
- The *collective layer* is concerned with the coordination of multiple resources and defines collections of resources that are part of a virtual organization. Popular examples of such services are directories for resource discovery and brokers for distributed task and job scheduling.
- The *application layer* comprises user applications that are used within a virtual organization.

Each of these layers may contain protocols, application programming interfaces, and software development kits to support the development of Grid applications and services. A benefit of this architecture is the ability to bootstrap a complex Grid framework while refining it successively on various levels. We emphasize that this architecture can be supported with an immensely rich set of already defined application interfaces, protocols, toolkits, and services provided through commodity technologies and developments within high-end computing. Reuse and extension of these standards, based on Grid-specific requirements, will support the development of Grids.

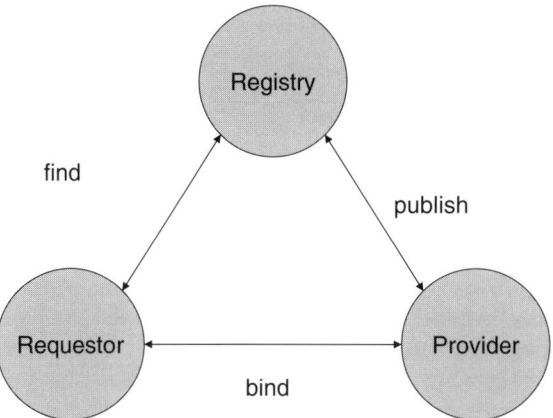

Fig. 5.4 The service model allows the description of a provider service that can be published in a registry and be found and bound by a requestor.

5.3.3 Service-Based Grid Architecture

In the near future we will observe a shift within information technologies toward service-oriented concepts. From the perspective of Grid computing, we define a service as a platform-independent software component, which is described with a description language and published within a directory or registry by a service provider (Figure 5.4). A service requester can locate a set of services with a query to the registry, a process known as *resource discovery*. A suitable service can then be selected and invoked, a process known as *binding* [37,41].

Definition: Service A platform-independent software component published within a directory or registry by a service provider.

The usefulness of the service-based Grid architecture can be illustrated by scheduling a task on a computer cluster. First, we locate a set of possible resources. Next, we select a compute resource from this set where we would like to schedule our task. A criterion to select such a resource could be cost or load balance among the resources. Once a suitable resource is selected, we bind the task of execution to this resource. Figure 5.3 shows the parties and message exchanges that define a service-based model. An important aspect of services is the possibility to compose new services easily while using existing ones. This is enabled by the standard description, not only of the protocol but also of the behavioral description of such a service.

Clearly, it is possible to develop complex flows between services. Since this service-based model deals with the use of asynchronous services, it will be important to deal appropriately with service guarantees in order to avoid deadlocks and other hazards. The service-based concept has been in wide use,

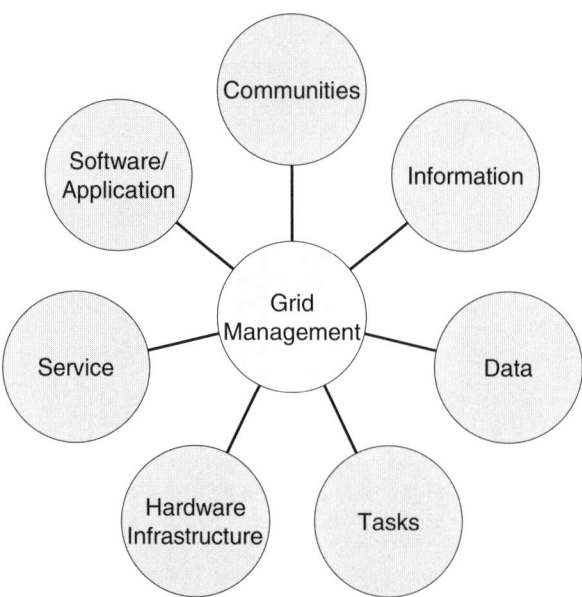

Fig. 5.5 The Grid approach must deal with a complex *management challenge* in many areas.

not only by the Grid community but also by the business community. This fact has led to recent collaborative efforts between the Grid and the business community. An example of such an activity is the creation of the Open Grid Services Architecture, which we describe in more detail in Section 5.5.2.

5.3.4 Grid Challenges

Whatever the form of a Grid, we must consider the dynamic, unpredictable properties of the Grid while providing a reliable and persistent infrastructure. Additionally, we would like to enable open collaborations without neglecting protection of the collaboration with appropriate security restrictions. These apparent contradictions—desire for reliability vs. a potentially unreliable infrastructure, or restricted vs. unrestricted access to information—provide complex challenges for Grids (Figure 5.5). For Grids to become a reality, we must develop infrastructures, frameworks, and tools that address these complex management challenges and issues.

5.4 GRID MANAGEMENT ASPECTS

A massively distributed and interconnected system entails management issues that go far beyond those of typical computers. Among these issues are the security of the system to maintain the overall integrity of the system; data and information management to ensure that the relevant data about users, systems,

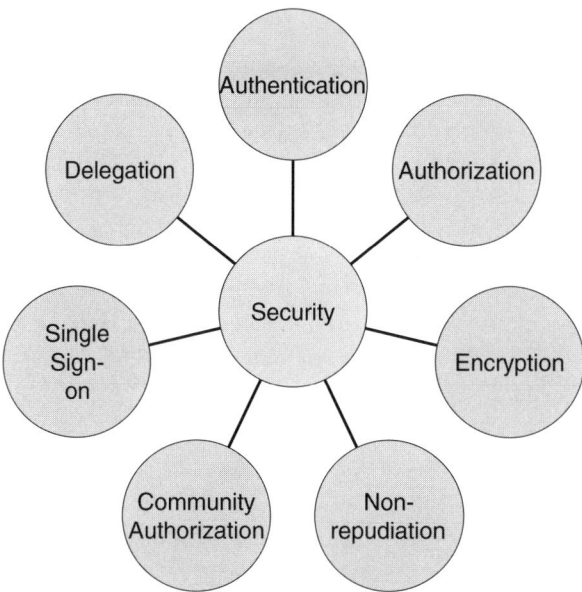

Fig. 5.6 Issues to be addressed in security.

and experiments is available to users and programs on the Grid; execution and resource management to handle the allocation of resources and ensure that tasks are executed in a timely matter; software management to handle deployment of software packages; and hardware management to ensure that the physical base of the Grid stays running. In this section we address these issues and their relationship to the Grid.

5.4.1 Managing Grid Security

Since the Grid approach deals with heterogeneous and dispersed resources and services, security aspects within Grids play an important role. Most commodity security services available today enable the interaction between two peers. The concepts used to enable this interaction are authentication, authorization, encryption, and nonrepudiation (Figures 5.6 and 5.7).

Authentication deals with verification of the identity of an entity within the Grid. Although this is commonly associated only with identification of a Grid user, the Grid also requires authentication of resources and services provided as part of the Grid.

Authorization deals with the verification of an action that an entity can perform after authentication was performed successfully. Thus, policies must be established that determine the capabilities of allowed actions. A typical example is the use of a batch queue by user A between 3 and 4 o'clock, with user B allowed to use the queue only from 5 to 6 o'clock. In general, policies determine *who* can do *what*, *when*, and at *which* resource.

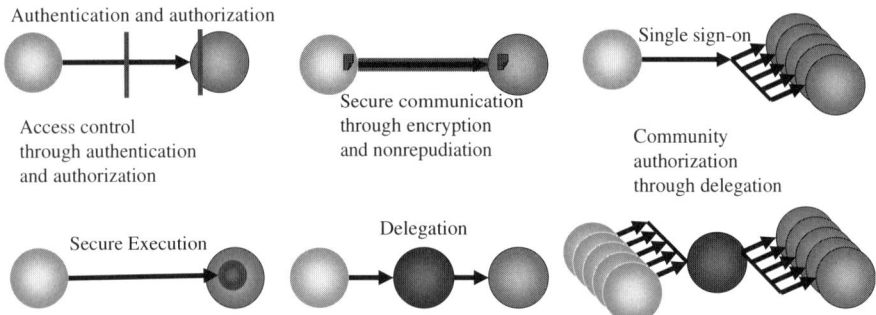

Fig. 5.7 Security concepts useful for Grids.

Encryption provides a mechanism for protecting the confidentiality of messages in transit between two peers.

Nonrepudiation in authentication services provides proof of the integrity and origin of data in an unforgeable relationship that can be verified by any third party at any time.

Besides these general security issues, the Grid infrastructure poses unique requirements. For instance, it is infeasible to authenticate via password challenges for a user on thousands of different resources.

Single sign-on is a mechanism that supports authentication to a large number of Grid resources on behalf of the user or resource by delegating the task of authentication to a service acting on behalf of the user (also called a *proxy service*). Such a service will typically create a temporary credential (often referred to as a *secure proxy*) that is used for authentication. An important factor to consider within single sign-on is that different domains may provide different local security mechanisms. Thus, any solution muse be able to deal with different identity mappings, such as UNIX accounts accessible through PKI or Kerberos.

Delegation is the process of one Grid entity acting on behalf of another Grid entity. Delegation must be performed carefully because it is possible to create delegation chains. A simple example of such a chain is the initiation of a process on a resource D, initiated by a resource A, and subsequently delegated through B and C($A {\hookrightarrow} B {\hookrightarrow} C {\hookrightarrow} D$). In general, we observe that the longer the chain, the greater the risk for misuse. Accordingly, it is desirable to create what we term *limited delegation*. This includes procurements for authentication restriction with more sophisticated Grid services. Thus, we can create a limited proxy that may, among other things, restrict use to a particular Grid resource.

Community authorization provides mechanisms for a virtual organization to define policies for groups of users that can be applied to enabling access control to resources by a community. This service is needed in case it is impossible or impractical to keep track of access to a resource on a user-by-user basis. An authority that establishes trust between the peers regulates inclusion in such a community. In this sense, community authorization enables single sign-on to resources while being delegated to a trusted authority.

Secure execution is desired in environments where the user community becomes too large to handle. In these cases it is important to provide a service that can run untrusted applications (those submitted by the users) in a trusted environment (the cluster at a compute center or a Grid); the concept of virtual machines is essential for such a service.

We must consider the user community when designing a security infrastructure for applications and services running in a Grid environment. Many users are unwilling to deal with obtrusive security procedures but at the same time expect a reasonable level of security. Hence, it is of utmost importance to present the security mechanisms to users in an easy and mostly transparent way. A minimum level of understanding by users is necessary so that they can specify their own security requirements and understand the security guarantees or risks of the Grid. In this respect, an *educational service* provided as part of the strategy of production Grids can offer the necessary explanations and guidance for accessing Grid resources and developing secure service.

5.4.2 Managing Grid Information

Within Grids, information about the users and the system is critical. User information helps to establish collaborative sessions, and system information helps users select the appropriate resources and applications. The availability of such information is important for the maintenance, configuration, and use of the heterogeneous and dynamically changing Grid infrastructure. Characteristics that must be imposed on such an information service to support Grids include

- Uniform, flexible access to information
- Scalable, efficient access to dynamic data
- Access to multiple information sources

The creation of such an information service must be an integral part of each Grid toolkit and application. In the past, distributed directories have provided such a service. Often, a centrally maintained relational database may serve the same purpose. In any case, the design of a scalable information service must consider the distributed nature of the Grid. Equally important is the fact that resource owners may not wish to export information about their systems to unauthorized users. Although restricted access to information is already possible, it is not addressed adequately in the first generation of prototype production Grids.

5.4.3 Managing Grid Data

Each program executed in a Grid is dependent on data, and the data requirements for applications running on the Grid are enormous. For example, gathering data for a meterological forecast requires processing and storage of petabytes of data each day. To compensate for limited storage capacities at remote sites, services that perform delivery on demand may augment the data with a lifetime to limit the amount of actual data in the Grid. If the calculation cannot be performed on the server where the data are located, the user must be able to replicate those data efficiently elsewhere. Thus, a reliable file transfer service must be provided to move the data between source and destination on behalf of the issuing client. Filters can be used to reduce the amount of data during a transfer, based on metadata attached with the file. If the data can be created with less effort than the actual data transfer, it may be advantageous to augment data with pedigree information about how to regenerate the data instead of storing them.

5.4.4 Managing Grid Execution and Resources

Calculations on resources within the Grid are controlled by execution services. The simplest execution service is part of the operating system and allows execution of jobs and tasks on a single resource. A Grid security infrastructure must be in place that provides authentication and authorization mechanisms to govern the use of this resource. Batch queuing systems provide a convenient way to extend such an execution service to a cluster, a parallel computer, or a supercomputer. In order to enable the use of multiple instances of such resources, a resource coallocation mechanism is needed. Such a mechanism will identify a suitable set of resources based on the Grid information service and verify that the resources selected are available (or fulfill the user's request if they are not), reserve the resources, and finally, execute the user's task on this agglomeration of resources.

Algorithms to control the collective use of such resources may be quite complex. Since the algorithmic implications for scheduling in such an environment are an NP-complete problem, heuristics may be used to solve the scheduling problem and to guarantee execution of the tasks. Researchers are currently exploring the use of combinatorial optimization strategies, stochastic sampling, economic models, and agent-based systems. Smart services are necessary that can deal with deadlock prevention, avoidance, and QoS guarantees on the local and global scales. Often, complicated workflows must be formulated as part of the complex interdisciplinary applications run by scientists on Grids. Thus, it is necessary to provide workflow management services that allow control of the flow of data and applications as part of the problem-solving process.

5.4.5 Managing Grid Software

Deployment of applications, components, and services in a distributed heterogeneous environment is a challenging problem. Of particular concern is guaranteeing interoperability between different versions of software and libraries on already installed and operational software and services. Use of the Grid service model described earlier offers a partial solution to this problem by providing metadata to each application and service installed on the Grid that can be queried through the Grid information service. In this way it is possible to include portability data within the infrastructure, which will be used as part of an authorization service to verify whether services or applications can interoperate.

5.4.6 Managing Grid Hardware

The resource providers are responsible for hardware management on the Grid. Notifications about downtimes and maintenance upgrades must be available through the information service in order to simplify the user's search for suitable resources with service guarantees. In general, hardware management must be augmented with an appropriate infrastructure on the hardware service provider side. Quality-of-service augmentations on the hardware level, such as networks, could provide a profound advantage for future Grid infrastructures.

5.5 GRID ACTIVITIES

We have organized our discussion of Grid projects into three classes: community activities, development toolkits, and applications (Figure 5.8). Within each class, we describe various activities in being performed by the Grid community.

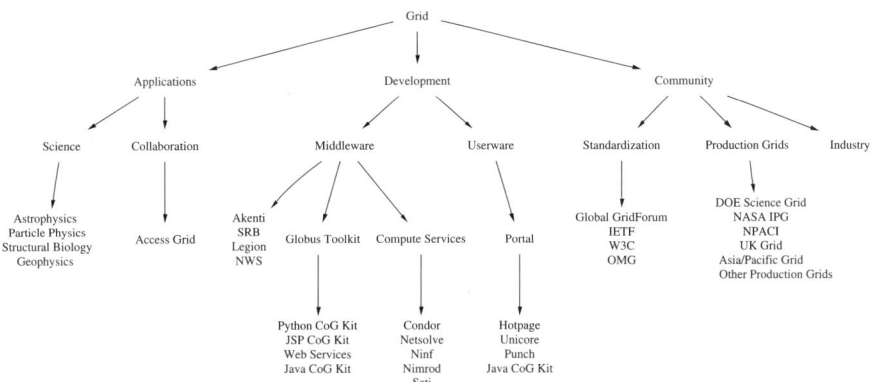

Fig. 5.8 Simple classification of Grid activities: community activities, development tools, and applications.

5.5.1 Community Activities

A variety of activities are performed by the community. Each of these activities has a profound impact on the development of Grids. We identify three basic Grid user communities and the activities they perform:

- *Development:* Grid programmers who develop services in a collaborative fashion for deployment in the Grid
- *Appication:* scientific or application users who access the services provided as part of the Grid
- *Community building:* administrators who deploy services and applications in production Grids in order to make them accessible to others

Whereas today's Grid users include mostly large-scale scientific application users and developers, we expect that with the availability of robust Grid toolkits the community will expand to the financial sector, the health care sector, small industries, and even the common household user needing access to services resources accessible through the Grid. Thus, the Grid will be instrumental in furthering the scientific discovery process [19] while developing the next generation of *community* problem-solving environments.

Global Grid Forum The Global Grid Forum (GGF) is an international community-initiated forum of individual researchers and practitioners working on various facets of Grids. The mission of the GGF is to promote and develop Grid technologies and applications through the development and documentation of "best practices," implementation guidelines and standards, with an emphasis on "rough consensus and running code." The objective is to support with such standards the creation of production Grids; address infrastructure obstacles inhibiting the creation of these Grids; perform educational outreach; and facilitate the use of Grid technologies within diverse application communities. Based on the Internet Engineering Task Force model, the GGF contains several area groups and, within these areas, working groups dealing with a particular Grid-related problem. The current areas are information services, security, scheduling and management, performance, architecture, data, and applications and models. Regular meetings arc held in which over 200 organizations from more than 30 countries are represented [25].

Production Grids A number of national and international community production Grids have been established in the past few years. Each is part of a virtual organization spanning multiple administrative domains and enabling access to high-end resources such as supercomputers, mass storage systems, and advanced instruments. A well-trained administrative staff is responsible for deploying services and components in such collectively maintained production Grids.

DOE Science Grid The Department of Energy (DOE) Science Grid is a pilot program to provide an advanced distributed computing infrastructure based on Grid middleware and tools to enable the degree of scalability in scientific computing necessary for DOE to accomplish its science missions. Emphasis is placed on making the construction and use of large-scale heterogeneous systems as easy as using today's desktop environments. The DOE Science Grid [40] is part of a large initiative entitled Scientific Discovery through Advanced Computing (SciDAC) [19], which was started in fiscal year 2001. The objective of SciDAC is to develop the scientific computing software and hardware infrastructure needed for terascale computers to advance DOE research programs in basic energy sciences, biological and environmental research, fusion energy sciences, and high-energy and nuclear physics.

TeraGrid The TeraGrid [21] project seeks to build and deploy the world's largest, fastest, most comprehensive distributed infrastructure for open scientific research. Upon completion, the TeraGrid will include 13.6 teraflops of Linux cluster computing power distributed at five sites: the National Center for Supercomputing Applications (NCSA) at the University of Illinois at Urbana–Champaign; the San Diego Supercomputer Center (SDSC) at the University of California–San Diego; Argonne National Laboratory in Argonne, Illinois; the California Institute of Technology (Caltech) in Pasadena; and the Pittsburgh Supercomputing Center in Pittsburgh. The TeraGrid will include other distributed facilities capable of managing and storing more than 450 terabytes of data, high-resolution visualization environments, and toolkits for Grid computing. A high-speed network, which will operate between 50 and 80 gigabits/second, will permit the tight integration of the components in a Grid. The $53 million project is funded by the National Science Foundation and includes corporate partners. The TeraGrid benefits from other Grid-related activities performed at the partner sites through the National Computational Science Alliance (Alliance) [9,10,76] and the National Partnership for Advanced Computational Infrastructure (NPACI) [11]. The Alliance and NPACI is supporting the TeraGrid activities through their partners and infrastructure/building activities and their current and future Grid infrastructures.

NASA Information Power Grid The NASA Information Power Grid project was initiated from a series of workshops in autumn of 1997. The goal is to provide seamless access to resources between NASA sites and a few selected NPACI sites for application development. These applications are likely to include aeronautics and other areas of interest to NASA, such as space sciences and earth sciences. The requirements that NASA will address first are seamless access to distributed legacy applications via networks, cross-platform computational and interactive visualization of large three-dimensional data sets, intelligent and distributed data mining across unspecified heterogeneous data sources, agent technologies, privacy and security, and tools for the development of multidisciplinary systems. Additionally, NASA must deal with a number of real-time requirements for aircraft operations systems [15]. The current hardware resources included in the prototype Information Power Grid are based on Globus Toolkit technology and comprise approximately 1500 CPU nodes in six SGI Origins distributed across several NASA centers. Also included are 10 to 50 terabytes of securely accessible mass storage, several workstation clusters with approximately 100 CPUs, and a Condor pool with 300 workstations.

EuroGrid EuroGrid [14] is an application testbed for the European Grid community. It is supported as a shared-cost research and technology development project between the European Commission and its 11 partner institutions. It will demonstrate the use of Grids in selected scientific and industrial communities, address the specific requirements of these communities, and highlight the benefits of using Grids. The objectives are to establish and operate a European Grid among several of Europe's high-performance computing centers. Besides developing Grid software and applying it within state-of-the-art applications such as biomolecular simulations, weather prediction, coupled CAE simulations, structural analysis, and real-time data processing, the alignment with commercial partners is intended to productize the software.

DataGrid The DataGrid [12] project is funded by the European Community. The objective is to enable next-generation scientific exploration that requires intensive computation and analysis of shared large-scale databases, from hundreds of terabytes to petabytes, across widely distributed scientific virtual communities. The initiative is led by CERN, the European Organization for Nuclear Research, together with five other main partners and 15 associated partners. Major application areas are quantum chromodynamics, Earth observation, and human health research.

ApGrid The ApGrid [13] is a partnership for Grid computing in the Asia/Pacific region. So far, it includes about 30 institutions. One of the important objectives of ApGrid is building an international Grid testbed. The current technology plan includes the Globus Toolkit as its underlying infrastructure.

5.5.2 Grid Middleware

The collection of APIs, protocols, and software that allow creation and use of a distributed system such as a Grid is called *middleware*. It is at a lower level than end-user applications, while being at a higher level than the underlying network transport methods. A variety of middleware packages are available, of which we examine a select few.

Globus Project Over the past few years, the Globus Project has contributed in many ways to the Grid effort. It has five thrust areas. First, the Globus Project conducts research on Grid-related issues such as resource management, security, information services, data management, and application development environments. Second, the Globus Project is developing open-source, open-architecture Grid software, called the Globus Toolkit. A growing number of research institutions and companies have committed to supporting this open source activity. Third, the Globus Project assists in the planning and building of large-scale testbeds, both for research and for production use by scientists and engineers. Fourth, the Globus Project collaborates in a large number of application-oriented efforts that develop large-scale Grid-enabled applications in collaboration with scientists and engineers. Fifth, the Globus Project is committed to community activities that include educational outreach and participation in defining Grid standards as part of the Global Grid Forum. The Globus Toolkit is modular, enabling users to choose the components needed for the development of Grid-enabled applications.

Security is an important aspect of the Globus Toolkit. The Grid Security Infrastructure (GSI) uses public key cryptography as the basis for its functionality. It enables security services such as mutual authentication, confidential communication, delegation, and single sign-on. GSI builds the core for implementing other Globus Toolkit services.

Communication within the Globus Toolkit is handled through the GlobusIO library, which provides TCP, UDP, IP multicast, and file I/O services with support for security, asynchronous communication, and quality of service. An important tool provided by the Globus Project is MPICH-G2, which supports MPI across several distributed computers. MPICH-G2 was used at SC2001 in an astrophysical calculation that received the Gordon Bell Prize [55].

Information about a Grid is handled through the Metacomputing Directory Service (MDS). The concept of a directory service for the Grid was first defined in [38] and later refined in [39]. The MDS manages information about entities in a Grid in a distributed fashion. The current implementation of MDS is based on the Lightweight Directory Access Protocol. This protocol enables uniform querying of system information from a variety of system components and can be used for constructing a uniform name space for resource information across a system that may involve many organizations.

Resource management within the Globus Toolkit is handled through a layered system in which high-level global resource management services are built on top of local resource allocation services. The current Globus Toolkit resource management system comprises three components: (1) an extensible resource specification language that serves as a method for exchanging information about resource requirements among all of the components in the Globus Toolkit resource management architecture; (2) a standardized interface to local resource management tools, including LSF, NQE, LoadLeveler, and Condor; and (3) a resource coallocation service that enables construction of sophisticated coallocation strategies that allow use of multiple resources concurrently.

Data management is supported by integration of the GSI protocol to access remote files through, for example, the HTTP and the FTP protocols.

Data Grids are supported through replica catalog services in the newest release of the Globus Toolkit. These services allow copying of the most relevant portions of a dataset to local storage for faster access. Installation of the extensive toolkit is enabled through a packaging toolkit that can generate custom-designed installation distributions.

Current research activities include the creation of a community access server, restricted proxies for placing additional authorization requests within the proxy itself, data Grids, quality of service, and integration within commodity technologies, such as the Java framework and Web services. Future versions of the Globus Toolkit will integrate the Grid architecture with Web services technologies.

Commodity Grid Kits The Globus Project provides a small set of useful services, including authentication, remote access to resources, and information services to discover and query such remote resource. Unfortunately, these services may not be compatible with the commodity technologies used for application development by software engineers and scientists. To overcome this difficulty, the Commodity Grid project is creating Commodity Grid Toolkits (CoG kits) that define mappings and interfaces between Grid services and particular commodity frameworks. Technologies and frameworks of interest include Java, Python, CORBA [77], Perl, Web Services, .NET, and JXTA.

Existing Java [78] and Python CoG kits provide the best support for a subset of the services within the Globus Toolkit. The Python CoG kit uses SWIG to wrap the Globus Toolkit C-API, while the Java CoG kit is a complete re-implementation of the Globus Toolkit protocols in Java. The Java CoG kit is done in pure Java and provides the ability to use a pure Java GRAM service. Although the Java CoG kit can be classified as middleware for integrating advanced Grid services, it can also be viewed both as a system providing advanced services currently not available in the Globus Toolkit and as a framework for designing computing portals [79]. Both the Java and Python CoG kits are popular with Grid programmers and have been used successfully in many community projects.

Open Grid Services Architecture One of the major problems facing Grid deployment is the variety of different "standards," protocols, and difficult-to-reuse implementations. This situation is exacerbated by the fact that much of the Grid development has been done separately from corporate-distributed computer development. As a result, a chasm has begun to appear [52].

The Open Grid Services Architecture (OGSA) is an effort to utilize commodity technology to create a Grid architecture. OGSA utilizes the Web service descriptions as a method to bring concepts from Web services into the Grid. In OGSA, everything is a network-enabled service that is capable of doing some work through the exchange of messages. Such "services" include computing resources, storage resources, programs, networks, databases, and a variety of tools. When an OGSA service conforms to a special set of interfaces and support standards, it is deemed a *Grid service*. Grid services have the ability to maintain their state; hence, it is possible to distinguish one running Grid service instance from another. Under OGSA, Grid services may be created and destroyed dynamically. To provide a reference mechanism for a particular Grid service instance and its state, each instance has a unique Grid service handler (GSH).

Because a Grid service instance may outlast the protocol on which it runs initially, the GSH contains no information about protocols or transport methods, such as an IP address or XML schema version. Instead, this information is encapsulated a Grid service reference (GSR), which can change over time. This strategy allows the instance to upgrade or add new protocols. To manipulate Grid services, OSGA has interfaces that handle and reference abstractions that make up OGSA. These interfaces can vary from service to service; however, the discovery interface must be supported on all services to allow the location of new Grid service instances.

Using such an object-oriented system offers several advantages. All components are virtualized, removing many dependency issues and allowing mapping of multiple logical resources into one physical resource. Moreover, because there is a consistent set of interfaces that all services must provide, construction of complex services is greatly simplified. Together these features allow for mapping of service semantics onto a wide variety of platforms and communication protocols. When OGSA is combined with CoG kits, a new level of ease and abstraction is brought to the Grid. Together, these technologies form the basis for the Globus Toolkit 3.0 [48].

Legion Legion is a Grid software project developed at the University of Virginia. Legion addresses Grid key issues such as scalability, programming ease, fault tolerance, security, and site autonomy. The goal of the Legion system is to support large degrees of parallelism in application codes and to manage the complexities of the physical system for the user. Legion seamlessly schedules and distributes the user processes on available and appropriate resources while providing the illusion of working on a single virtual machine.

As does other Grid middleware, Legion provides a set of advanced services. These include the automatic installation of binaries, a secure and shared virtual file system that spans all the machines in a Legion system, strong PKI-based authentication, flexible access control for user objects, and support of legacy codes execution and their use in parameter space studies.

Legion's architecture is based on an object model. Each entity in the Grid is represented as an active object that responds to member function invocations from other objects. Legion includes several core objects, such as computing resources, persistent storage, binding objects that map global to local process IDs, and implementation objects that allow the execution of machine code. The Legion system is extensible and allows users to define their own objects. Although Legion defines the message format and high-level protocol for object interaction, it does not restrict the programming language or the communications protocol. Legion has been used for parameter studies, ocean models, macromolecular simulations, and particle-in-cell codes. Legion is also used as part of the NPACI production Grid; a portal eases the interaction with the production Grid using Legion.

Storage Resource Broker The Storage Resource Broker (SRB) [20] developed by the San Diego Supercomputer Center is client-server middleware that provides a uniform interface for connecting to heterogeneous remote data resources and accessing replicated datasets. The SRB software includes a C client library, a metadata server based on relational database technology, and a set of Unix-like command line utilities that mimic, for example, ls, cp, and chmod. SRB enables access to various storage systems, including the Unix file system, archival storage systems such as UNITREE [8] and HPSS [6], and large database objects managed by various database management systems such as DB2, Oracle, and Illustra. SRB enables access to datasets and resources based on their attributes rather than their names or physical locations. Forming an integral part of SRB are collections that define a logical name given to a set of datasets. A Java-based client GUI allows convenient browsing of the collections. Based on these collections, a hierarchical structure can be imposed on data, thereby simplifying the organization of data in a manner similar to a Unix file system. In contrast to the normal Unix file system, however, a collection can encompass data that are stored on remote resources. To support archival mass storage systems, SRB can bind a large set of files (that are part of a collection) in a container that can be stored and accessed as a single file. Additionally, SRB supports three authentication schemes: GSI, SEA (an RSA-based encryption scheme), and plain text password. Furthermore, SRB can enable access control to data to groups of users. Other features of SRB include data replication, execution of user operations on the server, data reduction prior to a fetch operation by the client, and monitoring.

Akenti Akenti is a security model and architecture providing scalable security services in Grids. The project goals are to (1) achieve the same level of expressiveness of access control that is accomplished through a local human controller in the decision loop, and (2) accurately reflect existing policies for authority, delegation, and responsibilities. For access control, Akenti uses digitally signed certificates that include the user identity authentication, resource usage requirements (or use conditions), user attribute authorizations (or attribute certificates), delegated authorization, and authorization decisions split among on- and offline entities. All of these certificates can be stored remotely from the resources. Akenti provides a policy engine that the resource server can call to find and analyze all the remote certificates. It also includes a graphical user interface for creating use conditions and attribute certificates.

Network Weather Service Network Weather Service (NWS) [51] is a distributed monitoring service that periodically records and forecasts the performance of various network and computational resources over time. The service is based on a distributed set of performance sensors that gather the information in a central location. These data are used by numerical models to generate forecasts (similar to weather forecasting). The information also can be used by dynamic schedulers to provide statistical quality-of-service readings in a Grid. Currently, the system supports sensors for end-to-end TCP/IP performance measuring bandwidth and latency, available CPU percentage, and available nonpaged memory. The forecast models include mean-based methods, which use some estimate of the sample mean as a forecast; median-based methods, which use a median estimator; and autoregressive methods. While evaluating the accuracies of the prediction during run time, NWS is able to configure itself and choose the forecasting method (from those that are provided with NWS) that best fits the situation. New models can be included in NWS.

5.5.3 High-Throughput Computing

High-throughput computing is an extension of the concept of supercomputing. While typical supercomputing focuses on floating-point operations per second (flops), high-throughput systems focus on floating-point operations per month or year [24]. The projects listed in this section are projects that provide increased performance for long-term calculations by using distributed commodity hardware in a collaborative method.

Condor Condor is a system to utilize idle computing cycles on workstations by distributing a number of queued jobs to them. Condor focuses on high-throughput computing rather than on high-performance computing [75]. Condor maintains a pool of computers and uses a centralized broker to distribute jobs based on load information or preference associated with the jobs to be executed. The broker identifies, in the pool of resources, idle computers with available resources on which to run the program (thus, the metaphor of a condor soaring over the desert looking for food).

The proper resources are found through the ClassAds mechanism of Condor. This mechanism allows each computer in the pool to advertise the resources that it has available and to publish them in a central information service. Thus, if a job is specified to require 128 megabytes of RAM, it will not be placed on a computer with only 64 megabytes of RAM [24].

The ever-changing topology of workstations does, of course, pose a problem for Condor. When users return to their computers, they usually want the Condor processes to stop running. To address this issue, the program uses the checkpoints described above and restarts on another host machine. Condor allows the specification of elementary authorization policies, such as "user A is allowed to use a machine but not user B" and the definition of policies for running jobs in the background or when the user is not using the machine interactively. Such authorization frameworks have been used successfully in other projects, such as SETI@Home [42–44,56].

Today, Condor also includes client-side brokers that handle more complex tasks such as job ordering via acyclic graphs and time management features. To prevent monopolizing the resources by a single large application, Condor can use a fair scheduling algorithm. A disadvantage with the earlier Condor system was that it was difficult to implement a coallocation of resources that were not part of a workstation but were part of a supercomputing batch queue system. To also utilize batch queues within a pool, Condor introduced a mechanism that provides the ability to integrate resources for a particular period of time into a pool. This concept, known as glide-in, is enabled through a Globus Toolkit back end. With this technique, a job submitted on a Condor pool may be executed elsewhere on another computing Grid. Currently, Condor is working with the Globus Project to provide the necessary resource sharing [75].

Much of Condor's functionality results from the trapping of system calls by a specialized version of GLIBC that C programs are linked against. Using this library, most programs require only minor (if any) changes to the source code. The library redirects all I/O requests to the workstation that started the process. Consequently, workstations in the Condor pool do not require accounts for everyone who can submit a job. Rather, only one general account for Condor is needed. This strategy greatly simplifies administration and maintenance. Moreover, the special GLIBC library provides the ability to checkpoint the progress of a program. Condor also provides a mechanism that makes it possible to run jobs unchanged, but many of the advanced features, such as checkpointing and restarting, cannot be used. Additional Grid functionality has been included with the establishment of *Condor flocks*, which represent pools in different administrative domains. Policy agreements between these flocks enable the redistribution of migratory jobs among the flocks [42,43].

NetSolve NetSolve, developed at the University of Tennessee's Innovative Computing Laboratory, is a distributed computing system that provides access to computational resources across a heterogeneous distributed environment via a client-agent-server interface [16,33]. The entire NetSolve system is viewed as a connected nondirected graph. Each system that is attached to NetSolve can have different software installed on it. Users can access NetSolve and process computations through client libraries for C, Fortran, Matlab, and Mathematica. These libraries can access numerical solvers such as LAPACK, ScaLAPACK, and PETSc. When a computation is sent to NetSolve, the agent uses a "best-guess" methodology to determine to which server to send the request. That server then does the computation and returns the result using the XDR format [36]. Should a server process terminate unexpectedly while performing a computation, the computation is restarted automatically on a different computer in the NetSolve system. This process is transparent to the user and usually has little impact other than a delay in getting results.

Because NetSolve can use multiple computers at the same time through nonblocking calls, the system has an inherent amount of parallelism. This, in one sense, makes it easy to write parallel C programs. The NetSolve system is still being actively enhanced and expanded. New features included a graphical problem description file generator, Kerberos authentication, and additional mathematical libraries [26]. NetSolve's closest relative is Ninf (see below). Work has been done on software libraries that allow routines written for Ninf to be run on NetSolve, and vice versa. Currently, however, there are no known plans for the two projects to merge [33].

Ninf Ninf (Network Information Library for High Performance Computing) is a distributed remote procedure call system with a focus on ease of use and mathematical computation. It is developed by the Electrotechnical Laboratory in Tsukuba, Ibaraki, Japan.

To execute a Ninf program, a client calls a remote mathematical library routine via a metaserver interface. This metaserver then brokers various requests to machines capable of performing the computation. Such a client-agent-server architecture allows a high degree of fail safety for the system. When the routine is finished, the metaserver receives the data and transfers them back to the client.

The Ninf metaserver can also order requests automatically. Specifically, if multiple dependent and independent calculations need to take place, the independent ones will execute in parallel while waiting for the dependent calculations to complete. Bindings for Ninf have been written for C, Fortran, Java, Excel, Mathematica, and Lisp. Furthermore, these bindings support the use of HTTP GET and HTTP PUT to access information on remote Web servers. This feature removes the need for the client to have all of the information and allows low-bandwidth clients to run on the network and receive the computational benefits the system offers [63].

Several efforts are under way to expand Ninf into a more generalized system. Among these efforts are Ninflet, a framework to distribute and execute Java applications, and Ninf-G, a project designed a computational RPC system on top of the Globus Toolkit [69].

SETI@Home SETI@Home, run by the Space Science Laboratory at the University of California–Berkeley, is one of the most successful coarse-grained distributed computing systems in the world. Its goal is to integrate computing resources on the Web as part of a collection of independent resources that are plentiful and can solve many independent calculations at the same time. Such a system was envisioned as a way to deal with the overwhelming amount of information recorded by the Arecibo radio telescope in Puerto Rico and the analysis of the data. The SETI@Home project developed stable and user-appealing screen savers for Macintosh and Windows computers and a command-line client for Unix systems [56,61] that started to be widely used in 1999.

At its core, SETI@Home is a client-server distributed network. When a client is run, it connects to the SETI@Home work unit servers at the University of California–Berkeley and downloads a packet of data recorded from the Arecibo telescope. The client then performs a fixed mathematical analysis on the data to find signals of interest. At the end of analysis, the results are sent back to SETI@Home, and a new packet is downloaded for the cycle to repeat.

Packets of information that have been shown to have useful information are then analyzed again by the system to ensure that there was no client error in the reporting of the data. In this way, the system shows resiliency toward modified clients, and the scientific integrity of the survey is maintained [56]. To date, SETI@Home has accumulated more than 900,000 CPU-years of processing time from over 3.5 million volunteers around the globe. The entire system today averages out to 45 Tflops, which makes it the world's most powerful computing system by a big margin [34]. One of the principal reasons for the project's success is its noninvasive nature; running SETI@Home causes no additional load on most PCs, where it is run only during the inactive cycles. In addition, the system provides a wealth of both user and aggregate information and allows organizations to form teams for corporations and organizations, which then have their standings posted on the Web site. SETI@Home was also the first to mobilize massive numbers of participants by creating a sense of community and to project the goals of the scientific project to large numbers of nonscientific users.

SETI@Home was originally planned in 1996 to be a two-year program with an estimated 100,000 users. Because of its success, plans are now under way for SETI@Home II, which will expand the scope of the original project [28]. Multiple other projects, such as Folding@home, have also been started [4].

Nimrod-G Nimrod was originally a metacomputing system for parameterized simulations. Since then it has evolved to include concepts and technologies related to the Grid. Nimrod-G is an advanced broker system that is one of the first systems to account for economic models in scheduling of tasks. Nimrod-G provides a suite of tools that can be used to generate parameter sweep applications, manage resources, and schedule applications. It is based on a declarative programming language and an assortment of GUI tools.

The resource broker is responsible for determining requirements that the experiment places on the Grid and for finding resources, scheduling, dispatching jobs, and gathering results back to the home node. Internal to the resource broker are several modules:

- The *task-farming agent* is a persistent manager that controls the entire experiment. It is responsible for parameterization, creation of jobs, recording of job states, and communication. Because it caches the states of the experiments, an experiment may be restarted if the task-farming agent fails during a run.
- The *scheduler* handles resource discovery, resource trading, and job assignment. In this module are the algorithms to optimize a run for time or cost. Information about the costs of using remote systems is gathered through resource discovery protocols, such as MDS for the Globus Toolkit.
- *Dispatchers* and *actuators* deploy agents on the Grid and map the resources for execution. The scheduler feeds the dispatcher a schedule, and the dispatcher allocates jobs to the different resources periodically to meet this goal.

The agents are dynamically created and are responsible for transporting the code to the remote machine, starting the actual task, and recording the resources used by a particular project. The Nimrod-G architecture offers several benefits. In particular, it provides an economic model that can be applied to be metacomputing, and it allows interaction with multiple different system architectures, such as the Globus Toolkit, Legion, and Condor. In the future, Nimrod-G will be expanded to allow advance reservation of resources and use more advanced economic models, such as demand and supply, auctions, and tenders/contract-net protocols [30].

5.6 GRID APPLICATIONS

At the beginning of Section 5.5.1 we divided Grid projects into three classes: community activities, toolkits (middleware), and applications. Here we focus on three applications representative of current Grid activities.

5.6.1 Astrophysics Simulation Collaboratory

The Astrophysics Simulation Collaboratory (ASC) was originally developed in support of numerical simulations in astrophysics and has evolved into a general-purpose code for partial differential equations in three dimensions [1,31]. Perhaps the most computationally demanding application that has been attacked with ASC is the numerical solution of Einstein's general relativistic wave equations, in the context, for example, of the study of neutron star mergers and black hole collisions. For this purpose, the ASC community maintains an ASC server and controls its access through login accounts on the server. Remote resources integrated into the ASC server are controlled by the administrative policies of the site contributing the resources. In general, this means that a user must have an account on the machine on which the service is to be performed. The modular design of the framework and its exposure through a Web-based portal permits a diverse group of researchers to develop add-on software modules that integrate additional physics or numerical solvers into the Cactus framework.

The Astrophysics Simulation Collaboratory pursues the following objectives [32]:

- Promote the creation of a community for sharing and developing simulation codes and scientific results
- Enable transparent access to remote resources, including computers, data storage archives, information servers, and shared code repositories
- Enhance domain-specific component and service development supporting problem-solving capabilities, such as the development of simulation codes for the astrophysical community or the development of advanced Grid services reusable by the community
- Distribute and install programs onto remote resources while accessing code repositories, compilation, and deployment services
- Enable collaboration during program execution to foster interaction during the development of parameters and the verification of the simulations
- Enable shared control and steering of the simulations to support asynchronous collaborative techniques among collaboratory members
- Provide access to domain-specific clients that, for example, enable access to multimedia streams and other data generated during execution of the simulation

To achieve these objectives, ASC uses a Grid portal based on JSP for thin-client access to Grid services. Specialized services support community code development through online code repositories. The Cactus computational toolkit is used for this work.

5.6.2 Particle Physics Data Grid

The Particle Physics Data Grid (PPDG) [18] is a collaboratory project concerned with providing the next-generation infrastructure for current and future high-energy and nuclear physics experiments. One of the important requirements of PPDG is to deal with the enormous amount of data that is created during high-energy physics experiment and must be analyzed by large groups of specialists. Data storage, replication, job scheduling, resource management, and security components supplied by the Globus, Condor, STACS, SRB, and EU DataGrid projects [12] all will be integrated for easy use by the physics collaborators. Development of PPDG is supported under the DOE SciDAC initiative (Particle Physics Data Grid Collaboratory Pilot) [18].

5.6.3 NEESgrid

The intention of the Network for Earthquake Engineering Simulation grid (NEESgrid) is to build a national-scale distributed virtual laboratory for earthquake engineering. The initial goals of the project are to (1) extend the Globus Toolkit information service to meet the specialized needs of the community and (2) develop a set of services called NEESpop, along with existing Grid services to be deployed to the NEESpop servers. Ultimately, the system will include a collaboration and visualization environment, specialized NEESpop servers to handle and manage the environment, and access to external system and storage provided by NCSA [66].

One of the objectives of NEESgrid is to enable observation and data access to experiments in real time. Both centralized and distributed data repositories will be created to share data between different locations on the Grid. These repositories will have data management software to assist in rapid and controlled publication of results A software library will be created to distribute simulation software to users. This will allow users with NEESgrid-enabled desktops to run remote simulations on the Grid [65].

NEESgrid will comprise a layered architecture, with each component being built on core Grid services that handle authentication, information, and resource management but are customized to fit the needs of the earthquake engineering community. The project will have a working prototype system by the fourth quarter of 2002. This system will be enhanced during the next few years, with the goal to deliver a fully tested and operational system in 2004 to gather data during the next decade.

5.7 PORTALS

The term *portal* is not defined uniformly within the computer science community. Sometimes it represents integrated desktops, electronic marketplaces, or information hubs [49,50,71]. We use the term here in the more general sense of a community access point to information and services (Figure 5.9).

Definition: Portal A community service with a single point of entry to an integrated system providing access to information, data, applications, and services.

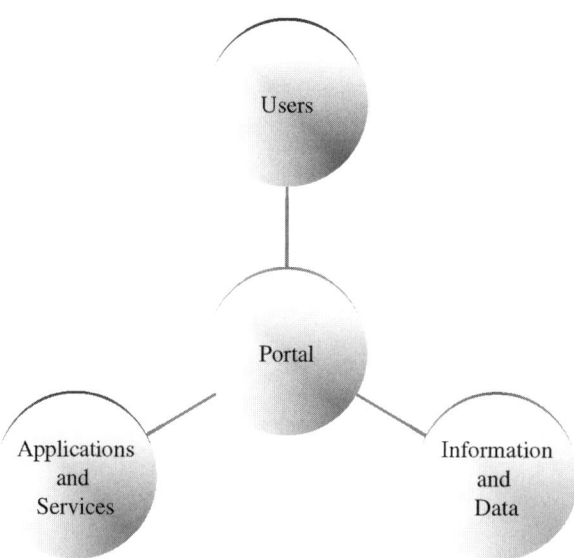

Fig. 5.9 Portals provide an entry point that helps to integrate information and data, application, and services.

In general, a portal is most useful when designed for a particular community in mind. Today, most common *Web portals* build on the current generation of Web-based commodity technologies, based on the HTTP protocol for accessing the information through a browser.

Definition: Web Portal A portal providing users ubiquitous access, with the help of Web-based commodity technologies, to information, data, applications, and services. The current generation of Web portals is accessed through HTTP and Web browsers.

A *Grid portal* is a specialized portal useful for users of production Grids. A Grid portal provides information about the status of the Grid resources and services. Commonly, this information includes the status of batch queuing systems, load, and network performance between the resources. Furthermore, the Grid portal may provide a targeted access point to useful high-end services, such as the generation of a compute- and data-intensive parameter study for climate change. Grid portals provide communities with another advantage: they hide much of the complex logic to drive Grid-related services with simple interaction through the portal interface. Furthermore, they reduce the effort needed to deploy software for accessing resources on production Grids.

Definition: Grid Portal A specialized portal providing an entry point to the Grid to access applications, services, information, and data available within a Grid.

In contrast to Web portals, Grid portals may not be restricted to simple browser technologies but may use specialized plug-ins or executables to handle the data visualization requirements of, for example, macromolecular displays or three-dimensional high-resolution weather data displays. A Grid portal may deal with different user communities, such as developers, application scientists, administrators, and users. In each case, the portal must support a personal view that remembers the preferred interaction with the portal at time of entry. To meet the needs of this diverse community, sophisticated Grid portals (currently under development) are providing commodity collaborative tools such as newsreaders, e-mail, chat and videoconferencing, and event scheduling. Additionally, some Grid portal developers are exploiting commodity technologies such as JavaBeans and JSP, which are already popular in Web portal environments. In the following sections we highlight several examples of well-known Grid portals and the toolkits being used to create these portals.

5.7.1 HotPage

HotPage [17] is a portal that provides a collective view of a distributed set of high-performance computing resources. The portal enables researchers easily to find information about each of the resources in the computational Grid. This information (which is stored in HTML) includes technical documentation, operational status, load and current usage, and queued jobs. Additionally, HotPage enables users to access and manipulate files and data and to submit, monitor, and delete jobs. Grid access is through the Globus Toolkit [22] or via the Network Weather Service [51]. The HotPage back end is accessed through Perl CGI scripts that create the pages requested. HotPage has been installed on a variety of production Grids, such as NPACI [11] and the NASA IPG [15].

5.7.2 Webflow and Gateway

Webflow and its successor, Gateway [35], are two influential projects in designing portals for Grids. They offer a programming paradigm implemented over a virtual Web-accessible Grid. An application is designed by a computational graph that is visually edited by the end user using Java applets. Nodes of the graph are reusable modules that written by the developers. Module users need not, however, be concerned with issues such as allocating and running the modules on various machines, creating connections among the modules, sending and receiving data across these connections, or running several modules concurrently on one machine. The Gateway system takes care of these management issues and coordinates the execution.

The Gateway system is based on a modern three-tiered architecture. Tier 1 is the high-level front end enabling visual programming, steering, runtime data analysis and visualization, and collaboration; this front end is based on Web technologies and object-oriented commodity standards. Tier 2 is formed by distributed object-based, scalable and reusable Web servers and object brokers and builds the middleware. Tier 3 comprises the back-end services such as execution services and data movement services.

5.7.3 XCAT

The XCAT Project [58] from Indiana University provides an implementation of the Common Component Architecture (CCA) [3] to assist in the assembly of applications using Grid resources. The CCA specification describes the construction of portable software components that can be reused in any CCA-compliant runtime frameworks. These frameworks are tuned for a variety of application environments and in some cases are designed for applications that run on massively parallel computers. Here components may be parallel objects (multiple component instances operating in synchrony and communicating with each other with MPI), or they may be highly multithreaded and run on large, shared memory multiprocessor servers. In other cases, the frameworks are designed to enable the construction of applications from components that are distributed over a Grid.

XCAT allows Grid application programmers to script complex distributed computations and package these applications with simple interfaces for others to use. Each user obtains a personal notebook for controlling the applications; the notebook is used as an elementary abstraction to package applications and data scripts and parameters as part of a Web page. The portal server has an integrated event service allowing application and Grid resource information to publish events through the Network Weather Service [51] and Autopilot [2]. XCAT has been tested on distributed simulation of chemical processes in semiconductor manufacturing and collaboratory support for x-ray crystallography. XCAT is based on the Globus Toolkit and uses the Java CoG Kit [53,78] for its core security and remote task creation, and RMI over XSOAP [60] as a communication protocol.

5.7.4 UNICORE

UNICORE (Uniform Interface to Computing Resources) [23] provides a vertical integration environment for Grids, including access to resources through a portal. It is designed to assist in the workflow management of tasks to be scheduled on resources that are part of supercomputing centers. UNICORE workflow comprises hierarchical assemblies of interdependent tasks, with dependencies that are mapped to actions such as execution, compilation, linking, and scripting according to resource requirements on target machines on the Grid. Besides strong authentication, UNICORE assists in compiling and running applications and in transferring input and output data. One of the main components of UNICORE is the preparation and modification of structured jobs through a graphical user interface that supports workflows. It allows submission, monitoring, and control of the execution as part of a client that gets installed on the user's machine. Originally, UNICORE supported Web browser plug-ins, but it is now distributed as a stand-alone application. UNICORE is being used as the Grid infrastructure for a research project known as UNICORE Plus. This project is enhancing the original UNICORE software with new functionality to handle system administration and management, modeling of dynamic and extensible resources, creation of application-specific client and server extensions, improved data and file management functions, and runtime control of complex job chains. Metacomputing support (e.g., reservation, co-scheduling, application-level communication, and performance analysis) is also under consideration. Development to utilize Globus Toolkit enabled resources within UNICORE is underway [5].

5.7.5 JiPANG

JiPANG (Jini-based Portal Augmenting Grids) [74] is both a portal system and a toolkit, providing a uniform interface layer for accessing a variety of Grid systems. JiPANG is built on top of the Jini distributed object technology. It functions as a higher-level management services to resources being managed by individual Grid systems such as Ninf [63], NetSolve [36], and the Globus Toolkit [22] via the Java CoG Kit [78]. A Java API provides the user with a uniform interface to the Grid. A specialized JiPANG browser allows interactive access to Grid resources and services.

5.7.6 PUNCH

PUNCH (Purdue University Network-Computing Hubs) is a distributed network computer that allows users to access text and graphical applications remotely via a Web browser. PUNCH provides the ability to define several community portals, each of which serves a specific set of users [27]. When users visit a community portal, they are presented with a menu of applications that they can execute. These applications range from CPU simulators to drawing programs to complex commercial electronic design automation and mathematical analysis packages. For text-based tools, an HTML interface is provided that forwards all commands to the actual application. This enables a quick integration of command line–based applications into PUNCH. For more complex graphical applications, systems such as VNC are used to transmit the display back to remote users [54]. Such a method has also been used by other Grid portal activities, including the Access Grid (see Section 5.7.7).

At the base of PUNCH is PVFS, the PUNCH virtual file system. By using a series of proxies over standard NFS protocols, PUNCH is able to allow near-native NFS performance over disparate networks. Also, the PVFS removes the need for individual user accounts. Instead, all files are owned by a system account with the PUNCH user of the file being identified by its position in the file system tree. This abstraction is taken further to the level of user maintenance. In a traditional distributed system, user account information would need to be propagated to all systems on the network. PUNCH solves this by maintaining a pool of UIDs on each server that are dynamically assigned to users when they begin execution of processes on a server. An accounting facility keeps track of the UIDs in use and reclaims UIDs automatically at the end of the user's session.

Based on these features, PUNCH allows different institutions to share computational resources and applications. Sharing is possible even across different administrative domains based on a limited-trust relationship that can be established between the domains. This feature allows users at multiple universities to have access to the same computer systems with small risk of exploitation [45].

5.7.7 Access Grid

The Access Grid (AG) project develops a package of Grid software and maintains a production Grid of resources that can be used to support human interaction. The goal of the Access Grid is to support large-scale distributed meetings, collaborative work sessions, seminars, lectures, tutorials, and training. It provides the ability to include multimedia display, presentation and interaction environments, and interfaces to Grid middleware and visualization environments. This focus on group communication is in contrast to desktop-based tools that focus much more on individual communication.

The environment is intended to foster both formal and informal group interactions. Large-format displays integrated with intelligent or active physical meeting rooms (also called *nodes*) are a central feature of the Access Grid. Such a physical meeting room contains the high-end audio and visual technology needed to provide a high-quality compelling user experience. A number of Access Grid nodes are deployed worldwide that are frequently used to conduct meetings, site visits, training sessions, and educational events [29].

5.7.8 Commercial Grid Activities

Many of the early Grid projects that started as research efforts are now also marketed commercially. Legion, for example, is currently marketed through Avaki (which was cofounded by the developers of Legion). Several companies have decided to include the Globus Toolkit in their Grid marketing strategies that are based on extensions or support models. Nevertheless, the Globus Toolkit will continue to be a free open-source toolkit.

Efforts such as IBM's commitment to the Web services framework, Microsoft's .Net [7], Sun's Web services [73] and JXTA framework [57] will be major drivers for the next generation of Grid software. The development of an Open Grid Services Architecture together with companies such as IBM promises to integrate business and research models and processes in order to leverage from each other's technologies. Much additional work is needed to extend this early work.

5.8 CONCLUSIONS

In this chapter we have identified a vision that motivates the creation of Grids and Grid-enabled systems. We have also examined a variety of projects that address some—but not all—of the issues that must be resolved before the Grid is truly universal. In addition to the development of middleware, interfaces are needed that can be used by the application scientists to access Grids. Commodity Grid toolkits enabling access to Grid functionality on an API level such as Fortran, Java, and Python are important. Portals must also be developed to hide the complex infrastructure of Grids and allow scientists to use this infrastructure in the daily scientific exploration. The tools and technologies discussed in this chapter are but the first step in the creation of a global computing Grid.

ACKNOWLEDGMENTS

This work was supported by the Mathematical, Information, and Computational Science Division subprogram of the Office of Advanced Scientific Computing Research, Office of Science, U.S. Department of Energy, under Contract W-31-109-Eng-38. DARPA, DOE, and NSF support Globus Toolkit research and development. We thank Ian Foster, Geoffrey C. Fox, Dennis Gannon, Xian-He Sun, and members of the Computing Portals Working Group, formerly known as Datorr and now active as part of the Grid Computing Environment working group of the GGF, for valuable discussions leading up to this work. The Globus Toolkit and Globus Project are trademarks held by the University of Chicago.

REFERENCES

1. ASC Portal, *http://www.ascportal.org*.
2. Autopilot, *http://www-pablo.cs.uiuc.edu/Project/Autopilot/AutopilotOverview.htm*.
3. Common Component Architecture Forum, *http://www.cca-forum.org/*.
4. Folding@home, *http://folding.stanford.edu/*.

5. Grid Interoperability Project, *http://www.grid-interoperability.org/*.
6. HPSS, *http://www.sdsc.edu/hpss/hpss1.html*.
7. Microsoft.NET, *http://www.microsoft.com/net/*.
8. Unitree, *http://www.unitree.com/*.
9. National Center for Supercomputing Applications, *http://www.ncsa.uiuc.edu/*, 1986.
10. Alliance on Track to Enhance Services, *http://archive.ncsa.uiuc.edu/datalink/0005/VMR.intro.html*, 2000.
11. National Partnership for Advanced Computational Infrastructure, *http://www.npaci.edu/*, 2000.
12. DataGrid Project, *http://www.eu-datagrid.org/*, 2000.
13. ApGrid: Partnership for Grid Computing in the Asia Pacific Region, *http://www.apgrid.org/*.
14. EUROGRID: Application Testbed for European Grid Computing, *http://www.eurogrid.org/*, 2001.
15. Information Power Grid Engineering and Research Site, *http://www.ipg.nasa.gov/*, 2001.
16. Netsolve, *http://www.cs.utk.edu/netsolve*, 2001.
17. NPACI HotPage, *https://hotpage.npaci.edu/*, 2001.
18. Particle Physics Data Grid, *http://www.ppdg.net/*.
19. Scientific Discovery through Advanced Computing (SciDAC), *http://www.sc.doe.gov/ascr/mics/scidac/*, 2001.
20. Storage Resource Broker (SRB), *http://www.npaci.edu/DICE/SRB/*, 2001.
21. TerraGrid, *http://www.teragrid.org/*, 2001.
22. Globus Project, *http://www.globus.org/*, 2001.
23. UNICORE, *http://www.unicore.de/*.
24. Condor, *http://www.cs.wisc.edu/condor/*, February 2002.
25. Global Grid Forum, *http://www.gridforum.org*, 2002.
26. NetSolve, *http://icl.cs.utk.edu/netsolve/*, February 2002.
27. PUNCH, *http://punch.ecn.purdue.edu/*, March 2002.
28. SETI@Home, *http://setiathome.ssl.berkeley.edu/*, February 2002.
29. Access Grid, *http://www-fp.mcs.anl.gov/fl/accessgrid/*, 2002.
30. D. Abramson, R. Buyya, and J. Giddy, A computational economy for Grid computing and its implementation in the Nimrod-G resource broker, *Future Generation Computer Systems*, Vol. 18, No. 8, October 2002.
31. G. Allen, W. Benger, T. Goodale, H. Hege, G. Lanfermann, J. Masso, A. Merzky, T. Radke, E. Seidel, and J. Shalf, Solving Einstein's equations on supercomputers, *IEEE Computer*, pp. 52–59, *http://www.cactuscode.org*, 1999.
32. G. Allen, W. Benger, T. Goodale, H.-C. Hege, G. Lanfermann, A. Merzky, T. Radke, E. Seidel, and J. Shalf, The Cactus code: A problem solving environment for the Grid, in *High-Performance Distributed Computing, 2000, Proceedings of the 9th IEEE International Symposium on High-Performance Distributed Computing*, Pittsburgh, August 2000, IEEE Press, New York, pp. 253–260.
33. D. Arnold, S. Agrawal, S. Blackford, J. Dongarra, M. Miller, K. Sagi, Z. Shi, and S. Vadhiyar, *Users' Guide to NetSolve V1.4*, Technical Report CS-01-467, Computer Science Department, University of Tennessee, Knoxville, TN, July 2001.

34. G. Bell and J. Gray, What's next in high-performance computing, *Communications of the ACM*, Vol. 45, No. 2, pp. 91–95, February 2002.
35. D. Bhatia, V. Burzevski, M. Camuseva, G. C. Fox, W. Furmanski, and G. Premchandran, WebFlow: A visual programming paradigm for Web/Java based coarse grain distributed computing, *Concurrency: Practice and Experience*, Vol. 9, No. 6, pp. 555–577, 1997.
36. H. Casanova and J. Dongarra, NetSolve: A network server for solving computational science problems, *International Journal of Supercomputer Applications and High Performance Computing*, Vol. 11, No. 3, pp. 212–223, October 1997.
37. E. Christensen, F. Curbera, G. Meredith, and S. Weerawarana, Web Services Description Language (WSDL) 1.1, *http://www.w3.org/TR/wsdl*, March 15, 2001.
38. S. Fitzgerald, I. Foster, C. Kesselman, G. von Laszewski, W. Smith, and S. Tuecke, A directory service for configuring high-performance distributed computations, *Proceedings of the 6th IEEE Symposium on High-Performance Distributed Computing*, Portland, OR, August 1997, IEEE Press, New York, pp. 365–375.
39. K. Czajkowski, S. Fitzgerald, I. Foster, and C. Kesselman, Grid information services for distributed resource sharing, *Proceedings of the 10th IEEE International Symposium on High-Performance Distributed Computing*, San Francisco, August 2001, IEEE Press, New York, pp. 181–184.
40. DOE Science Grid, *http://www.doesciencegrid.org/*.
41. D. Ehnebuske, D. Box, G. Kakivaya, A. Layman, H. Frystyk, N. N. Mendelsohn, S. Thatte, and D. Winer, Simple Object Access Protocol (SOAP) 1.1, *http://www.w3.org/TR/SOAP*, 2000.
42. D. H. J. Epema, M. Livny, R. van Dantzig, X. Evers, and J. Pruyne, *A Worldwide Flock of Condors: Load Sharing among Workstation Clusters*, Technical Report DUT-TWI-95-130, Delft University of Technology, Delft, The Netherlands, 1995.
43. X. Evers, J. F. C. M. de Jongh, R. Boontje, D. H. J. Epema, and R. van Dantzig, *Condor Flocking: Load Sharing between Pools of Workstations*, Technical Report DUT-TWI-93-104, Delft University of Technology, Delft, The Netherlands, 1993.
44. S. Fields, Hunting for wasted computing power: New software for computing networks puts idle PC's to work, *University of Wisconsin Research Sampler*, 1993.
45. R. J. Figueiredo, N. H. Kapadia, and J. A. Fortes, The PUNCH virtual file system: Seamless access to decentralized storage services in a computational Grid, *Proceedings of the 10th IEEE International Symposium on High-Performance Distributed Computing*, San Francisco, August 2001, IEEE Press, New York.
46. I. Foster, The anatomy of the Grid: Enabling scalable virtual organizations, *International Journal of High-Performance Computing Applications*, Vol. 15, No. 3, pp. 200–222, August 2001.
47. I. Foster, The Grid: A new infrastructure for 21st century science, *Physics Today*, Vol. 55, No. 22, pp. 42–47, 2002.
48. I. Foster, C. Kesselman, J. Nick, and S. Tuecke, The physiology of the Grid: An open Grid services architecture for distributed systems integration, *http://www.globus.org/research/papers/ogsa.pdf*, February 2002.

49. G. C. Fox, *Portals for Web Based Education and Computational Science*, http://new_npac.csit.fsu.edu/users/fox/documents/generalportalmay00/exdeportay.html, 2000.
50. G. C. Fox and W. Furmanski, High performance commodity computing, in I. Foster and C. Kesselman, eds., *The Grid: Blueprint for a New Computing Infrastructure*, Morgan Kaufmann, San Francisco, 1999.
51. B. Gaidioz, R. Wolski, and B. Tourancheau, Synchronizing network probes to avoid measurement intrusiveness with the Network Weather Service, *Proceedings of the 9th IEEE High-Performance Distributed Computing Conference*, pp. 147–154, http://www.cs.ucsb.edu/rich/publications/, August 2000.
52. D. Gannon, K. Chiu, M. Govindaraju, and A. Slominski, An analysis of the Open Grid Services Architecture, http://www.extreme.indiana.edu/gannon/OGSAanalysis3.pdf, March 2002.
53. V. Getov, G. von Laszewski, M. Philippsen, and I. Foster, Multi-paradigm communications in Java for Grid computing, *Communications of the ACM*, Vol. 44, No. 10, pp. 119–125, 2001.
54. N. H. Kapadia, R. J. Figueiredo, and J. A. Fortes, PUNCH: Web portal for running tools, *IEEE Micro*, Vol. 20, No. 3, pp. 38–47, May–June 2000.
55. N. Karonis, MPICH-G2 Web page, http://www.hpclab.niu.edu/mpi/, 2001.
56. E. Korpela, D. Werthimer, D. Anderson, J. Cobb, and M. Lebofsky, SETI@home: massively distributed computing for SETI, *Computing in Science & Engineering*, Vol. 3, No. 1, pp. 78–83, January–February 2001.
57. N. Krishnan, The Jxta solution to P2P.
58. S. Krishnan, R. Bramley, D. Gannon, M. Govindaraju, R. Indurkar, A. Slominski, B. Temko, R. Alkire, T. Drews, E. Webb, and J. Alameda, The XCAT science portal, *Proceedings of SC2001*, November 10–16, 2001, http://www.sc2001.org/papers/pap.pap287.pdf.
59. J. Licklider and R. W. Taylor, The computer as a communication device, http://memex.org/licklider.pdf, 1968.
60. P. M. Lyster, L. Bergman, P. Li, D. Stanfill, B. Crippen, R. Blom, C. Pardo, and D. Okaya, CASA gigibit supercomputing network: CALCRUST three-dimensional real-time multi-dataset rendering, presented at Supercomputing '92, Minneapolis, MN, November 17–20, 1992.
61. D. Molnar, The SETI@home problem, *ACM Crossroads*, Vol. 1, Fall 2000, http://www.acm.org/crossroads/columns/onpatrol/september2000.html.
62. G. E. Moore, Cramming more components onto integrated circuits, *Electronics*, Vol. 38, No. 8, pp. 114–117, April 19, 1965.
63. H. Nakada, M. Sato, and S. Sekiguchi, Design and implementations of Ninf: Towards a global computing infrastructure, *Future Generation Computing Systems*, Vol. 15, No. 5–6, pp. 649–658, 1999.
64. The seven layers of the OSI model, http://www.iso.org and http://www.webopedia.com/quick_ref/OSL_Layers.html.
65. T. Prudhomme, C. Kesselman, T. Finholt, I. Foster, D. Parsons, D. Abrams, J.-P. Bardet, R. Pennington, J. Towns, R. Butler, J. Futrelle, N. Zaluzec, and J. Hardin, *NEESgrid: A Distributed Virtual Laboratory for Advanced Earthquake Experimentation and Simulation: Scoping Study*, NEES Technical Report 2001-02, February 2001.

66. T. Prudhomme and K. D. Mish. *NEESgrid: A Distributed Virtual Laboratory for Advanced Earthquake Experimentation and Simulation: Project Execution Plan*, NEES Technical Report 2001–02, June 2001.
67. F. N. C. Resolution, Definition of "Internet," *http://www.itrd.gov/fnc/Internet_res.html*, October 24, 1995.
68. L. F. Richardson, *The Collected Papers of Lewis Fry Richardson*, 2 volumes, Cambridge University Press, Cambridge, 1993.
69. S. Sekiguchi, Ninf Project home page, *http://ninf.apgrid.org/*, February 2002.
70. F. G. Shuman, History of numerical weather prediction at the NMC, *Weather and Forecasting*, Vol. 4, p. 286, 1989.
71. L. Smarr, Infrastructures for science portals, *http://www.computer.org/internet/v4n1/smarr.htm*, 2001.
72. R. C. Somerville, *The Forgiving Air: Understanding Environmental Change*, University of California Press, Berkeley, CA, 1996.
73. Sun Microsystems, Web services made easier, *http://java.sun.com/xml/webservices.pdf*.
74. T. Suzumura, S. Matsuoka, and H. Nakada, A Jini-based computing portal system, *http://matsu-www.is.titech.ac.jp/ suzumura/jipang/*.
75. C. Team, *Condor Version 6.2.2 Manual*, University of Wisconsin–Madison, Madison, WI, 2001.
76. J. Towns, The Alliance virtual machine room, *http://archive.ncsa.uiuc.edu/SCD/Alliance/VMR/*, 2001.
77. S. Verma, J. Gawor, G. von Laszewski, and M. Parashar, A CORBA commodity Grid kit, *Proceedings of the 2nd International Workshop on Grid Computing in Conjunction with Supercomputing 2001 (SC2001)*, Denver, CO, November 12, 2001, *http://www.globus.org/cog*.
78. G. von Laszewski, I. Foster, J. Gawor, and P. Lane, A Java commodity Grid kit, *Concurrency and Computation: Practice and Experience*, Vol. 13, No. 8–9, pp. 643–662, 2001.
79. G. von Laszewski, I. Foster, J. Gawor, P. Lane, N. Rehn, and M. Russell, Designing Grid-based problem solving environments and portals, *34th Hawaiian International Conference on System Science*, Maui, HI, *http://www.mcs.anl.gov/laszewsk/papers/cog-pse-final.pdf*, 2001.
80. V. A. Vyssotsky, F. J. Corbat, and R. M. Graham, Structure of the Multics supervisor, *Joint Computer Conference, AFIPS Conference Proceedings 27*, p. 203, *http://www.multicians.org/fjcc3.html*, 1965.

CHAPTER 6

Software Development for Parallel and Distributed Computing

M. PARASHAR

Department of Electrical and Computer Engineering, Rutgers University, Piscataway, NJ

S. HARIRI

Department of Electrical and Computer Engineering, University of Arizona, Tucson, AZ

6.1 INTRODUCTION

In this chapter we study the software development process in high-performance parallel and distributed computing (HPC) environments and investigate the nature of support required at each stage of development. Our objective is to illustrate the significance of tools and environments discussed in this book during software development. In what follows we first highlight some of the issues that must be addressed during HPC software development. The HPC software development process is then described. A parallel stock option pricing model is used as a running example in this discussion. Finally, some existing tools applicable at each stage of the development process are identified.

6.2 ISSUES IN HPC SOFTWARE DEVELOPMENT

In this section we highlight some of the issues that arise during HPC software development and that must be addressed by any software development environment. The first set of issues (Sections 6.2.1 to 6.2.5) focus primarily on efficient software development and high performance. This set includes issues pertaining to computational models, application description media, algorithm

---

Tools and Environments for Parallel and Distributed Computing, Edited by Salim Hariri and Manish Parashar
ISBN 0-471-33288-7 Copyright © 2004 John Wiley & Sons, Inc.

development issues (classification, evaluation, and mapping), implementation/runtime issues and visualization and animation support. In addition to these issues, there exists another set of equally important issues (Sections 6.2.6 to 6.2.8) that needs to be addressed. These issues involve the maintainability, reusability, and reliability of the developed application. Some of these issues have been addressed in [4,7,8,10,14,27–29].

6.2.1 Models for Parallel Computation

Computational models serve as a basis for specifying algorithms and as a means to gauge their computational complexity. Existing models for parallel computation can be classified as either general models such as the PRAM or the circuit model, or models bound to specific machines or architectural classes. General models abstract a large number of different architectures. However, these models do not represent the actual operation of any real machine, and algorithms developed based on them have to be further optimized for the target system. Algorithms developed using architecture (or machine)-specific models, on the other hand, are not portable and have to be separately developed for each such model. Although it may not be possible to have a single computational model applicable to all existing architectures, it will be helpful to minimize the number of distinct models and to investigate interrelations between different existing models.

6.2.2 Portable Application Description Medium

Existing (or proposed) application description media that are capable of describing parallelism can be classified as either *parallel extension* or *parallel languages*. The former class consists of classical languages such as C, Fortran, or Pascal with appropriate language extensions to handle parallel processes, communication, and synchronization. These languages make it easier to port existing applications to HPC systems. However, parallelism is introduced as an afterthought in these languages. As a result, it may not be possible to fully express the parallelism present in the application or to exploit the potential of the underlying hardware. Parallel languages are specifically designed with parallelism in mind and provide primitives to express application parallelism and exploit parallel architectures. Using these languages, however, would require redevelopment of complete applications. Most existing application description media are tied to a particular machine and its computational model. For example, CMFortran and C* are specific languages for the Connection Machines (TMC), MP-Fortran is targeted to the DECmpp's (DEC), while Occam has been designed for transputer-based systems. HPC requires a portable and flexible application description medium that provides the capability of expressing application parallelism and that can be implemented efficiently on diverse HPC architectures.

6.2.3 Parallel Algorithm Development

The utilization of HPC systems depends on the availability of efficient parallel algorithms. Parallel extensions or implementations of existing sequential algorithms are not able to exploit the parallelism inherent in the problem because this information usually is lost (or hidden) during development of the sequential version. Consequently, high-performance software warrants the development of new algorithms which are specifically designed to exploit parallelism at every level. Issues related to parallel algorithm development include:

- *Algorithm classification:* the ability to classify algorithms on the basis of their computational and communication characteristics so that algorithms can be matched with target HPC architectures during software development
- *Algorithm evaluation:* the ability to evaluate an algorithm to obtain a realistic estimate of its complexity or potential performance, enabling the developer to evaluate different algorithms for a problem and to make an appropriate selection
- *Algorithm mapping:* the assignment of the parallel algorithm to an appropriate HPC system based on algorithm classification and system specifications

6.2.4 Program Implementation and Runtime

Program implementation issues address system specific decisions made during program development, such as synchronization strategies, data decomposition, vectorization strategies, pipelining strategies, and load balancing. These issues define the requirements of a parallel programming environment, which include parallel language support, syntax-directed editors, intelligent compilers and cross-compilers, parallel debuggers, configuration management tools, and performance evaluators. Runtime issues include providing efficient parallel runtime libraries, dynamic scheduling and load-balancing support, as well as support for nonintrusive monitoring and profiling of application execution.

6.2.5 Visualization and Animation

Since HPC systems can process large amounts of information at high speeds, there is a need for visualization and animation support to enable the user to interpret this information. Further, visualization and animation enable the user to obtain insight into the actual execution of the application and the existing inefficiencies.

6.2.6 Maintainability

Maintainability issues include ensuring that the software developed continues to meet its specifications and handling any faults or bugs that might surface during its lifetime. It also deals with the evolution and enhancement of the software.

6.2.7 Reliability

Reliability issues include software fault tolerance, fault detection, and recovery. Multiple processing units operating simultaneously and possibly in an asynchronous fashion, as is the case in a HPC environment, make these issues difficult to address.

6.2.8 Reusability

Software reusability issues, as with sequential computing, deal with software development efficiency and costs. Designing software for reusability promotes modular development and standardization.

6.3 HPC SOFTWARE DEVELOPMENT PROCESS

The HPC software development process is described as a set of stages that correspond to the phases typically encountered by a developer. At each stage, a set of support tools that can assist the developer are identified. The stages can be viewed as a set of filters in cascade (Figure 6.1) forming a development pipeline. The input to this system of filters is the application description and specification which is generated from the application itself (if it is a new problem) or from existing sequential code (porting of dusty decks). The final output of the pipeline is a running application. Feedback loops present at some stages signify stepwise refinement and tuning. Related discussions pertaining to parallel computing environments and spanning parts of the software development process can be found in [4,7,28]. The stages in the HPC software development process are described in the following sections. Parallel modeling of stock option pricing [20] is used as a running example in the discussion.

6.4 PARALLEL MODELING OF STOCK OPTION PRICING

Stock options are contracts that give the holder of the contract the right to buy or sell the underlying stock at some time in the future for an agreed-upon striking or exercise price. Option contracts are traded just as stocks, and models that quickly and accurately predict their prices are valuable to the traders. Stock option pricing models estimate the price for an option contract

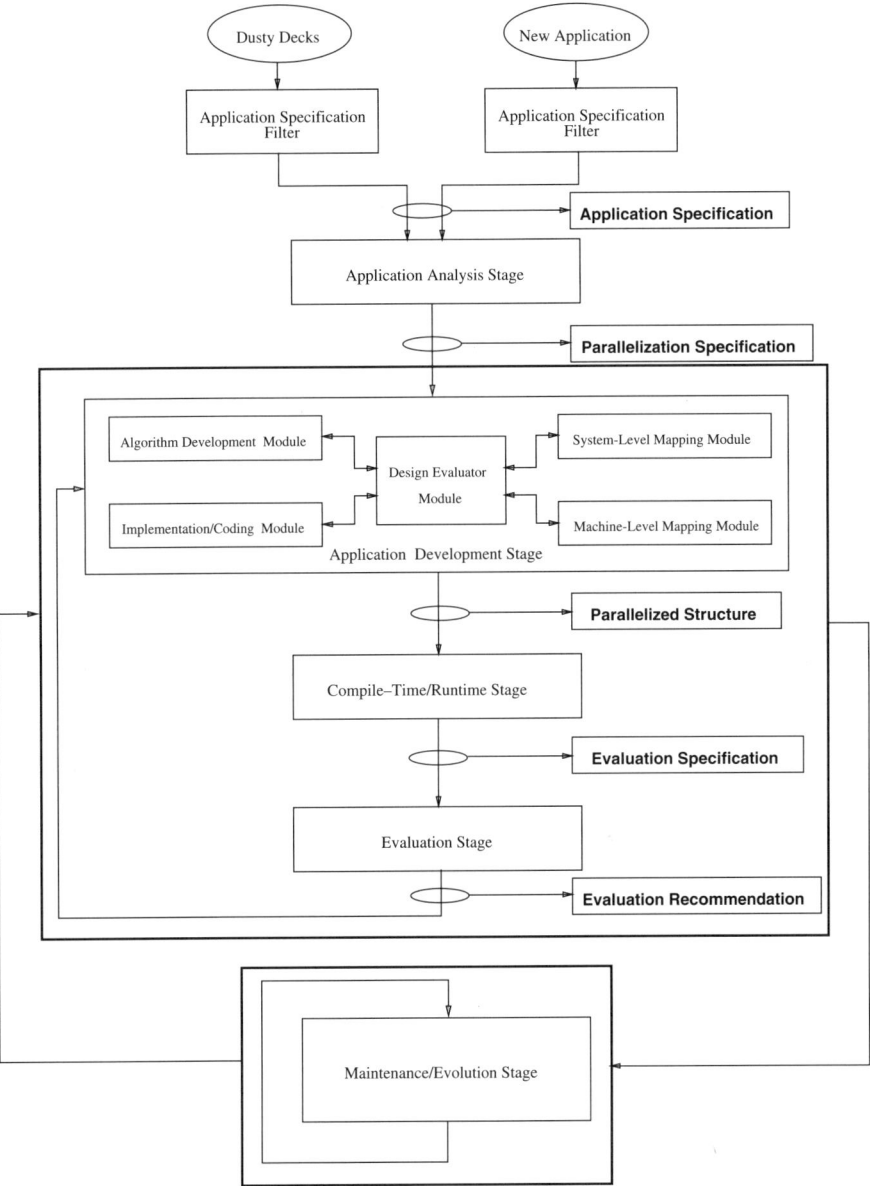

Fig. 6.1 HPDC software development process.

based on historical market trends and current market information. The model requires three classes of inputs:

1. *Market variables*, which include the current stock price, call price, exercise price, and time to maturity.

2. *Model parameters*, which include the volatility of the asset (variance of the asset price over time), variance of the volatility, and the correlation between asset price and volatility. These parameters cannot be observed directly and must be estimated from historical data.
3. *User inputs*, which specify the nature of the required estimation (e.g., American/European call, constant/stochastic volatility), time of dividend payoff, and other constraints regarding acceptable accuracy and running times.

A number of option pricing models have been developed using varied approaches (e.g., nonstochastic analytic models, Monte Carlo simulation models, binomial models, and binomial models with forced recombination). Each of these models involves a set of trade-offs in the nature and accuracy of the estimation and suit different user requirements. In addition, these models make varied demands in terms of programming models and computing resources.

6.5 INPUTS

The HPC software development process presented in this chapter addresses two classes of applications:

1. *"New" application development.* This class of applications involves solving new problems using the resources of a HPC environment. Developers of this class of applications have to start from scratch using a textual description of the problem.
2. *Porting of existing applications (dusty decks).* This class includes developers attempting to port existing codes written for a single processor to a HPC environment. Developers of this class of applications start off with huge listings of (hopefully) commented source code.

The input to the software development pipeline is the application specification in the form of a functional flow description of the application and its requirements. The functional flow description is a very high-level flow diagram of the application outlining the sequence of functions that have to be performed. Each node (termed *functional modules*) in the functional flow diagram is a black box and contains information about (1) its input(s), (2) the function to be performed, (3) the output(s) desired, and (4) the requirements at each node. The application specification can be thought of as corresponding to the user requirement document in a traditional lifecycle model.

In the case of new applications, the inputs are generated from the textual description of the problem and its requirements. In the case of dusty decks, the developer is required to analyze the existing source code. In either case, expert system–based tools and intelligent editors, both equipped with a knowledge base to assist in analyzing the application, are required. In Figure 6.1, these tools are included in the "Application Specification Filter" module.

The stock price modeling application comes under the first class of applications. The application specifications based on the textual description presented in Section 6.3, is shown in Figure 6.2. It consists of three functional modules: (1) The input module accepts user specification, market information, and historical data and generates the three inputs required by the model; (2) the estimation module consists of the actual model and generates the stock option pricing estimates; and (3) the output module provides a graphical display of the estimated information to the user. The feedback from the output module to the input module represents tuning of the user specification based on the output.

6.6 APPLICATION ANALYSIS STAGE

The first stage of the HPC software development pipeline is the application analysis stage. The input to this stage is the application specification as described in Section 6.5. The function of this stage is to analyze the application thoroughly with the objective of achieving the most efficient implementation. An attempt is made to uncover any parallelism inherent in the application. Functional modules that can be executed concurrently are identified, and dependencies between these modules are analyzed. In addition, the application analysis stage attempts to identify standard computational modules, which can later be matched with a database of optimized templates in the application development stage. The output of this stage is a detailed process flow graph called the *parallelization specification*, where the nodes represent functional components and the edges represent interdependencies. Thus, the problems dealt with in this stage can be summarized as (1) the module creation problem (i.e., identification of tasks which can be executed in parallel), (2) the module classification problem (i.e., identification of standard modules), and (3) the module synchronization problem (i.e., analysis of mutual interdependencies). This stage corresponds to the *design phase* in standard software life-cycle models, and its output corresponds to the *design document*.

Tools that can assist the user at this stage of software development are: (1) smart editors, which can interactively generate directed graph models from the application specifications; (2) intelligent tools with learning capabilities that can use the directed graphs to analyze dependencies, identify potentially parallelizable modules, and attempt to classify the functional modules into standard modules; and (3) problem specific tools, which are equipped with a database of transformations and strategies applicable to the specific problem.

The parallelization specification of the running example is shown in Figure 6.3. The Input functional module is subdivided into two functional compo-

196 SOFTWARE DEVELOPMENT FOR PARALLEL AND DISTRIBUTED COMPUTING

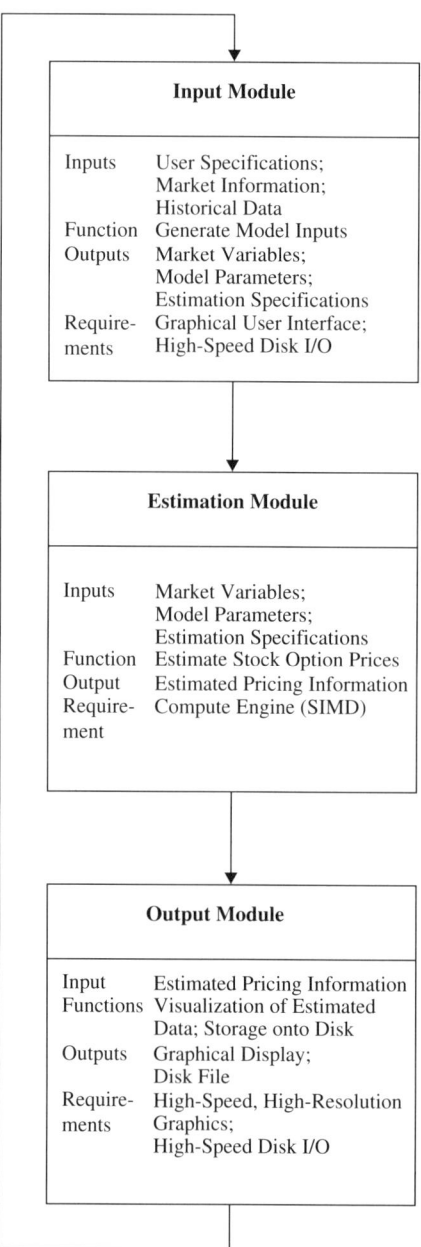

Fig. 6.2 Stock option pricing model: application specifications.

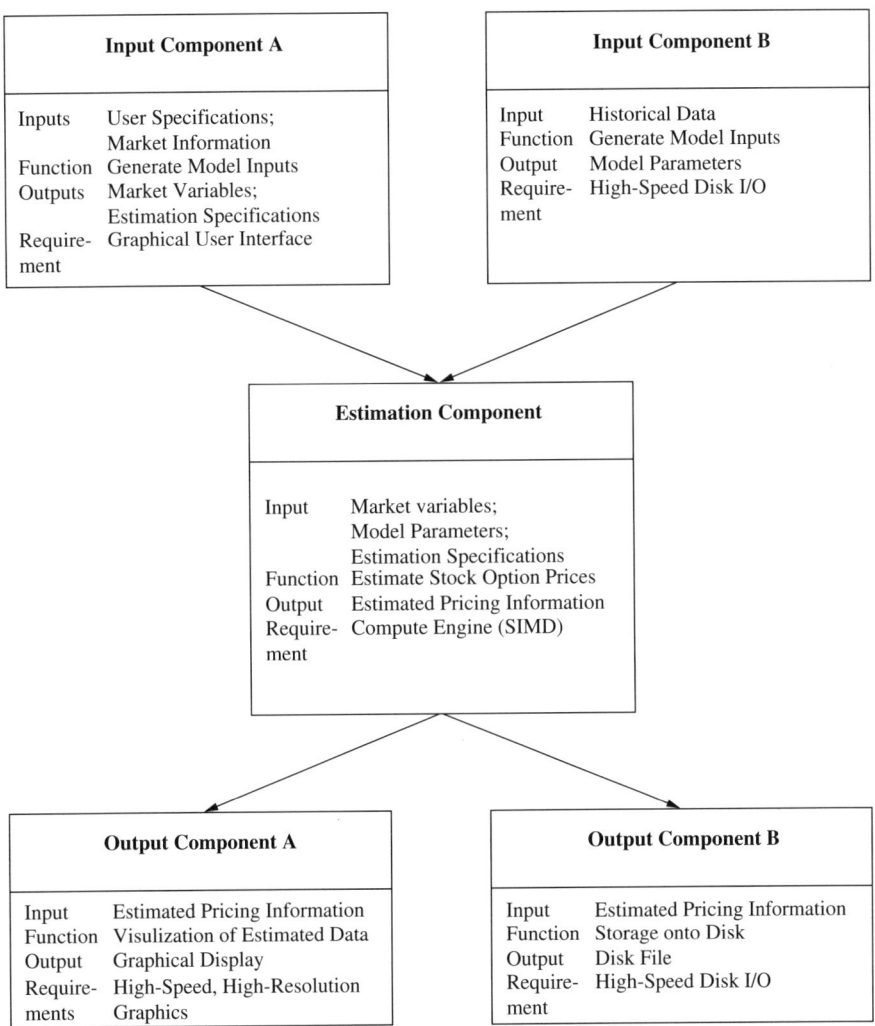

Fig. 6.3 Stock option pricing model: parallelization specifications.

nents: (1) analyzing historical data and generating model parameters, and (2) accepting market information and user inputs to generate market variables and estimation specifications. The two components can be executed concurrently. The estimation module is identified as a standard computational module and is retained as a single functional component (to avoid getting into the details of financial modeling). The output functional module consists of two independent functional components: (1) rendering the estimated information onto a graphical display, and (2) writing it onto disk for subsequent analysis.

6.7 APPLICATION DEVELOPMENT STAGE

The application development stage receives the parallelization specifications as its input and produces the parallelized structure, which can then be compiled and executed. This stage is responsible for selecting the right algorithms for the application, the best-suited HPC system (from among available machines), mapping the algorithms appropriately onto the selected system, and then implementing or coding the application. Correspondingly, the stage is made up of five modules: (1) algorithm development module, (2) system-level mapping module, (3) machine-level mapping module, (4) implementation/coding module, and (5) design evaluator module. These modules, however, are not executed in any fixed sequence or a fixed number of times. Instead, there is a feedback system from each module to the other modules through the design evaluator module. This allows the development as well as the tuning to proceed in an iterative manner using stepwise refinement. A typical sequence of events in the application development stage are outlined as follows:

- The algorithm development module uses an initial system-level mapping (possibly specified via user directives) to select appropriate algorithms for the functional components.
- The algorithm development module then uses the services of the design evaluator module to evaluate candidate algorithms and to tune the selection.
- The system-level mapping module uses feedback provided by the design evaluator module and the algorithm development module to tune the initial mapping.
- The machine-level mapping module selects an appropriate machine-level distribution and mapping for the particular algorithmic implementation and system-level mapping. Once again, feedback from the design evaluator module is used to select between alternative mappings.
- This process of stepwise refinement and tuning is continued until some termination criterion is met (e.g., until some acceptable performance is achieved or up to a maximum time limit).
- The algorithm selected, system-level mapping, and machine-level mapping are realized by the implementation/coding module, which generates the parallelized structure.

6.7.1 Algorithm Development Module

The function of the algorithm development module is to assist the developer in identifying functional components in the parallelization specification and selecting appropriate algorithmic implementations. The input information to this module includes (1) the classification and requirements of the components specified in the parallelization specification, (2) hardware configuration information, and (3) mapping information generated by the system-level mapping module. It uses this information to select the best algorithmic implementation and the corresponding implementation template from its database. The algorithm development module uses the services of the design evaluator module to select between possible algorithmic implementations. Tools needed during this phase include an intelligent algorithm development environment (ADE) equipped with a database of optimized templates for different algorithmic implementations, an evaluation of the requirements of these templates, and an estimation of their performance on different platforms.

The algorithm chosen to implement the estimation component of the stock option pricing model (shown in Figure 6.3) depends on the nature of the estimation (constant/stochastic volatility, American/European calls/puts, and dividend payoff times) to be performed and the accuracy/time constraints. For example, models based on Monte Carlo simulation provide high accuracy. However, these models are slow and computationally intensive and thereby cannot be used in real-time systems. Also, these models are not suitable for American calls/puts when early dividend payoff is possible. Binomial models are less accurate than Monte Carlo models but are more tractable and can handle early exercise. Models using constant volatility (as opposed to treating volatility as a stochastic process) lack accuracy but are simple and easy to compute. Modeling American calls wherein the option can be exercised anytime during the life of the contract (as opposed to European calls which can only be exercised at maturity) is more involved and requires a sophisticated and computationally efficient model (e.g., binomial approximation with forced recombination). The algorithmic implementations of the input and output functional components must be capable of handling terminal and disk I/O at rates specified by the time constraint parameters. The output display must provide all information required by the user.

6.7.2 System-Level Mapping Module

The system-level mapping module is responsible for selecting the HPC system best suited for the application. It achieves this using information about algorithm requirements provided by the algorithm development module and feedback from the design evaluation module. System-level mapping can be accomplished in an interactive mapping environment equipped with tools for analyzing the requirements of the functional components, and a knowledge base consisting of analytic benchmarks for the various HPC systems.

The algorithms for stock option pricing have been implemented efficiently on architectures like the CM2 and the DECmpp-12000 [20]. Consequently, an appropriate mapping for the estimation functional component in the parallelization specification in Figure 6.3 is an SIMD architecture. The input and output interfaces (input/output component A) require graphics capability with support for high-speed rendering (output display) and must be mapped to appropriate graphics stations. Finally, input/output component B requires high-speed disk I/O and must be mapped to an I/O server with such capabilities.

6.7.3 Machine-Level Mapping Module

The machine-level mapping module performs the mapping of the functional component(s) onto the processor(s) of the HPC system selected. This stage resolves issues such as task partitioning, data partitioning, and control distribution, and makes transformations specific to the particular system. It uses the feedback from the design evaluator module to select between possible alternatives. Machine-level mapping can be accomplished in an interactive mapping environment similar to the one described for the system-level mapping module, but equipped with information pertaining to individual computing elements of a specific computer architecture.

Performance of the stock option pricing models is very sensitive to the layout of data onto the processing elements. Optimal data layout is dictated by the input parameters (e.g., time of dividend payoff, and terminal time) and by the specification of the architecture onto which the component is mapped. For example, in the binomial model, continuous time processes for stock price and volatility are represented as discrete up/down movements forming a binary lattice. Such lattices are generally implemented as asymmetric arrays that are distributed onto the processing elements. It has been found that the default mapping of these arrays (i.e., in two dimensions) on architectures like the DECmpp 12000, lead to poor load balancing and performance, especially for extreme values of the dividend payoff time [19]. Further, the performance in case of such a mapping is very sensitive to this value and has to be modified for each set of inputs. Hence, in this case, it is favorable to map the arrays explicitly as one-dimensional arrays. This is done by the machine-level mapping module.

6.7.4 Implementation/Coding Module

The function of the implementation/coding module is to handle code generation and code filling of selected templates so as to produce a parallel program that can then be compiled and executed on the target computer architecture. This module incorporates all machine-specific transformations and optimized libraries, handles the introduction of calls to communication and synchronization routines, and takes care of the distribution of data among the processing elements. It also handles any input/output redirection that may be required.

With regard to the pricing model application, the implementation/coding module is responsible for introducing machine-specific communication routines. For example, the binary estimation model makes use of the "end-of-shift" function for its nearest-neighbor communication. The corresponding function calls in the language used (e.g., C* on the CM2 or MPL on the DECmpp-12000) are introduced by this module. A machine-specific optimization that would be introduced by this module is the reduction of communication through use of in-processor arrays. This optimization can improve performance by about two orders of magnitude [20].

6.7.5 Design Evaluator Module

The design evaluator module is a critical component of the application development stage. Its function is to assist the developer in evaluating different options available to each of the other modules, and identifying the option that provides the best performance. It receives information about the hardware configuration, application structure, requirements of the algorithms and mappings selected, and uses this information to estimate the performance of the selection on the target system. It also provides insight into the computation and communication costs, the existing idle times, and the overheads. This information can be used by the other modules to identify regions where further refinement or tuning is required. The effects of different runtime scenarios can be evaluated (e.g., system load, network contention) to enable the developer to account for them during design. The keys features of this module are (1) the ability to provide evaluations with the desired accuracy, with minimum resource requirements, and within a reasonable amount of time; (2) the ability to automate the evaluation process; and (3) the ability to perform an evaluation within an integrated workstation environment without running the application on the target computers. Support applicable to this module consists primarily of performance prediction and estimation tools. Simulation approaches can also be used to achieve some of the required functionality.

6.8 COMPILE-TIME AND RUNTIME STAGE

The compile-time/runtime stage handles the task of executing the parallelized application generated by the development stage to produce the output required. The input to this stage is the parallelized source code (parallelized structure). The compile-time portion of this stage consists of optimizing compilers and tools for resource allocation and initial scheduling. The runtime portion of this stage handles runtime functions such as dynamic scheduling, dynamic load balancing, migration, and irregular communications. It also enables the user to (nonintrusively) instrument the code for profiling and debugging and allows checkpointing for fault tolerance. During the execution of the application, it accepts outputs from the various computing elements and directs them for proper visualization. It intercepts error messages generated and provides proper interpretation.

Compile-time and runtime issues with regard to the stock option pricing model include allocation of the functional modules to processing elements, communicating input data and information between these modules, collecting and visualizing the estimated output, forwarding outputs for storage, and finally, interactively modifying model parameters.

6.9 EVALUATION STAGE

In the evaluation stage, the developer retrospectively evaluates the design choices made during the development stage and looks for ways to improve the design. In this stage a thorough evaluation is performed of the execution of the entire application, detailing communication and computation times, communication and synchronization overheads, and existing idle times. Further, this information is provided at all required granularities of the application. This evaluation is then used to identify regions of the implementation where performance improvement is possible. The evaluation methodology enables the developer to investigate the effect on performance of various runtime parameters such as system load and network contention, as well as the scalability of the application with machine and problem size. The key feature of this stage is the ability to perform evaluation with the desired accuracy and granularity while maintaining tractability and nonintrusiveness. Support applicable to the evaluation stage includes various analytic tools, monitoring tools, simulation tools, and prediction/estimation tools.

6.10 MAINTENANCE/EVOLUTION STAGE

In addition to the stages described above, encountered during the development and execution of HPC applications, there is an additional stage in the life cycle of this software which involves its maintenance and evolution. Maintenance includes monitoring the operation of the software and ensuring that it continues to meet its specifications. It involves detecting and correcting bugs as they surface. The maintenance stage also handles the modifications needed to incorporate changes in the system configuration. Software evolution deals with improving the software, adding additional functionality, and incorporating new optimizations. Another aspect of evolution is the development of more efficient algorithms and corresponding algorithmic templates and the incorporation of new hardware architectures. To support such a development, the maintenance/evolution stage provides tools for the rapid prototyping of hardware and software and for evaluating the new configuration and designs without having to implement them. Other support required during this stage includes tools for monitoring the performance and execution of the software, fault detection and recovery tools, system configuration and configuration evaluation tools and prototyping tools.

TABLE 6.1   HPC Software Development Stages: Support Requirements

Development Stage	Tools Required
Application specification filter	SA/SD CASE tools
Application analysis stage	Intelligent editors, problem-specific databases
Application development stage	
(a) Algorithm development module	Intelligent ADEs, databases, optimized templates
(b) System-level mapping module	Intelligent mapping tools, analytic benchmarks
(c) Machine-level mapping module	Same as system-level mapping
(d) Implementation/coding module	Code generation tools, code optimizers
(e) Design evaluator module	Performance prediction tools
Compile-time/runtime stage	Intelligent optimizing compilers, dynamic load-balancing tools, debuggers, profilers, visualization tools, error-handling support, etc.
Evaluation stage	Performance analysis tools, performance monitoring tools, performance simulation tools, performance prediction tools
Maintenance/evolution stage	Monitoring tools, fault detection/recovery tools, system configuration tools, prototyping tools, predictive evaluation tools

6.11   EXISTING SOFTWARE SUPPORT

In this section we identify existing tools that provide support at different stages of the software development process. Our objective is twofold: (1) to demonstrate the nature of support needed at each stage of the HPC software development process; and (2) to illustrate the fact that although a large number of individual tools or systems have been developed, there is a lack of an integrated environment which can support the developer through the entire software development process. Table 6.1 summarizes the support required at each stage of the HPC software development process developed in this chapter. Some existing tools applicable to the different stages are discussed briefly below.[1]

6.11.1   Application Specifications Filter

The SAMTOP tool, which is proposed to be a part of the TOPSYS [5] system, will provide the functionality required by this stage. In addition, existing

---

[1] An extensive survey of tools and systems for high-performance parallel/distributed computing can be found in [11,31].

SA/SD (structured analysis/structured design) CASE tools can be used at this stage.

6.11.2 Application Analysis Stage

The Sigma editor, which is part of the FAUST [15] parallel programming environment, provides the support required by this stage for shared memory architectures. It provides intelligent, interactive editing and parallelizing capabilities and incorporates a performance predictor. Another system applicable to this stage is Parafrase-2 [25]. The SAMTOP tool discussed above will also provide some analysis capabilities.

6.11.3 Application Development Stage

At the application development stage, tools such as SCHEDULE [13] and SKELETONS assist the user during algorithm development while MARC, Paralex [23], and TEACHER 4.1 [17] provide mapping support. SKELETONS and MARC are part of an integrated application development and runtime environment for transputer-based systems [7]. Existing approaches which provide some of the functionality of the design evaluator module include methodologies proposed by Balasundaram et al. [2], Sussman [30], and Gupta and Banerjee [16]. Support for implementation and coding is provided by SUPERB [32] and by the system proposed by Bhatt et al. [6]. Other tools providing support during application development include the CODE parallel programming environment [9], ParaScope [3], and SPADE [7]. SAMTOP and Sigma systems also provide some functionality required by this stage.

6.11.4 Compile-Time and Runtime Stage

Support required by this stage of software development is provided by the FAUST and TOPSYS systems discussed above. TOPSYS provides debugging support (DETOP), while FAUST incorporates a compile-time and runtime environment. Another tool applicable to this stage is the Parafrase-2 [25] system, which provides compile-time support for shared memory architectures.

6.11.5 Evaluation Stage

Existing evaluation systems include PATOP and VISTOP from TOPSYS, the Pablo performance analysis environment [26], the IPS-2 system [18], the SIMPLE environment [22], and RPPT [12]. FAUST and RPPT [12] specifically provide evaluation support for the CEDAR computer system.

6.11.6 Maintenance/Evolution Stage

The PAWS systems [24] presents an approach for machine evaluation and can be used during the maintenance/evolution stage. System prototyping capabilities are provided by SiGLe [1] and Proteus [21].

REFERENCES

1. F. Andre and A. Joubert, Sigle: an evaluation tool for distributed systems, *Proceedings of the International Conference on Distributed Computing Systems*, pp. 466–472, 1987.
2. V. Balasundaram, G. C. Fox, K. Kennedy, and U. Kremer, An interactive environment for data partitioning and distribution, *Proceedings of the 5th Distributed Memory Computing Conference*, Charleston, SC, pp. 1160–1170, April 1990.
3. V. Balasundaram, K. Kennedy, U. Kremer, K. McKinley, and J. Subhlok, The parascope editor: an interactive parallel programming tool, *Supercomputing '89*, Reno, NV, November 1989.
4. V. R. Basili and J. D. Musa, The future engineering of software: a management perspective, *IEEE Computer*, Vol. 24, No. 9, pp. 90–96, September 1991.
5. T. Bemmerl, A. Bode, P. Braun, O. Hansen, T. Treml, and R. Wismüller, *The Design and Implementation of TOPSYS-Ver 1.0*, Technische Universität München, Institut Für Informatik, Munich, July 1991.
6. S. Bhatt, M. Chen, C.-Y. Lin, and P. Liu, *Abstractions for Parallel n-Body Simulations*, Technical Report DCS/TR-895, Yale University, New Haven, CT, 1992.
7. J. E. Boillat, H. Burkhart, K. M. Decker, and P. G. Kropf, Parallel computing in the 1990's: attacking the software problem, *Physics Report* (review section of Physics Letters), Vol. 207, No. 3–5, pp. 141–165, 1991.
8. G. Booch, *Software Engineering with Ada*, 2nd ed., Benjamin/Cummings, San Francisco, 1986.
9. J. C. Browne, M. Azam, and S. Sobek, Code: a unified approach to parallel programming, *IEEE Software*, July 1989.
10. J. P. Cavano, Software development issues facing parallel architectures, *Proceedings of the 12th Annual International Computer Software and Applications Conference*, pp. 300–301, 1988.
11. D. Y. Cheng, *A Survey of Parallel Programming Languages and Tools*, Technical Report RND-93-005, NAS Systems Development Branch, NASA Ames Research Center, Moffett Field, CA, March 1993.
12. R. C. Covington, S. Madala, V. Mehta, J. R. Jump, and J. B. Sinclair, *The Rice Parallel Processing Testbed*, ACM 0-89791-254-3/88/0005/0004, pp. 4–11, 1988.
13. J. J. Dongarra and D. C. Sorensen, Schedule: tools for developing and analyzing parallel Fortran programs, in L. H. Jamieson, D. B. Gannon, and R. J. Douglas, eds., *The Characteristics of Parallel Algorithms*, MIT Press, Cambridge, MA, 1987.
14. G. C. Fox, Issues in software development for concurrent computers, *Proceedings of the 12th Annual International Computer Software and Applications Conference*, pp. 302–305, 1988.

15. D. Gannon, Y. Gaur, V. Guarna, D. Jablonowski, and A. Malony, FAUST: an integrated environment for parallel programming, *IEEE Software*, pp. 20–27, July 1989.
16. M. Gupta and P. Banerjee, Compile-time estimation of communication costs in multicomputers, *Proceedings of the 6th International Parallel Processing Symposium*, Beverly Hills, CA, March 1992.
17. A. Ieumwananonthachai, A. N. Aizawa, S. R. Schwartz, B. W. Wah, and J. C. Yan, Intelligent mapping of communicating processes in distributed computing systems, *Proceedings of Supercomputing '91*, pp. 512–521, 1991.
18. B. P. Miller, M. Clark, J. Hollingsworth, S. Kierstead, S.-S. Lim, and T. Torzewski, Ips-2: the second generation of a parallel program measurement system, *IEEE Transactions on Parallel and Distributed Systems*, Vol. 1, No. 2, pp. 206–217, April 1990.
19. K. Mills, G. Cheng, M. Vinson, and G. C. Fox, *Expressing Dynamic, Asymmetric, Two-Dimensional Arrays for Improved Performance on the decmpp-12000*, Technical Report SCCS-261, Northeast Parallel Architectures Center, Syracuse University, Syracuse, NY, October 1992.
20. K. Mills, G. Cheng, M. Vinson, S. Ranka, and G. C. Fox, Software issues and performance of a parallel model for stock option pricing, *Proceedings of the 5th Australian Supercomputing Conference*, Melbourne, Australia, December 1992.
21. P. H. Mills, L. S. Nyland, J. F. Prins, J. H. Reif, and R. W. Wagner, Prototyping parallel and distributed system in proteus, *Proceedings of the 3rd IEEE Symposium on Parallel and Distributed Processing*, 1991.
22. B. Mohr, Simple: a performance evaluation tool environment for parallel and distributed systems, *Proceedings of the 2nd European Distributed Memory Computing Conference (EDMCC2)*, pp. 80–89, April 1991.
23. Ö. Babaoğlu, L. Alvisi, A. Amoroso, R. Davoli, and L. A. Giachini, *Paralex: An Environment for Parallel Programming in Distributed Systems*, Technical Report, Department of Mathematics, University of Bologna, Bologna, Italy, 1991.
24. D. Pease, A. Gafoor, I. Ahmad, D. L. Andrews, K. Foudil-Bey, T. E. Karpinski, M. A. Mikki, and M. Zerrouki, Paws: a performance evaluation tool for parallel computing systems, *IEEE Computer*, pp. 18–29, January 1991.
25. C. D. Polychronopoulos, M. Girkar, M. R. Haghighat, C. L. Lee, and B. Leung, Parafrase-2: an environment for parallelizing, partitioning, synchronizing and scheduling programs on multiprocessors, *Proceedings of the International Conference on Parallel Processing*, Vol. 2, pp. 39–48, August 1989.
26. D. A. Reed, R. A. Aydt, T. M. Madhyastha, R. J. Noe, K. A. Shield, and B. W. Schwartz, *An Overview of the Pablo Performance Analysis Environment*, Technical Report, University of Illinois, Urbana, IL, November 1992.
27. J. H. Reif, ed., *Synthesis of Parallel Algorithms*, Morgan Kaufmann, San Francisco, 1993.
28. L. Russell and R. N. C. Lightfoot, Software development issues for parallel processing, *Proceedings of the 12th Annual International Computer Software and Applications Conference*, pp. 306–307, 1988.
29. D. B. Skillicorn, Models for practical parallel computation, *International Journal of Parallel Programming*, Vol. 20, No. 2, pp. 133–158, 1991.

30. A. Sussman, *Execution Models for Mapping Programs onto Distributed Memory Parallel Computers*, Technical Report 189613, Institute for Computer Applications in Science and Engineering, NASA Langley Research Center, Hampton, VA, March 1992.
31. L. H. Turcotte, *A Survey of Software Environments for Exploiting Networked Computing Resources*, Technical Report, Engineering Research Center for Computational Field Simulation, Mississippi State, MS, June 1993.
32. H. Zima, H. Bast, and M. Gerndt, Superb: a tool for semi-automatic SIMD/MIMD parallelization, *Parallel Computing*, Vol. 6, pp. 1–18, January 1988.

INDEX

Accumulators, 73
Active Message, 23
Adaptive Communication Systems:
  Adaptive Group Communication Service, 29
  Application-Aware Multicasting, 44–48
  Control Plane, 24, 25
  Data Plane, 25, 26
  Multiple Communication Interfaces, 28
  Multithread Communication Service, 24
  Programmable Communication, Control and Management Service, 26–28
  Resource Aware Scheduling Algorithm (RAA), 29, 49, 50
  Separation of Data and Control Functions, 24
Alewife, 67, 68
Algorithm development module, 198, 199
Application specification filter, 193, 195, 196, 203
ASCOMA, 66
Authentication, 159
Availability, 2

Back-propagation neural network (BPNN), 39, 42
Barriers, 71, 74, 75
Binomial models, 194, 199, 200
BOA, 83, 144
Brazos, 71, 72

Cache coherence, directory-based, 59, 60
Capacity miss, 66
CC-NUMA, 64
client.policy, 94
Client-side, 88, 89
COMA, 65
Commercial Grid activities, 182
Commodity Grid kits, 168
Community authorization, 160
Community production Grid, 153
Compression, 72
Conflict miss, 66
Consumer, 103
CORBA, 79, 81–84, 87, 88, 90, 95, 103, 109, 126, 144
Cost-effectiveness, 2
Critical section, 71
CRL (C Region Library), 74, 75

DCOM, 79, 85–87, 89, 90, 99, 100, 103, 114, 136, 144
Delegation, 160
Design document, 195
Design evaluator module, 201
Diff, 71
DII, 83
Directory header, 69
Distributed-object computing, 79
Distributed pointer protocol, 60
Distributed shared memory, 12
Distributed shared memory (DSM) systems:
  architecture, 61, 62
  hardware-based, 63–69

Tools and Environments for Parallel and Distributed Computing, Edited by Salim Hariri and Manish Parashar
ISBN 0-471-33288-7 Copyright © 2004 John Wiley & Sons, Inc.

mostly software page-based, 63, 69–72
properties, 58
software/object-based, 63, 72–76
taxonomy, 58, 63
Distributed system design framework, 6, 7
DSI, 84
Dusty decks, 192, 194
Dynamic copyset reduction, 71

Encryption, 160
Estimation module, 197
Event flags, 75
Extendibility, 2

False sharing, 70, 72
Fast Fourier Transform (FFT), 39, 40, 42
Fault tolerance, 2
FAUST, 204
FLASH, 68, 69
Functional module, 194, 195, 197

Gestalt of the Grid, 150
Global Grid Forum, 164
Globus Project, 167
Grid, 149, 150, 153
Grid appliance, 154
Grid applications:
  Astrophysics Collaboratory, 175
  NEESgrid, 177
  Particle Physics Data Grid, 176
Grid approach, 149, 152
Grid architecture:
  N-tiered architecture, 155
  role-based architecture, 155
  service-based architecture, 157
Grid challenges, 158
Grid community activities, *see* Commercial Grid activities; Grid middleware; Portals; Production Grids
Grid layers:
  application layer, 156
  collective layer, 156
  connectivity layer, 156
  fabric, 155
  resource layer, 156

Grid management aspects:
  data, 161
  execution, 162
  hardware, 163
  information, 161
  resources, 162
  security, 159
  software, 162
Grid middleware:
  Akenti, 170
  Commodity Grid kits, 168
  Globus Project, 167
  Legion, 169
  Network Weather Service, 171
  Storage Resource Broker, 170
Grid plane, 154

High-level packet blasting, 72
High-performance distributed system, 4
High-throughput computing:
  Commodity Grid kits, 168
  Condor, 171
  Netsolve, 172
  Nimrod-G, 174
  Ninf, 173
HPC software development:
  application analysis, 195, 196, 204
  application development, 198–201, 204
  compile-time and runtime, 201, 202, 204
  evaluation stage, 202, 204
  inputs, 194, 195
  issues, 189–192
  maintenance/evolution, 202, 205
  process, 192, 193
  software support, 203–205

IDL, 83, 84, 88, 95, 109, 126, 142, 143
idl2java, 95
Implementation/coding module, 200, 201
In-process activation, 85
IUnknown, 86, 89

java.rmi.remote, 87, 104, 115
Joint Photographic Experts Group (JPEG), 39, 40, 43

Latency, 5, 6
Linear equation solver, 49

INDEX

Locks, 71, 74, 75
Lockup-free caches, 68

Machine-level mapping module, 200
Madeleine I and II, 22, 23
MAGIC chip, 69
Makefile, 93, 98, 108, 114, 125, 135
Market variables, 193
Matrix, 118
Memory consistency models:
  entry consistency, 61, 74
  processor-consistency, 61
  release consistency, 61, 76
  scope consistency, 60, 72
  sequential consistency, 60, 73, 74
Message-Passing Interface (MPI), 21, 22
Message-passing tools:
  Active Message, 23
  classification, 15–19
    hardware-based approach, 17
    software-based approach, 17–19
      high-performance API, 18, 19
      middleware, 19
      multithreading, 17, 18
  desirable features, 13–15
  experimental results and analysis, 29–51
  model, 12–13
  socket-based, 19–20
  see also Adaptive Communication Systems; Madeleine I and II; Message-Passing Interface; Nexus; Parallel Virtual Machine; p4
Metacomputer, 152
MIDL, 85, 89, 100, 143
Midway, 74
Mirage+, 72
MIT Alewife Machine, 67, 68
Modality of operation, 152
Moniker, 81, 103, 145
Monte Carlo models, 194, 199
Multicomputers, 62

Naming, 80
Networking technology, 5
Nexus, 22
NUMA, 62, 64, 65

OMA, 82
OMG, 81
Open Grid Services Architecture, 168
Orca, 73
Out-of process activation, 85

Panda, 73
Parallel algorithms, 191
Parallel computation models, 190
Parallel sorting with regular sampling (PSRS), 39, 41, 43
Parallel Virtual Machine (PVM), 20, 21
Parallelization specification, 193, 195, 197
PAWS, 205
POA, 83, 88, 96, 133, 134, 144
Portals:
  Access Grid, 182
  Commodity Grid Kit, 168
  Gateway, 179
  Grid Portal, 179
  Hotpage, 179
  JiPang, 181
  Punch, 181
  UNICORE, 180
  Webflow, 179
  Web Portal, 178
  XCAT, 180
Processing technology, 5
Producer, 103
Production Grid, 152
Production Grids:
  ApGrid, 166
  DataGrid, 166
  DOE Science Grid, 165
  EuroGrid, 166
  NASA Information Power Grid, 165
  TeraGrid ,165
p4, 20

regedit, 101
Reliability, 2
Remote reference, 80
RMI, 79, 80, 87, 88, 90, 103, 104, 119, 144
RMIREGISTRY (also rmiregistry), 80, 88, 94, 143
RMI Security Manager, 88, 106, 107, 123, 124, 145
R-NUMA, 65

SAM, 73, 74
SAMTOP, 203
Secure execution, 161
Serialization, 81
Servant, 82
server.policy, 94
Server-side, 87, 89
Service, 157
Shared miss, 75
Sharing of resources, 2
Shasta, 75, 76
Sigma editor, 204
Single sign-on, 160
Skeleton, 81, 83
SKELETONS, 204
Software tools and environments, 6
Stanford FLASH multiprocessor, 68, 69
Stock option pricing model, 192–203
Stub, 81, 83
Synchronization operations, 61
System-level mapping module, 199, 200
S-COMA, 65

Thrashing, 65
TOPSYS, 203, 204
TreadMarks, 70, 71
Twin, 71
Type library, 89, 101, 103

UMM, 146, 147
UnicastRemoteObject, 87, 104, 106, 115, 121

Values, 73
Vector, 118
Virtual Organization, 154
Voting application, 39, 41, 44, 49

Write protocols:
　multiple-writer, 70, 71
　single-writer, 70
　write-invalidate, 70, 72, 75
　write-update, 70, 74